The Everlasting Staircase

The Everlasting Staircase:

A History of the Prison Officers' Association, 1939–2009

DAVID EVANS with SHEILA COHEN

www.plutobooks.com

in association with the

PRISON OFFICERS' ASSOCIATION

First published 2009 by the
PRISON OFFICERS' ASSOCIATION
Cronin House, 245 Church Street, Edmonton, London N9 9HW
and distributed by Pluto Press
345 Archway Road, London N6 5AA

www.plutobooks.com

British Library Cataloguing in Publication Data
A catalogue record for this book is available from the British Library

ISBN   978 0 7453 2963 5   paperback

Library of Congress Cataloging in Publication Data applied for

10   9   8   7   6   5   4   3   2   1

Designed and produced for the Prison Officers' Association by
Chase Publishing Services Ltd, Sidmouth, England
Printed and bound in the European Union

This book is dedicated to those men and women who have worked for and sustained the union for over 70 years.

Without the dedication of local branch officials the achievements of national representatives would not have been possible.

David Evans

CONTENTS

ABBREVIATIONS

ACTO	Advisory Council on the Treatment of Offenders
ASDA	Additional Staff Daytime Allowance
ASLs	Agreed Staffing Levels
CCSU	Council of Civil Service Unions
CCT	compulsory competitive tendering
CAC	Central Arbitration Committee
CNA	Certified Normal Accommodation
CDCs	Continuous Duty Credits
CSAT	Civil Service Arbitration Tribunal
CSC	Correctional Services Corporation
CSCA	Civil Service Clerical Association
CSH	contract supplementary hours
CWA	Common Working Agreement
CWS	Common Working System
ETL	Essential Task List
FBU	Fire Brigades Union
FGS	Functional Group Systems
FTA	Failure To Agree
G4S	Group 4 Security
GALIPS	Gays And Lesbians In the Prison Service
GCHQ	Government Communications Head Quarters
GMB	General, Municipal and Boilermakers union
HOPD	Home Office Prison Department
HR	Human Resources
IIP	Investors In People
ILO	International Labour Organisation
IRA	Irish Republican Army
IRPA	Industrial Relations Procedure Agreement
JIRPA	Joint Industrial Relations Procedural Agreement
KPIs	Key Performance Indicators
KPTs	Key Performance Targets

LSIs	Long Service Increments
MPT	Manpower Project Team
MUFTI	Minimum Use of Force Tactical Intervention
NAPO	National Association of Probation Officers
NEC	National Executive Committee
NHS	National Health Service
NOMS	National Offender Management Service
NTS	Notice To Staff
NUM	National Union of Mineworkers
NUPPO	National Union of Police and Prison Officers
OME	Office of Manpower Economics
PAR	Parva Against Racism
PCS	Public and Commercial Services union
PFF	Prison Force Federation
PFI	Private Finance Initiative
POA	Prison Officers' Association
POF	Prison Officers' Federation
PORB	Prison Officers' Representative Board
PPS	Premier Prison Services
PRB	Pay Review Body
PROP	Preservation of the Rights Of Prisoners
PSMB	Prison Service Management Board
PSNPP	Public Service Not Private Profit
PSPRB	Prison Service Pay Review Body
PSU	Prison Service Union
PWC	PricewaterhouseCoopers
RMT	Rail, Maritime and Transport workers union
SBCS	Strategy Board for Correctional Services
SLA	Service Level Agreement
SNP	Scottish National Party
SPOA	Scottish Prison Officers' Association
SPS	Scottish Prison Service
STCs	Secure Training Centres
TOIL	Time Off In Lieu
TUC	Trades Union Congress
UDR	Ulster Defence Regiment
UKDS	UK Detention Services

VA	Voluntary Agreement
VERSE	Voluntary Early Retirement and Severance scheme
VIRA	Voluntary Industrial Relations Agreement
WFM	Workforce Modernisation
YOI	Young Offenders' Institution

ACKNOWLEDGEMENTS

The following are gratefully acknowledged for their help with the production of this history:

Steve Lewis, POA Research Officer, for statistics, information and in-depth research;

the following POA officers, NEC members and activists for their contributions through interviewing and other sources:

John Boddington, NEC Member (retired) Honorary Life Member
Angela Burgess, POA Wormwood Scrubs (retired)
Brian Caton, POA General Secretary
Steve Gillan, POA Finance Officer
Bryan Goodman, POA Honorary Life Member
Dave Melrose, Area Chairman POA Scotland
Colin Moses, POA National Chairman
John Renton, General Secretary Scottish POA (retired)
Tom Robson, NEC Member
Finlay Spratt, Area Chairman Northern Ireland
Dave Turner, POA Pentonville
Derek Turner, Assistant Secretary POA Scotland ...

... and many, many more, including the staff in all three POA offices ...

AND ALL OUR LOYAL AND DEDICATED MEMBERS.

PLATES

Plates 1–15 archives of Prison Officers' Association
Plate 16 courtesy of *Islington Tribune*

THE NATIONAL UNION OF POLICE AND PRISON OFFICERS

EXECUTIVE COMMITTEE 1919

1. The Executive Committee of NUPPO, 1919 (note 'E.R. Ramsay' – far right, second row – is identified as 'Magazine Editor')

2. Banner of the Lambeth branch of NUPPO during the 1919 dispute

3. Jack Hayes, General Secretary of NUPPO, 1919

4. Len White of the CSCA

6. Painting of Harley Cronin, first General Secretary of the POA, which hangs in the General Secretary's office

5. Bill Brown of the CSCA

7. Northern Ireland Prison Service Role of Honour which hangs in Cronin House

8. Leadership board that hangs in Cronin House identifying all National Chairmen and General Secretaries and their terms in office

P.O.A.
ESTABLISHED 1939

NATIONAL CHAIRMEN		GEN. SECRETARIES
Mr A.J. RICKARD 1939-1945	Mr M. HEALY 1997-2001	Mr H. CRONIN M.B.E. 1939-1963
Mr H. BIESTY 1945-1948	Mr A. DARKEN 2001-2002	Mr F.G. CASTELL M.B.E. 1963-1972
Mr A.J. RICKARD 1948-1949	Mr C. MOSES 2002	Mr K.A. DANIEL 1972-1981
Mr J.F. LAWRIE 1949-1957		Mr D.M. EVANS B.A. 1981-2000
Mr J. SWAINSTON 1957-1962		Mr B. CATON 2000-
Mr D. J. VILLER 1962-1964		
Mr N. COWLING 1964-1968		
Mr S. POWELL 1968-1976		
Mr F.W. NONELY 1976-1978		
Mr P. NAUGH 1978-1980		
Mr C.D. STEEL 1980-1987		
Mr J. BARTELL 1980-1995		
Mr J. BODDINGTON 1995-1997		

9. The destruction left after the Strangeways riot in 1990

10. POA delegates to the 1999 TUC Black Workers' Conference (left to right: Tom Robson, David Uduehi, Roland Biosah, Colin Moses, Tom Appaddo, Clover Copeland and Tim Dastoor)

11. POA delegates to the 2001 TUC Women's Conference (left to right: Mandy Booth, Carmen Garaway, Giannina Maina and Lisa Persey)

12. Scenes at Winson Green Birmingham during the first ever national walkout by prison officers on 29 August 2007

13. Wakefield on 29 August 2007

14. Prison officers outside HMP Holloway on 29 August 2007

15. POA Leaders with Brendan Barber at the Speak Up for Public Services rally, 2007

16. Colin Moses with Holloway Branch Chairman Simon Peters and branch members at a union meeting against Workforce Modernisation in February 2009

INTRODUCTION: 'SLAVES OF SIBERIA'

Prisons, prisoners and prison officers go back a long way before the formation of the Prison Officers' Association (POA) in September 1939. As one of the few histories on the subject[1] tells us, institutions resembling the modern prison and employing what were then called 'warders' (a hated term finally abolished in 1921) began during the early period of industrialisation in the first half of the nineteenth century. The 1865 Prisons Act finally eliminated the old, piecemeal system of Elizabethan 'bridewells' and prison hulks, transportation, county and convict prisons, by decisively placing overall administration in the hands of central government.

Up to this point 'the salaried gaoler was a rarity',[2] but the 1865 Act established a staffing structure expected to include a gaoler, a chaplain, a surgeon and a matron (in women's prisons). Job specifications were set out in great detail, and, significantly, it was forbidden to employ prisoners as staff – previously a widespread practice.

Prisons were further centralised in an 1877 Act which set up a new body, the Prison Commission, to operate every aspect of prison administration under the watchful eye of the Home Secretary. Its first Chair, Edmund du Cane, has been identified with a 'harsh' rather than rehabilitative approach to the treatment of prisoners. However, his generally authoritarian approach, and the power then vested in his position, meant at least that it was totally clear to prison officers where the central power lay.

In J.E. Thomas' words, 'There was ... a need for strong leadership. At the head of the service du Cane provided this; at the local level power was delegated to the governor and he was expected to exercise it. As a result the staff were able to identify the person who exercised authority.'[3] As Thomas also points out, this was something that was to become less obvious in later years.

Such leadership did not, however, reduce the degree of conflict in this early period. Though strike action and associated radicalism were not yet as widespread as they would become in the late 1880s,[4] at the time of the centralisation of local prisons in 1877 'the emerging radical spirit among workers was affecting the attitude of some staff, and there was a new militancy in their dealings with the [prison] Directors'.[5]

During the 1880s, dissatisfaction among staff increased, mainly over low pay and long hours. 'Agitation' over these issues, mainly via clandestine lobbying of MPs or anonymous letters to the press, resulted in two major inquiries: that of the Rosebery Committee in 1883, and the Gladstone Committee, eleven years later.

The Rosebery inquiry proved a disappointment. Though the committee considered petitions from staff at Wormwood Scrubs, Pentonville, Portsmouth, Parkhurst, Brixton, Portland and Dartmoor, in which they unanimously asked for an eight-hour system of work, an increase in annual leave, a readjustment of pay and allowances and increased superannuation, its response was 'overtly hostile' to these requests. As well as assuming that the officers' complaints were unfounded, given that the service was still able to attract 'a sufficient supply of capable men', Committee members resented the fact that 'the officers ... have preferred the method of public agitation' to more formal channels of complaint.[6]

This familiar criticism reflected a broader reaction by the authorities against the radical climate of the times. As Thomas explains: 'This was the first major protest which the staff had made, and ... it is likely that the new militancy was regarded as something which had to be quashed. At the time the growth of union activity ... was causing great concern to the ruling classes.' A year later, du Cane expressed concern about prison officers who might become 'a tool of agitators'.[7]

In 1885 a new Prison Service Chairman, Sir Evelyn Ruggles-Brice, succeeded Edmund du Cane and was 'even less sympathetic' to prison officers' concerns. While leaning towards the reform of conditions for prisoners more than his predecessor, his lack of concern for the needs of prison staff was signalled by his opposition to a new grade of 'chief warder in charge' established in the same year. The elevation of 'warders' to this position was proposed as a reaction against the 'disproportionate rates' paid to the governors of small prisons. Asked whether he favoured this small but significant improvement in prison officers' prospects, Ruggles-Brice replied, 'No, I do not think I am; in fact, I may say emphatically that I am not.'[8]

Objections by 'establishment' figures like Ruggles-Brice to any suggested promotion of prison officers were rooted in sheer snobbery. Rather than arguing that the proposed 'chief warder' would be unable to deal effectively with prisoners, it was suggested that the officer would be unable to deal with other prison officials 'who are really his superiors ... by reason of their higher social position'. In fact, the Gladstone Committee recommended changing the title 'chief warder', to 'Governor Class V', a change which 'underlined the feeling that socially, emotionally and intellectually, warders could not be effective governors'.[9] This shift was underlined by the gradual growth of 'direct entry' to the governor grade from outside, rather than promotion from within.

The issue of 'chief warders' was one of those discussed by the Gladstone Committee, which was set up in 1894 primarily to look at the prison system as it affected prisoners rather than at issues concerning staff. Nevertheless, evidence to the Committee included 'derogatory remarks about the subordinate ranks', particularly with reference to the military background of many prison officers; William Tallack, a leading advocate of prison reform, felt that although 'military warders are better for discipline, civilians have a higher moral character than the soldiers ... a larger proportion [of prison officers] should be civilians'.[10]

Another concern raised regarding basic-grade prison officers was the inadequacy of their training. At the time, officers were given three months' on-the-job training and only then were allowed to take charge of prisoners, but in local prisons at least trainees were often placed in charge of prisoners before the three months were up in the event of staff shortages. Concern was also expressed over the training given by local staff who might 'not themselves be qualified to instruct'. In the light of these concerns, the committee recommended a number of important changes leading to the setting up of training schools and the introduction of ongoing 'In-Service Training'.

Although it mentioned a few other minor issues connected with staff, the main impact of the Gladstone Committee Report was to set in motion a philosophy of 'reformation', in opposition to the previous emphasis on control and deterrence within the Prison Service. This approach, which was to dominate most of the decades that followed, was bitterly resented at the time by many prison officers. Placed as they now were in a highly contradictory position in which they were expected both to restrain and to rehabilitate prisoners, uniformed staff found themselves at the centre of 'the organisational confusion which has dogged the twentieth-century prison service'. Under the new regime, 'control was undermined, Governors and prisoners were drawn together, and participation of the warders in the new developments was restricted'. All this represented 'the substance of an overall change in the operation of the prison service, which was to create a profound sense of alienation' amongst already embittered officers.[11]

'Like policemen, sailors and soldiers ...'

In this context of resentment at the apparent priority of prisoners' needs over their own, coupled with the unresolved issues of pay, hours and leave which had been submitted to the Rosebery Committee, it was not surprising that many prison officers began to look to some form of organisation that could better represent their views. In fact, as another study of the prison officer history by Steven R. Thomas points out,[12] the need for independent representation was strengthened precisely by the loss of direct communication with governors and thus Prison Commissioners available within the 'paramilitary' chain of command existing within the service before its restructuring by the Gladstone Committee.

Submissions to the various committees and inquiries themselves favoured organisation; as J.E. Thomas points out, the petitions presented by prison staff to such committees 'bore evidence of communication between staffs in different prisons',[13] and in 1895, evidence of service-wide discontent was shown by the first attempt to publish a prison officers' magazine. However, this collapsed after one issue, and the years that followed, with high levels of unemployment and severe legal judgments against strike action, were not favourable to the cause of trade unionism in Britain.

In 1906, however, the Trades Disputes Act granted immunities against lawsuits for workers involved in strike action, improving conditions for organised labour, and in the same year the question of a union for prison officers was mentioned for the first time in Parliament.[14] On 15 March, Winston Churchill, then Home Secretary, was asked about 'the alleged grievances of warders' and whether he would allow them the same right to 'federation' as postal employees now had. Churchill, as was usual with politicians at his level, knew nothing of prison officers' grievances, and he deferred any decision on federation. However, on 5 April he announced a Standing Order (No. 805) whereby, with the sanction of the governor, prison staff could 'meet and discuss among themselves questions relating to their duties and position in the prison service'.

As with so many of the 'great and the good' during this period, Winston Churchill's 'reformative enthusiasm on behalf of the prisoners had no counterpart in his handling of staff affairs. His wish to improve the conditions of one, and his refusal to do the same for the other was, for staff, the most typical and depressing feature of Home Office rule after 1906.'[15] Two years after the minor concession of the Standing Order, a further question was asked in Parliament as to whether that ruling meant that prison staff had the same rights of association as other 'workmen', but this question never received an answer.

Despite the Home Secretary's ignorance of them, prison officers did indeed have grievances; as well as rigorous discipline resulting in frequent fines, staff endured dismal living quarters, excessive hours and, of course, inadequate pay. Despite occasional concessions such as the abolition of night duty and some improvements in pensions, dissatisfaction was widespread, spurring prison officers on in their quest for organisation and representation. In 1910, another attempt at founding a publication aimed at uniting and mobilising prison officers was successful, leading to a new voice for staff which, though officially entitled the *Prison Officers' Magazine*, came to be known as the 'Red-Un'. While at first this epithet was due more to the colour of its cover than the radicalism of its views – in its early years the *Magazine* 'could be said to have been restrained in its tone' – from 1915, when the notorious 'E.R. Ramsay' took over as editor, its more fiery content became well deserving of the term.

The enormous significance of the *Magazine* in the history of the Prison Officers' Association is shown both in its declared objective of 'provid[ing] a means of communication between the staffs scattered about all over the country' and also in the fact that its price rapidly had to be increased from 4d to 6d a copy 'after improvements in layout and presentation had been made at the request of officers who were keenly interested in improving the bad conditions under which they were employed'.[16]

The following year saw another move forward in the progress towards organisation, sparked by another question in Parliament. When Churchill was asked whether the 1906 Standing Order could be altered to allow prison officers to hold one general meeting a year and to give them more opportunity to present grievances, he replied that prison officers 'were like policemen, soldiers and sailors. It was inappropriate for them to form unions ....'[17] A proposed meeting in a London hotel, bringing staff together from different prisons, was banned as contrary to the Standing Order.

In response to this repression, Churchill was warned that the officers would organise in secret. In fact, an abortive attempt to form a Prison Officers' Federation (POF) took place the following year, in 1912; this failed within a year largely because of the rival claims of the National Union of Police and Prison Officers (NUPPO), formed in 1913. There was discussion in the *Magazine* in October 1914 about a 'furious fight going on over unionism, which was not simply a struggle between old officers and young officers'. Despite these clear warnings of prison staff mobilisation, when Churchill was asked again in December 1915 whether the 'warders' could meet, he again refused.

As predicted, in that same year the underground POF was formed. In fact, the intention to form the POF had been announced in the *Prison Officers' Magazine* in May 1915. With regard to the rival NUPPO, it was suggested that prison officers had never favoured association with the police and wanted their own representation. Nevertheless, 'there was still a certain amount of support among officers for NUPPO, especially at Pentonville … The new Federation hoped for harmonious relations with the older union.'[18]

Despite what was by now the exit of many prison officers to the armed forces as the First World War entered its second year, by July 1915 at least 500 out of a staff of about 4,000 were reported to have joined the POF. But soon after, there were signs of trouble in the organisation. By 1916, several prisons had withdrawn their support, and the failure of a petition for a war bonus made by the Federation led to many officers refusing to subscribe. The editor asked in the May issue of the *Magazine* why there appeared to be a reluctance to join the Federation:

> He believed that it was a 'fear' of the consequences, even though the membership list was secret … [but] part of the reason was the customary reluctance of people to support staff associations, particularly if, as was the case with the Federation, the association is entirely unofficial and is not recognised by the employers. Another reason arose from the peculiarities of the Prison Service. Many officers supported the view that this was a 'discipline' service and were hesitant about going 'behind the backs of superior officers', not through fear, but because they believed it was underhand.[19]

Although in December 1916 the editor claimed that 'almost every prison' was represented, with density ranging from 90 per cent in two or three prisons to about a dozen in one or two, it was becoming 'increasingly obvious', according to Thomas, that 'the Federation was not going to flourish'.[20] Then, just as the ongoing First World War neared its end, prison officers' independent attempt at organisation was overtaken by historic events. In August 1918, NUPPO called its members out on strike.

This action, sparked by massive resentment over the decline in police pay relative to other occupations during the war,[21] was restricted to a two-day walkout of Metropolitan Police officers in London; but its implications for prison officers, as will be seen in the next chapter, were enormous.

Not surprisingly, the government was terrified by the outbreak of militancy amongst its guardians of law and order. Among other things, rumours were spreading that troops sent to take over police duties in guarding government buildings 'were fraternising with the strikers, and pledging that they would never act against them'.[22] The Prime Minister, Lloyd George, was perhaps accurate in stating that 'the country was nearer to Bolshevism that day than any time since'.[23]

For that very reason, the government acted quickly in receiving a delegation from NUPPO. Lloyd George, nicknamed the 'Welsh Wizard' for good reason, offered the NUPPO committee what appeared to be categorical assurances of the right to form a union, which, along with increases in pay and pensions, was one of the strikers' central demands. As Sellwood puts it, 'The police representatives had come into Number ten like angry lions and had gone out – if not as lambs – at least with ... a feeling of satisfaction that justice ... was being granted ....'[24] In fact, those assurances were fatally flawed, fenced around with conditions rapidly expressed in a 'corrective statement' from the Home Office, which confirmed the Prime Minister's promise of an 'authoritative organisation' but added: 'of course, this is quite a different thing from a union in the ordinary sense'.[25]

This crucial caveat was lost in the general jubilation. The strikers' leader, Jim Marston, proclaimed to a victory meeting at Tower Hill: 'The effect of Mr Lloyd George's reception of the Executive committee of the Police Union is Government recognition of the union ....' The delegates announced acceptance of the terms with 'a show of hands, which shot up as thick as a forest'.[26] Later, 96 per cent of all London police officers attended a celebratory meeting at Holborn Town Hall.

In the wake of this apparent success, prison officers gave up their attempt at separate organisation. In November 1918, the POF announced that it would amalgamate with NUPPO. The *Prison Officers' Magazine* ceased publication, and its then editor, 'E.R. Ramsay', became editor of the *Police and Prison Officers' Magazine* instead.

The 'Bolshie' at the *Prison Officers' Magazine*

Perhaps the best ending to this brief introduction is a summary of the early career of this much-loved figure, whose fiery diatribes played such a vital role in the formation and early history of the POF. Born Hubert Witchard, he joined the Prison Service at Dartmoor in 1903 as a member of the Works staff. By 1915, his identity by necessity concealed under the lifetime pen-name of 'E.R. Ramsay', Witchard had become editor of the *Prison Officers' Magazine* after its first editor, Fred Ludlow, resigned in the face of the multitude of 'petty victimisations' visited on his subscribers and contributors.

Within a short space of time, the vigorous opinions expressed in the *Magazine* had

> the powers-that-be concentrat[ing] all their efforts on trying to locate the 'Bolshie' who had taken over as Editor of the 'Red-Un'. They would clearly never associate this demon with the quiet, unassuming clerical gent [who] sat ... at his Dickensian type desk in the Foreman of Works office at Dartmoor with a friendly smile for all and sundry ... [W]hen night came he was to be found, with a blanket to muffle the sound of his typewriter, busily working against time to meet the printer's deadline.[27]

Needless to say, combining a full-time job with such strenuous and surreptitious labour proved a struggle. Despite severe financial difficulties, 'E.R.' managed to buy the copyright of the *Magazine* for £75 in 1916 and then moved from Bristol to London in order to be near the House of Commons and the Home Office. It is here that we learn the origin of the mysterious parliamentary questions which were to embarrass the Home Secretary: 'With information obtained from the latter he bombarded the former with Parliamentary questions pertaining to the conditions of employment of the Prison Service, bringing injustices to light and always seeking to improve the lot of the Prison Officer.'[28]

The 'Bolshie' tag now attached to the *Magazine* clearly had its origins in Ramsay's style, so much at odds with the 'quiet, unassuming' personality described above. As J.E. Thomas writes: 'Ramsay expressed all the smouldering anger of the uniformed staff about "class" ....'[29] But Ramsay was at his most 'venomous', according to Thomas, when contrasting the conditions of prisoners with those of prison officers: 'Article after article, cartoon after cartoon, had as their themes the contrast between the increasing freedom of the prisoners and the continued restrictions on the staff – the "Slaves of Siberia".'[30]

While liberal objections might be raised to Ramsay's apparent antipathy to prisoners, his unstinting championship of staff made him 'a folk hero' to early union activists and prison officers in general. Ramsay 'was known throughout the length and breadth of the British Isles wherever Prison Officers congregated over a period of years stretching from 1915 to 1949'.[31] And it was roughly halfway through that period, and due in no small part to his untiring efforts, that those prison officers were able to build an effective, independent Association. The story of that process will now be told in the next chapter.

1

1919–39: THE BLUE GLISS HALL

After 1919 ...

As might have been predicted by the vagueness of the assurances Lloyd George had given the NUPPO committee after the initial 1918 protests, 1919 brought complete betrayal with a Police Act forbidding police officers from joining a union. The government's prime concern was with the police as immediate protectors of property and state power, but 'the Act's fallout involved the prison service ... the Home Office insisted on applying its provisions and restrictions to prison officers', according to an account by the future General Secretary of the Prison Officers' Association[1] (see below).

NUPPO called a strike in response to this betrayal in the August of 1919, but support was badly undermined by 'a mixture of intimidation ... and bribery'.[2] Those who took part were threatened with the sack, while extra rewards were offered to those who 'stayed loyal'. Ultimately, only about 700 London policemen took action, with supporters from Birmingham, Birkenhead and Liverpool subjected to extreme violence and victimisation;[3] of prison officers, about 70 from Wormwood Scrubs and a much smaller number from Birmingham joined the strike. The result was utter defeat. Every prison officer on strike was instantly dismissed, and all attempts to secure their reinstatement over the ensuing years failed. As Thomas writes: 'Their treatment is one of the blackest episodes in English trade union history ....'[4]

After the strike the government set up consultative machinery in the form of the Prison Officers' Representative Board (PORB) as a sop to prison officers' emergent militancy. Unfortunately, as shown below, this body was almost totally ineffectual in addressing their basic concerns. An underlying streak of rebellion, however, continued: in 1920 the *Prison Officers' Magazine* resumed publication under the editorship of the famous 'E.R. Ramsay' and, due partly to the colour of its cover but also almost certainly to its somewhat subversive politics, became universally known as the 'Red-Un'.

As an early symptom of this alleged radicalism, Ramsay had to defend himself frequently against the charge that he had encouraged the Wormwood Scrubs prison officers to join the strike. This 'accusation' was made by officers prominent in NUPPO who were now leaders of the PORB – which organisation Ramsay consistently opposed for its ineffectiveness (see below).

So, as with so many organisations, early relationships within the grouping that would eventually become the POA were by no means harmonious. External relations were little better; the newly-formed Labour Party, itself set up by trade unions in 1906, greatly disappointed prison officers when it became clear that reinstatement of the strikers would not be taken up by the party, a betrayal confirmed when Labour finally gained office in 1924.

As a result, after 1919 'relations with the Labour Party were very frail', according to Thomas, who also draws attention to a break with the Howard League generated by Ramsay's vitriolic attacks on the League and other prison reform groups in the *Prison Officers' Magazine*. Some idea of the official suspicion of the radicalism Ramsay was suspected as sowing can be drawn from Prison Commissioner Ruggles-Brice's description of the ineffectual PORB as 'The Soviet', a wild exaggeration belied by the challenge to the state posed by revolutionary workers' soviets in Russia 15 years earlier. Significantly, in 1922 the *Magazine* opposed the appointment as Prison Commissioner of Sir Alexander Paterson, whose humane approach compared to his aggressive predecessor Ruggles-Brice is said to have signalled a 'golden age of prison reform'.[5]

The Golden Age? Borstal and the Dartmoor Mutiny

Two major episodes in the history of prison management during this period pointed to the growing dominance of 'reform' perspectives: the development of the borstal system in the early 1930s, and the 1932 mutiny at Dartmoor. Both, while largely separate from the processes leading to prison officer trade union organisation, are significant for raising issues of staff–prisoner relations and their impact on the daily lives of prison officers at the time.

While the borstal system had been introduced by the combative Ruggles-Brice in 1921, its management by reform-minded Commissioner Paterson indicated a very different approach to the treatment of young offenders. Paterson had initially indicated, in his first (1922–23) Report,[6] that the objective of such treatment was now 'a system of training such as will fit the prisoner to re-enter the world as a citizen', and borstal was seen as the avenue through which this approach was to be introduced into the prison system generally.

While idealistic, this approach did seem to gain a notable degree of success. Thomas describes 'one of the most remarkable events in penal history' when a group of staff and borstal boys marched in stages from Feltham Borstal in Middlesex to Lowdham Grange in Nottinghamshire, where they set about building an open borstal – the first open prison of any kind in England. Similar marches and activities followed, with staff and borstal inmates jointly building two further open borstals at Boston (North Sea Camp) and Hollesley Bay in Suffolk. Though the experience was arduous and the work extremely hard, these experiments symbolised 'all that was challenging in borstal ... [and] a rejection of the torpor and misery of the treadmill'.[7]

Clearly, the prison officers involved in these innovative events would themselves have experienced something very different from the 'torpor and misery' of much conventional prison life. Paterson's approach, which 'made England a world centre of the prison reform movement',[8] centrally involved prison staff, who were detached for periods of duty to many different countries to spread the word on these innovative policies, and in 1936, courses began to be held in England for overseas prison staff.

The Dartmoor mutiny signalled a very different and much darker side to prison life in the 1930s, and was seen at the time as a major challenge to Paterson's reformative regime. The mutiny, which had been signalled by 'ominous' finds of coshes and hacksaw blades among prisoners, erupted in January 1932 on the prison's parade ground when, after a series of incidents, a 'ringleader' gave his fellow-prisoners the order: 'Draw your sticks.' Staff, heavily outnumbered by prisoners, were unable to control them in the fight that followed, which became extremely dangerous with the prospect of prisoner escapes and the possible 'sacking' of the nearby town. However, police called in by a gate officer helped to prevent any escapes, and staff were able to drive the prisoners back to their cells.

While a subsequent inquiry dismissed suggestions that more 'humane' treatment of prisoners had been a factor in the riot, Thomas argues that reforms introduced into the prison had 'created an inmate community, able to communicate, and thus able to organise'.[9] This came about through the encouragement of association between prisoners. While clearly more humane than the original practice of forbidding prisoners to talk to each other or 'associate' in any way – the traditional pre-reform policy – the loosening of such rules under the Paterson regime is said to have created new sets of problems for both prisoners and prison officers. Thus the origins of the Dartmoor mutiny, according to Thomas, 'lay in the social dynamics which association initiates. New stresses arise among prisoners, and between prisoners and staff, which are difficult to ease in the secure prison. There has to be an outlet ....'[10]

Prison officers of the time would certainly have agreed with this argument and its implied doubts about some aspects of 'reform'. The *Prison Officers' Magazine* of April 1932, discussing the mutiny, brusquely dismissed the 'so-called reformer type, most of whose followers are of the conscientious objector type who sees red in any man in blue whether he is a prison or police officer. Borstalising in prisons will not do.'

Perhaps more importantly, the June issue of the *Magazine* attributed the riot to reduced numbers of staff, for which the Prison Commissioners were held responsible. But the resentment of prison reform and its implications, not only in terms of reduced safety but also what was perceived as the comparative lack of consideration for staff versus inmates, continued to limit prison officers' sympathy for such approaches.

As late as 1938, E.R. Ramsay was drawing attention in the *Magazine* to the interaction between 'reform' and worsening conditions for prison officers:

> An important point seems to be overlooked by the Prison Department and the Home office generally, that with the ever increasing changes incumbent on Prison reform, with a limited staff, the position is more worrying and less secure than it has been for 20 years. Two out of three officers are suffering from 'nerves' – the strain is intense on the officers ....[11]

The Objectionable Bell Scales ...

This resentment of the implications of 'reform' spilled over on to key issues affecting the working lives of prison officers, such as the notorious 'Bell Scales' that regulated prison officers' working hours:

> Through the objectionable Bell Scales involving the split system and irregular meal times, gastric and kindred stomach troubles are common. Matters are rendered worse by a shortage of staff ... *The officers of all ranks have twice as much to do as formerly. The Services are not as mechanical as they used to be.* As far as a layman can, the officers have to be psychologists; they must be able to understand the men in their care ....[12]

Describing the impact on staff, Ramsay wrote in April 1938 that:

> These scales are causing seething discontent throughout the Service. We spoke to an officer recently after he had finished his evening tour of duty. He did not answer, but simply undid his tunic. From the top of his shoulders to the waist his underclothes were wringing wet. We call upon the Secretary of State to abandon this method of slavery, or employ sufficient staff to allow that each officer has the time in which to do one job and not, as at present, try to cope with four or five in the time that it takes to do the one job correctly ....[13]

A letter to the same year's *Prison Officers' Magazine* underlined the point:

> How often have we heard the Prison Service spoken of as 'second to none' – words which are in effect 'sounding brass and tinkling cymbals' when we remember the Bell-Scale that destroys the body and soul of [staff]. It is a monstrosity to see day by day the hurry and scurry of this hounded element of humanity ... plodding along for a period spread over fourteen hours a day ....[14]

The treatment of night patrol officers, a group which continually suffered inferior terms and conditions within the service until their abolition decades later, was also cited as evidence of the allegedly greater sympathy shown for the needs of prisoners than for those of prison staff:

> The position of night patrols is positively disgusting; just imagine these officers having to work ten hours per shift in the half-dark and dreary prison halls of this country. The pay is also disgusting. The most amazing fact is that the people who defend this form of mental slavery ... do about six hours themselves, and then under better conditions.[15]

As shown in the introduction, prison officers' resentment against the sympathy extended to prisoners, given the poor quality of their own conditions, was a longstanding grievance, and this now merged with generally oppositional attitudes among much of the working class in the tumultuous post-First World War period. As Thomas puts it:

> The warders, like other working class groups at the time, were becoming increasingly impatient of the equation of ability with 'class'. They had a long history of being regarded as inferior, and their status and prospects had suffered because of the assumption that men of their 'class' could not be relied upon to take on responsible jobs ....[16]

The recent abolition of direct entry to the governor grades sharpened this understandable resentment, which had always simmered below the surface. In article after article, Ramsay criticised the contrast between the increasing 'reformative' freedoms afforded to prisoners and the continued restrictions on staff, receiving wholehearted support from his readers. In 1924 Ramsay resigned from the Howard League because 'reform had been too one-sided'. Yet, while understandable, the breach with the Howard League and other prison reform organisations, left officers with very little contact with any influential organisation. The loss of contact with respected public bodies, accentuated by the breach with the Labour Party, meant that for the next 20 years or so, until the formation of the POA in 1939, the relatively ineffective PORB was the only official channel of communication between prison officers and government bodies like the Prison Commission.

'The Board ... is a Washout'

Given the evidence, it seems that E.R. Ramsay was justified in his consistent attacks on this purely 'representative' rather than negotiating body. Ramsay argued that prison staff were 'indifferent' to the Board and that it was 'too closely identified with the commissioners', this being 'inevitable' because the PORB officials were all prison officers and 'had to consider their future in the service'. The PORB had no full-time official.

While the Board may be seen to have had one notable success in securing the agreement of the Prison Commissioners to the abolition of the hated term 'warder' and substitution of 'Officer' in 1922, little else can be said in its favour. Although, the following year, the PORB tried to challenge the conclusions of the 1923 Stanhope Report, which had argued that 'the present rates of pay of the subordinate ranks ... are generally adequate', its inability to intervene to any effect simply further 'damaged [its] image as a negotiating body'.[17] The Report had galvanised the PORB, which condemned it as a 'farce', yet the Treasury in its turn attacked the Board for 'bringing pressure when it had no case'.

In general, the Board proved powerless to gain even minor concessions from an arrogant and unsympathetic Prison Commission. The Minute Book kept between 1926 and 1935 by PORB Representative Officer W.W. Waldron demonstrates a callous disregard for even the most humble and reasonable requests. For example, at a meeting in February 1928 it was minuted that 'we respectfully ask that the Commissioners attention be drawn to the recent retirements of the Swansea staff and Officers that have not been awarded the Imperial Service Medal possibly this has been overlooked'. In answer they were informed 'that these cases were not overlooked. It is not all Officers with 25 years or more service to whom it is possible to award the I.S. Medal and the Comms. regret that they were unable to recommend the Officers referred to for this distinction.'

Arguments on more everyday issues like the administration of the 'Bell Scales' and staffing were treated just as brusquely. In June 1927, officers carried a resolution 'That the prisoners be allowed 20 minutes' exercise before breakfast ... and to be given 40 minutes' after dinner ... At present: it is all hustle and bustle and the time allowed is not sufficient for Officers to perform their duties with satisfaction and go to breakfast at Bell Scale.' The unsympathetic response was that 'This is a step in the wrong direction. It is against the speeding up and efficiency of the establishment ... I think the time is sufficient and everyone lives in these days by hustle as you call it.'[18]

There was no shortage of anger and resentment among prison officers over pay and conditions; a Minute from July 1928 documents:

> the following resolution to be forwarded to Chairman of P.O.R.B. re pay question: That this meeting of the Swansea staffs are profoundly disturbed at the low salary of all Prison Officers. To maintain their position and give them a decent existence. This cannot be too strongly emphasised. We ask that immediate attention should be given to the promise made in 1920 [the year the PORB was established].[19]

But the appeal was in vain, as were others on staffing. To a resolution that 'The Commissioners be asked to increase the staff to its former strength ie two additional officers who were taken from us. Prop. Morgan, Sec. Quelch', the abrupt reply was 'The Commissioners will not consider this.'

The utter futility of 'representation' through the PORB is reflected in accounts of the growth of prison officer organisation in Northern Ireland, at Belfast and other prisons and 'youth training schools' in the province. After the instigation of the Ulster regime in 1922, 'a similar set-up' to the PORB 'was imposed on prison staffs in the six counties'. Yet here, too,

> Positive (or successful) representations were virtually unknown, not surprisingly so in view of the fact that there was no avenue of appeal available ... In these circumstances it was inevitable that the unfairness of the [PORB] system and the frustration against the injustices which it threw up should create a feeling of bitterness amongst the staffs of all penal establishments in the Northern Ireland Prison Service.[20]

As late as 1938, feelings about the 'washout' of PORB representation continued to run high, as a letter from one 'Z.Z.' to the *Prison Officers' Magazine* demonstrates:

> Sir, I'd like to tell the subscribers to the good old magazine, Mr Ramsay, what the fellows at my prison said about the last P.O.R.B. Minutes, but I daren't, for your magazine is for the expression of restrained thoughts, and I am certain that you would not publish them! But I'll tell you this: the Board, as a workable medium, is a washout. Please help us to get a meeting with some neutral people so that we can get our complaints, apart from pay, etc, looked into.[21]

The problems were not necessarily attributable to the prison officer representatives themselves. As Ramsay commented much later: 'In spite of much hard work put in by the representatives of the Board System, it is too isolated to deliver valuable goods ....'[22]

While prison officers today may sometimes feel equal resentment and frustration at the shortage of sympathy emanating from official quarters, a crucial difference is clear in these accounts – that the PORB lacked the essential element of independence from management, and ability to apply sanctions, characteristic of even the most moderate forms of trade unionism.

It was this need for accessibility to those in power, along with 'neutrality' and independence in negotiating, that was noted by a young prison officer who was to become the first General Secretary of the POA less than ten years later.

Had the Tolpuddle Martyrs Won their Fight?

When Harley Cronin first joined the Prison Service in 1927, conditions were 'very different' from those of 1967, when his memoir was published. 'The prison officer fought his battles alone ... Not even in the army ... when discipline was pretty strict, were the cards anything like so unfairly stacked against other ranks vis-à-vis commissioned officers as they were in my early days ... between the prison officer and his superiors.'[23]

Nevertheless, Cronin relates how, behind the scenes, 'the old Police and Prison Officers' Union ... had been growing in strength'. This was 'despite a persecution of its members ... which made one wonder whether the Tolpuddle Martyrs had ... won their fight. The slightest slip up ... by any prison officer who was a union member and he was out.' Dues had to be collected by hiding them under an approved religious periodical called the 'On and Off', shorthand for its official title *On and Off Duty*: 'The collector would place [a copy] before each union member ... The member would hand over the price of the periodical, one penny, but beneath the penny there would nestle, concealed, a two-shilling piece, his monthly union subscription!'

Interestingly for students of trade union democracy, during this period the union official's routine complaint of 'membership apathy' was not to be heard: 'There were no lukewarm or apathetic members in a union which operated in these conditions ... An inactive member of the old Police and Prison Officers' Union was as improbable as a phoney Christian in the period when adherents of that faith ran the daily risk of being fed to the lions ....'[24]

Cronin himself first began to find his trade union feet when he was transferred from what was then the relatively repressive Horfield Prison in Bristol to London's Wormwood Scrubs, notable for the participation and subsequent victimisation of its officers in the 1919 strike and also for its more progressive and 'reha-bilitative' regime under the influence of Sir Alexander Paterson (see above). Cronin, more sympathetic to this approach than many other prison officers, describes 'the Scrubs' as a 'Laboratory of Reform'.

It was here that the future General Secretary first began to 'find [himself] in the company of others ... with similar ideas'. What most infuriated the embryo trade unionists thus gathered was 'the utter futility of the Representative Board system', allied to the fact that, alone among the civil servants with whom they were classed, prison officers were not only banned from joining a union but denied even the right to arbitration.

The powerlessness of the Board system is conveyed vividly in words which echo the sad frustration of the Minutes cited above: 'It was so impossible ... to get a fair hearing ... with all the effective power vested in the nominees of the Prison Commission, that the majority of officers looked upon the Board and all its works as a grim joke.' In this context, suggestions that representation on the Board could or should be a channel for change were 'received with ... apathy, when not jeered at'. If a proposal made to the Board by prison officers' representatives was not immediately dismissed by their 'betters', it had to go to the Prison Commission itself for consideration, a process which would take at least six months; on its final return to the Board, that body would take another six months to agree on and draft its response. 'And so on, ad infinitum, or until the almost inevitable final ukase was received: "The Commissioners regret ...." And that was that. There was no appeal. No arbitration.'[25]

In the meantime, circumstances were not improving for prison officers. Rates of pay, already 'scandalously' low, had remained static with the implementation of a policy of so-called 'equality of sacrifice', introduced in 1931 by Ramsay MacDonald's National Government, which took the shape of a 10 per cent pay cut in the wages and salaries of all civil servants. Thus, while Cronin had earned £3 2s 6d a week when taken on as a prison officer in 1927, weekly pay packets in 1936 ranged from £2 10s 6d to £3 10s.

The appalling level of prison officers' pay, and the apparent inability of the PORB to do very much about it, is emphasised by the ever-vigilant E.R. Ramsay in a later edition of the *Prison*

Officers' Magazine. Since the late 1920s the Board had 'passed 26 resolutions requesting a radical improvement in pay'. Nothing worth mentioning had been achieved, as Ramsay made clear: 'We will not mention that contemptible "improvement" of the pay scales in connection with the "consolidation" of January, 1936, in which some officers got a few coppers.' In a foreshadowing of the complexities of some of today's bureaucratic efforts, this scheme 'took several foolscaps of type to explain and … was the best cross-word puzzle of the type we have encountered for over 20 years'. What it did not achieve, evidently, was a living wage increase for prison officers. Even by April 1938, 'There is not one new candidate who would tolerate the poor pay and conditions any longer than he or she was obliged; if he (or she) saw a better job, he would get out, as many have done and as many are contemplating.'[26]

By 1936, however, the beginnings of change were in sight. It was in this year that Harley Cronin was elected as representative to the Central Board of the PORB. This met twice a year in London and considered resolutions and issues raised by the four 'prison districts': North, East, Midlands and South. It was perhaps appropriate that the Wormwood Scrubs officers, motivated by the fact that 'I had been shooting my mouth off … for years', should elect Cronin to this more influential body on the grounds that, in his words '"All right, if he's so clever, let's see what he can do about it."'[27]

Cronin's participation in his first meeting as Central Board representative clearly did have an unprecedented impact. His account of the occasion deserves reproducing in full:

> After the reading of the previous minutes, and after we'd listened to a whole stack of regrets by the Prison Commission that nothing could be done about most of the matters raised therein, my opportunity came. I rose to my feet and proposed that application be made for a substantial increase in what I made no bones about describing as our disgraceful rates of pay.
>
> I was heard in dead … silence. When I sat down the chairman favoured me with an icy stare. He doubted, he said, whether this was either the time

or the place to raise a matter of this kind. It was, in any case, quite out of the question [due to] the country's current economic difficulties ....

[The Chairman] concluded his remarks, and turned to the Secretary to know the next business ... 'Mr Chairman, sir,' I appealed to him, and got on my feet again.

The prison officers present ... looked at me as if they thought I'd gone mad. The official members of the Board stared straight ahead, as if they feared ... to witness my humiliation. Or maybe they were just plain embarrassed by what, in a session of the Central Board, almost amounted to an ugly scene ....

'Mr Chairman,' I said, 'the rules of good debate allow the proposer of a motion the right of reply.' And without pausing I told the Board what I thought of the Chairman's ruling ... By the Police Act of 1919, I said, prison officers had been quite illegally ... banned from the normal union activity which was permitted to every other civil servant ... 'Officers', I said, 'had been fobbed off for too many years with the sort of reply which the Chairman had given.'

I sat down. There was a long silence which ... you could have cut with a knife ... I think my colleagues around the table half expected see me [struck] dead at any moment, for this defiance of the Chairman's divine right to say when the last word had been spoken ....

... 'Blimey!' said one of the prison officer representatives, when the door had closed behind us, 'You'll be for it!' Some of them obviously thought I'd ... made matters worse ....

I was unrepentant. 'Somebody's got to start something sometime', I told them. 'Why not now?'[28]

As Cronin himself notes, his spectacular challenge to protocol did nothing to make him popular with existing Board representatives, who almost by definition were a cautious and conservative group. Fortunately, the reign of the incumbent officers did not last long. At about the time Cronin was elected in 1936, a 'clean sweep' brought a new group into office who, like Cronin, were tired of the Board's 'flabby acquiescence' and determined to make a stand. Backed by this more radical tendency, Cronin was elected as Assistant Secretary of the PORB Staff Side.

Brown and White

As with most pioneering efforts to establish effective trade union organisation, campaigning and strategic planning took place both on and off 'the job'. Cronin relates how:

> One of those who canvassed for me most enthusiastically was a tough young officer called Rickard (inevitably 'Tex'). We began to meet frequently, over a few drinks and otherwise, to discuss ways and means of beating down the barriers that stood between us and a fair deal. 'If only', we used to say to each other, 'we had leaders to fight for us of the calibre of Bill Brown and Len White of the Civil Service Clerical Association ....'[29]

The leading role of these two formidable activists, prominent within Civil Service trade unionism for their abilities as negotiators and representatives on arbitration boards, cannot be excluded from any account of the origins and subsequent development of the Prison Officers' Association. Clearly, their reputation went before them within trade union circles in the Civil Service and beyond. As Cronin recounts:

> One evening in the winter of 1936 Tex Rickard turned up at the officers' club in Wormwood Scrubs ... obviously very excited about something. 'Great news!' he whispered to me ... I telephoned Len White of the C.S.C.A. He wants to see you.' Great news indeed. The Civil Service Clerical Association was among the strongest and most influential of the unions representing government employees. If we could get the backing of its brilliant leadership – if we could get Brown and White in our corner – brother ... we were on our way!
>
> Rickard and I met Len White the following evening in the Horse and Groom, a Belgravia pub near C.S.C.A. headquarters. Later we were to meet his redoubtable chief, Bill Brown. It was the beginning of an entertaining as well as, for prison officers, a profitable acquaintanceship.[30]

Under the aegis of Brown and White, a strategy emerged of which the crucial component was the demand for access to independent arbitration. A series of secret meetings were held, from which emerged the first effective challenge to the dictatorial methods of the authorities that had confronted them for nearly twenty years.

From today's persepctive, that challenge seems harmless enough. It was no more than demands to the then Home Secretary, Sir Samual Hoare, that prison officers should have the right to appeal to an Independent Arbitration Board against the authorities' refusal to improve the officers' intolerably bad conditions, and that officers be assisted in the presentation of their case by persons not in the employment or under the control of the authorities. This demand proved to be very well-timed.

'The Freedom to Manoeuvre towards a Trade Union'

By January 1938, it seemed that what E.R. Ramsay describes as 'the concession to go to arbitration which should have been conceded 10 years ago' had at last been won. What was more, members of the PORB were themselves, by now, more than ready for a fight. As Ramsay reported in that month's issue of the *Prison Officers' Magazine*: 'We are quite sure now, after years of real bitterness on the vexed pay question, that the Department realise that something will have to be done; hence the recourse to arbitration. Long, long overdue!' Progress was hastened by the fact that the Home Secretary, proclaiming his 'strong desire to improve prisoners' conditions', was currently on the point of introducing a Criminal Justice Bill which would grant prisoners increased privileges and rights. It was suggested to him by Brown and White that some of his reforming 'zeal' in the interests of prisoners could be directed towards improving the conditions of 'the men and women on whom the very difficult daily task of administering the prisons fell'.

As the indefatigable Ramsay put it:

> Much has been said, and promised, with reference to the ardent desire to penetrate the core of contributory causes of crime and the application of … treatment towards its perpetrators. Nothing has been said, attempted or even hinted at, regarding the conditions of those operatives utilised by the State in its application of those 'Humane methods'.[31]

A defeated Home Secretary conceded the argument, 'and so was gained the freedom to manoeuvre towards a union'.

Given the championing of their cause by Civil Service Clerical Association leaders Brown and White, the most appropriate body to provide independent arbitration on prison officers' demands and grievances would clearly be the Civil Service Arbitration Tribunal (CSAT). As Cronin records the process: 'First, we had to win access to the Arbitration Tribunal, and then, in snaky and underhand fashion, [win] permission to have outside assistance in presenting our case. Only when both objectives had been conceded by the Home Office did we, so to speak, tear off the false whiskers of our outside assistants and disclose them to be Bill Brown and Len White!'[32] And it was Brown and White, also, who used their undoubted eloquence to conclusively wrest from Hoare the right for prison officers to process their claims through the CSAT.

The Blue Gliss Hall

To celebrate, a meeting was held on 5 April 1938 in the Blue Gliss Hall, Acton, an occasion which, for POA historians, 'will always stand out as one of the highlights in this struggle. Men and women came from all the prisons in London ... colleagues were present in force from Broadmoor. The enthusiasm born of new hope was tremendous. Officers who had suffered intolerable conditions for many years knew that at long last changes were being made.'[33]

The May 1938 issue of the *Prison Officers' Magazine* records in detail Brown's speech to the mass meeting. Headed 'Officers' Mass Meeting: Enthusiasm at Blue Gliss Hall!', the transcript reads:

> You are starting at the beginning of the equivalent of the post-war phase of the Civil Service, that is, you are now beginning to win those rights and privileges which we won towards the beginning of the post-war phase but which are only now becoming available to you. I think that the worst part of your struggles is over ....
>
> There is no doubt that the right to arbitration has been won in the past few months, and the right to be represented outside the Service ... we have got the right to appeal to an independent body and we are going to get a substantial increase for the Service ....

> We have in the Civil Service a grade known as Record Keepers. Their job is to look after records and files. They work in no smell [unlike 'the very smell of the prison itself', to which Brown had referred earlier]. There is plenty of fresh air, and they get 84s. a week. The prison officer gets from 50s. to 70s. a week for looking after prisoners, for filing also, and he does this work in a prison cell ....

Brown continued on the vexed question of (lack of) promotion for prison officers:

> Ninety-three per cent of you do not get promoted because when you are young there are no vacancies, and when there are, you are too old ... Having satisfied [a number of] tests, the seven per cent who get promoted will then pass through to a higher scale of pay from 72s. 6d. by 2s. 6d., rising to 85s. a week. I believe you get a bit of gold braid, but you can't eat that ....

It was hardly surprising that this champion of the underdog was cheered to the rafters, along with his colleague L.C. White, by prison officers ecstatic at finally facing the prospect of effective, independent trade unionism.

In May 1938, a claim for improved pay was presented to an independent arbitration board, argued by Brown and White on the first occasion in their long history as advisors to prison officer representatives processing such demands. The claim was opposed by the Chairman of the Prison Commission at this hearing, but he faced unprecedented opposition: 'The court was crowded by staff from establishments all over the country, enthused by the new situation in which their rights could be publicly demanded, and those who were denying those rights [were] compelled in public to justify their actions.'[34]

Perhaps as a result, on 1 June 1938 – 'the next red letter day in the developments' – the Arbitration Tribunal announced an award amounting to a 10 per cent increase. The minimum of the Prison Officer pay scale (50 shillings) was increased by five shillings a week, and the minimum of the Chief Officer pay scale (110 shillings) by 15 shillings a week, and there were increases in allowances.

The *Magazine* trumpeted in response:

> It is a distinct victory … It goes to show what can be done by sticking at it in spite of set-backs … It also shows what can be done by solidarity – the uniting of all forces for progress.
>
> Whilst it is not all for which we have fought, the Award is very acceptable to the whole staffs … Like Bill Brown, we are not satisfied. The award is accepted as a first stage – a stepping stone to better things ....[35]

As the editorial suggested, even this partial victory, like many such stepping-stones to effective organisation, 'led to staff adopting an even firmer resolve to have the right to association granted them'. Prison officers across the service would be swept up in the impending change: 'We have no doubt that the Broadmoor … and Scottish prison staffs will ultimately benefit, and we hope our comrades in Northern Ireland will also have their scales assimilated with the new scales awarded by the Arbitration Board for England and Wales.'[36]

'The Good Ship "Real Representation" …'

According to the *Magazine*, at the next (July) meeting of the Prison Commissioners, a resolution was to be put requesting the withdrawal of Standing Order No. 805, introduced in 1906 (see introduction) to allow prison staff, 'with the sanction of the Governor', to 'meet and discuss among themselves questions relating to their duties and position in the Prison Service'. Withdrawal of the Standing Order would 'permit the P.O.R.B. to be assisted in negotiating by persons not employed by the Prison Service' – a crucial alteration allowing Civil Service Clerical Association (CSCA) officials Brown and White to play a full part in negotiations.

Although the Home Secretary, Winston Churchill, was asked in 1911 to modify the Standing Order to give, he refused – an act of obstinacy which was said to have provoked the formation of the underground Prison Officers' Federation. But in this sense, as Ramsay's editorial argued, the prison officers' barrier to trade union membership appeared to have been imposed by an administrative decision of the Home Office and not, as was the case for the police, by an Act of Parliament – a crucially important difference which, much later, was recognised by the Home Office as part of its eventual, reluctant acceptance of the right of prison officers to independent organisation (see below).

In the midst of these conflicting and confusing circumstances, the PORB now recommended in a resolution that it 'should not be compelled to continue to function in circumstances which are definitely unfavourable' to representing prison staff. Such circumstances included 'lack of knowledge of changes in the conditions of Civil Servants', and the fact that 'up to now the P.O.R.B. has not been permitted in negotiations to be assisted by those knowledgeable of Civil Service matters'. The resolution was based on the argument that issues for negotiation could in principle be referred to the Civil Service Arbitration Tribunal (CSAT) and that all negotiations should now be based on full knowledge of 'outside Civil service conditions'.[37]

Coming from the hitherto moderate and undemanding PORB, this comes across as a considerably more assertive claim on the part of prison officers to be allowed to participate in some kind of trade union-related bargaining structure, even with the kind of limited remit permitted to civil servants at the time. The intention of the resolution is clearly towards gaining more independent negotiating rights than the PORB had until then possessed.

Indeed, this was confirmed in the editorial of the August edition of the *Prison Officers' Magazine* for that year. Under the heading 'Board Matters', E.R. Ramsay wrote: 'The good ship "Real Representation" has at last been launched, and will be setting out on its maiden voyage in the next few months ....' Reporting on the most recent PORB meeting, he continued: 'The Board Meeting was an outstanding one for the Service representatives. First we had the advice ... of an outside advocate ... Secondly, we were offered the right to have the Service "case" presented to the Commission by [Brown and White] ....'

In the same issue of the *Magazine*, an article by W.J. Brown himself pledged to win even greater gains than those of the recent arbitration award, and elaborated the other, equally pressing concerns and injustices under which prison officers had laboured for so long. In 'The Award – and After', he proclaimed:

> Let no one ... imagine that we shall be content with the revised scales. They are as much as we can get for the moment – but only for the moment ... As soon as circumstances permit we shall return to the attack with a view to securing a further bettering of ... pay ....
>
> Meantime, we are turning our hands to other aspects of prison conditions which require amendment no less than rates of pay.
>
> In the first place there is the question of hours of labour. A 96 hour fortnight exclusive of meal times is far too long – even when the arrangement of the hours is regular day by day. With the additional strain of irregular shifts due to the Bell Scales, a 96 hour fortnight is still more wrong ... We are claiming a 44 hour inclusive week ....[38]

Expressing an awareness in advance of his time for today's 'work–life balance' approach, Brown went on to say:

> Strictly speaking, there is no 'hours problem' in the Prison Service. What there is is a 'staffing problem'. Given enough staff, working upon a reasonable shift system, I see no reason why the domestic and social life of the prison officer need be mutilated in the way that it is at the present time. Hours could be regular each day ... And given the necessary money and staff, there is no reason why the prison officers should not be able to lead a regular life – instead of being 'battledored and shuttlecocked' about as they are now.

Of course, this raised the question, as always, as to how willing the authorities would be to provide the 'necessary money and staff'. Brown's scepticism on the issue of resources and Home Office priorities was expressed with his usual dry humour:

> Of course, this would mean a big increase in staff, and increases in staff cost money ... But then the Prison Service will have to get used to the fact that in future they will have to spend more money on the Prison Staffs. Lots of money! Doubtless they will get used to this idea in time, even if they need a little education at first ....

Going on to the equally vexed question of 'allowances ... first [their] amount ... and second [their] pensionability', Brown listed the various different types of allowances then received by prison officers, including 'instructional', 'rent' and 'inconvenience', among many others. Comparing the Prison Service to the Civil Service, 'where the allowance is so regular that ... it becomes part of the officer's normal emolument [and] is counted as pay for pension purposes', he pointed out that while there were Prison Officers who had been drawing allowances for up to 20 years before their retirement, 'not a penny is allowed to count towards superannuation assessment. That is highly ridiculous, and it must not continue.'

Next in Brown's tireless list of lost causes, soon to be 'found' for prison officers under his energetic leadership, were annual leave and the still more deeply-felt issue of promotion (or the lack of it):

> It is bad enough that many of the staff should be unable to take their leave in the summer months – but that may be inevitable in such a service. But what is not at all inevitable is that the amount of annual leave should be so restricted ...
>
> Then there is the group of problems that are associated with 'promotion' ....

But he concluded on a highly optimistic note:

> Here are some ... of the issues which we shall try to deal with ... facilitated by the new right which has been won since the Arbitration Award ... the right of the P.O.R.B. to be assisted by outside 'counsel' – not only in Arbitration proceedings when negotiations have failed but *during* the negotiations between the P.O.R.B. and the Prison Commissioners ....

This would mean that 'hereafter Prison Staffs will not be placed at a disadvantage by comparison with Civil Servants elsewhere in the matter of negotiations with their employers'.

And indeed, by September 1938 it could be reported (by L.C. White) that 'Progress Continues'. The Arbitration Award had now been extended to Scottish prison staffs and to Broadmoor (prison staff from Northern Ireland were fully integrated into the system by 1939 – see below). As White wrote in the *Prison Officers' Magazine*, since the award had been granted, along with 'the agreement of the Home Office to a continuation of the arrangement under which Mr Brown and I are available to assist Prison Officers in negotiation and arbitration ... essential preliminary steps have been taken towards remedying certain of the more serious grievances'.[39]

For example, the PORB had now raised with the Prison Commissioners the question of hours and pensionability of allowances. Yet, while White emphasised that 'A very important principle ... has now been established. If the question of pay can be referred to arbitration then so also can the matters of allowances and general conditions of service', the PORB was still a long way from being a truly representative body. White mentions the persistent lack of consultation of the PORB over building new prisons as 'merely one example of the distance we have to travel before we are able to say, in the Prison Service, that we have achieved a representative position equal to that prevailing elsewhere'. In order to achieve this position, White urged his troops, it was 'essential that the P.O.R.B.s ... be given whole-hearted support', such as had been given during the weeks preceding the arbitration case.

Charabancs Fighting through the Fog ...

By October, the *Prison Officers' Magazine* could refer to 'the near future when the New Association comes into being'. Ramsay predicted that 'This Association will be run on constitutional lines, like any other Civil Service Association ....'[40] In the same issue, L.C. White wrote of still 'Further Progress' for the Board in the direction of independent unionism, as already practiced within the Civil Service. He announced a new agreement whereby the PORB could now seek outside help – for example, legal counsel – in any matters affecting conditions of service, and compared this to the longstanding 'Whitley' system already existing within the Civil Service and many other areas of the public sector. Within this system employees were represented by a 'Staff Side' which regularly met employers represented by the 'Official Side' in order to discuss and negotiate terms and conditions of employment.[41]

White was now able to argue that 'This new arrangement will place the P.O.R.B. in a position somewhat similar to that of departmental Whitley Committees within the Civil Service ... The official side of the Whitley Council (which is another name for the Treasury) has made an agreement with the Staff Side which ... as far as the Prison Service is concerned over-rides any antiquated dictum of 30 years ago' – a clear reference to the Standing Order of 1906 which, as shown above, forbade prison officers from combining or negotiating in any way over pay or other conditions affecting them at work.

The PORB Sub-Committee itself, in a Report included in the *Magazine*, underlined the growing pace of the movement towards independent organisation:

> During the coming months it is hoped that it will be possible to arrange another Mass Meeting of the Prison Staffs. The interest shown in the last one was such that the sub-committee felt that it was their duty to propose this course. At the last meeting nearly 600 persons were present, but we hope that 1,000 will not be too high to aim at this time ... These meetings will do much to foster, strengthen and maintain the present unity shown by almost the whole of the subordinate staff.[42]

As the Northern Ireland POA history points out, by this point 'Arbitration had been finally conceded, a pay claim had been prepared and was largely successful ....' Given these concessions, now:

> the Treasury thinking appeared to be 'If the prisons' staffs are to be enabled to go to the Arbitration Tribunal let them go at their own expense, not through the P.O.R.B. for which we (the Treasury) have to pay.' This [thinking] provided an opportunity too good to miss, meetings were organised and decisions were taken to try to form a completely independent organisation to represent prison officers.[43]

Perhaps as a result of this logic, but undoubtedly also through the newly-strengthened activism of prison officers ably assisted by their remarkable Civil Service allies, truly decisive change was now on the agenda. On 25 October 1938, once again at the Blue

Gliss Hall, 'an enthusiastic mass meeting was held to launch the final push … towards a Prison Officers Association'.[44]

A vivid description of this historic meeting is provided in a letter to the *Magazine* on 'The New Movement' from the PORB Sub-Committee. Headed 'Charabancs Fighting Through the Fog to Reach London', it reports:

> The meeting at the Blue Gliss Hall on October 25th was well attended in spite of the dense fog that hung over West London. Several charabancs could not travel … others had to turn back. About 600 men and women put in an appearance. The enthusiasm was remarkable … A fine meeting; and were it not for the fog we doubt if the hall would have held all who intended coming ….[45]

'Now or Never …'

By November 1938, a *Prison Officers' Magazine* editorial could confidently claim that 'Very soon a proper association will be formed on normal Trade Union lines, like the associations in the Civil Service generally.' Not only matters of pay, but 'the questions of hours, including the objectionable Bell Scales, which make the hours of duty so irksome and impossible, overtime and leave' were already being considered: 'We will not make too much comment on these matters as they are being dealt with, as will be noted.'

In the same issue, an article by W.J. Brown focused on the negotiating machinery which would now be necessary. Interestingly, this did not yet mention the possibility of an independent prison officers' union:

> During the period since the Arbitration Tribunal's Award on Wage Scales, we have been negotiating with the Prison Commissioners as to the form which negotiating machinery should take in the future. It is plain that some machinery is necessary which will operate much more quickly than half-yearly meetings of the P.O.R.B. … Accordingly, it has been agreed between us and the Commissioners … that there should in future be a small negotiating body representing the prison staffs, consisting of myself and [White] plus the officers of the P.O.R.B. … This … would have the right of discussing staff issues with the Commissioners at any time. Its

conclusions would be reported to the P.O.R.B., with whom the final word
... would rest.

The negotiation and arbitration machinery of the Prison Service will
then ... be as good as that obtaining in the Public Service as a whole: and
more than that we cannot ask.[46]

Yet at the same time, a letter in the same issue of the *Magazine*
vociferously championed prison officers' actions in asking for
rather more. Under the heading 'Hell Scales', an 'Open Letter'
described the level of organising activity, mentioning for what
appears to be the first time a future POA:

Several local meetings have taken place, and we recently had the privilege
of attending one at a large London prison ... A large gathering was present.
They were quite prepared to go to any lengths to support and help in the
formation of a strong and vigorous Prison Officers' Association ... There was
an almost complete absence of trivialities which have been so prevalent
in past P.O.R.B. history.

Looking back to the events leading up to this historic series of
events, the letter continued:

We shall not forget the scene of enthusiasm at the Board meeting when
contact with Mr. Brown and Mr. White was announced. That enthusiasm
was communicated to the Service, and culminated in the pay award. We ask
you not to forget that the result was only made possible by a unity never
before experienced in the history of the Prison Service.

The New 'Association of Prison Officers'

By December 1938, it could be claimed by a *Prison Officers'
Magazine* editorial that

Over 90 per cent of the staffs in England and Wales have intimated their
willingness and readiness to support the New Association ...We urge the
Officers to back the New Movement which will be worked on constitutional lines.

IF YOU HAVE NOT PUT YOUR NAME ON THE LIST OF NEW MEMBERS ASK YOUR
REPRESENTATIVE TO DO SO AT ONCE.

> The great opportunity is with us now. We respectfully and earnestly
> appeal to you to
> GRASP THE OPPORTUNITY NOW
> – Now or Never.

In the same issue, an article headed 'Progress' reported that 'over 2,000 officers of all ranks have intimated their intention of supporting the new "Association of Prison Officers"'. Not surprisingly, the writer claimed that 'This augurs well for the ultimate success of the enterprise ....'

However, the article went on to raise the important issue of funding the new organisation:

> In the matter of the amount of ... contributions ... to the new Association,
> some are agreed in principle, but say the amount is too much! Can this
> really be so? Would it be fair and consistent with our claims of 'under-
> payment' in the Arbitration Court recently, if we said that those charged
> with the Management of the Association should never receive any reward
> for their services?

As the argument continued:

> Even when all these matters have been considered, this does not entirely
> exhaust the necessity of establishing a sum of money over and above the
> 'bare necessities' margin ... Therefore, brother and sister officers, you are
> asked to fully consider these matters of general welfare, and ... put aside
> any prejudices that you may have and register your support at once for the
> new Association, remembering always, that 'Unity is strength.'

The call was clearly answered. By 1939, in the words of the Northern Ireland POA history, 'the "Prison Officers' Association" was in full swing, branches were formed in every penal establishment, the Treasury issued a "Certificate of Approval" (necessary under the provisions of the 1927 Act), rates of subscriptions were fixed (and approved at the First Annual Conference in 1940)'.[47]

The Primary Object ...?

The full story of the final establishment of the POA will be told in the next chapter. In the meantime, it is worth examining the reactions of 'the enemy' as revealed in Home Office correspondence, between November 1938 and March 1939, on what was clearly turning into an independent association for prison officers.

The first of these letters, dated 16 November 1938, is from W.H. Waddams of the Prison Commission, and suggests rather misleadingly that 'the proposed Association would not be an organisation of which the primary object was to influence or affect the remuneration and conditions of its members, but merely a business Association for the purposes indicated in its Constitution'.

If this was not the case – that is, if the Association was a genuine union – it would be 'necessary to obtain Treasury authority for the recognition of the Association under Section 5 of the Trades Disputes Act 1927'. Waddams sought advice on whether the proposed Association 'falls within Section 5 of the Act, and, if not, whether the Commissioners can deal with the request without submitting the matter formally to the Treasury'.

This initially rather misleading view of the Association had been obtained through a letter from L.C. White, 'who, with the Commissioners' authority, advises the Prison Officers' Representative Board (P.O.R.B) on matters of general Service interest'. White's letter, dated 15 November, had stated that 'the purpose of the Association [was] to collect and disperse funds in connection with (i) the Prison Officers' Magazine, and (ii) the arrangements which the Commissioners have agreed for negotiation and arbitration on questions affecting the conditions of service of the Discipline Staffs'.

In the case of 'an ordinary Civil Service organisation' (that is, union or staff association) no difficulty would arise with this because 'officers are appointed to run this side of the organisation'. But the position of the PORB 'is somewhat different and does not permit of this sort of machinery'. White therefore requests 'some special arrangement', that is, that 'Stewards' be authorised to deduct the subscription to the new Association 'from the wages of those Prison Officers who so desire'.

Even this mild request created suspicions in the minds of the Home Office. On 23 November, Waddams wrote to another official, a Mr R.J.P. Harvey:

> The question of whether this new 'Association' falls within Section 5 of the Trades Disputes Act 1927 is for you, but it seems to me that if one of its objects is the collection of funds for financing negotiations and related activities of the P.O.R.B. (including presumably the conduct of claims before Arbitration Tribunals), there is very little to distinguish it from an ordinary Staff Association.

Harvey comments: 'I rather agree, but we shd. have the views of the Registrar of Friendly Societies. I have written to Mr Roberts.' However, 'As regards the proposal that subscriptions should be collected by means of deductions from salaries and wages, even subject to the Association meeting the cost ... [this] is open to many objections and I think we must refuse at once.' His suspicions confirmed, Waddams replied: 'I quite agree ... My impression is that this is a manoeuvre on the part of Mr White to get the principle established that Staff association subscriptions may be collected in this way.'

On 28 November, Harvey wrote to F.W. Roberts at the Registry of Friendly Societies, enclosing a copy of Waddams' letter of the 16th and explaining that 'The point at issue is whether the Prison Officers' Association, if it is to function, ought to be approved under the Civil Service (Approved Association) Regulations, 1927.' Up to the present time, he informed Roberts, the PORB had been the 'organisation which has represented the views of the staff'. Although 'the new Prison Officers' Association' was 'apparently a business association for the purpose of collecting funds for the activities of the P.O.R.B.', Harvey was cautious: 'It may well be that, as the result of the formation of the new Association, the Board will be more active than it has been in the past.' Then came the crunch: 'My personal view is that as the main purpose of the new association is the collecting of funds for "staff side" purposes, the distinction between the new association and a staff association is pretty thin, and I am inclined to think that the Association ought to apply to you for recognition under the 1927 Regulations.'

On 6 December, Roberts replied: 'I surmise that the primary objective of the P.O.R.B may be to influence remuneration etc', a judgement which seemed to indicate that even the humble PORB might be classed as a trade union. However, 'The provisions of the [Trades Disputes] Act are not applicable to it [because] it is merely a body of representatives ... and not an Association ... which would require approval under the [Act's] Regulations.' On the other hand, 'If this is correct, it seems that the proposed Prison Officers' Association would not materially alter the situation ....' Roberts, however, was not taken in by this: 'But financing is hardly an object in itself ... On the information before me, therefore, I am inclined to think that the Association ought to apply for approval.'

On 8 December, Harvey notes: 'The correspondence (Mr Fox's letter of 18.10.27) supports that Prison Officers may not (as a condition of their employment) belong to any Union or Association –. If that is still the position it is a question whether the Prison Commission should allow the Association to be formed at all ....' On the same date, he wrote to Waddams, arguing that:

> It seems to us that the proposed Association, in conjunction with the P.O.R.B., virtually constitutes a Staff Association of the normal type ... [Its] primary object would clearly be to affect the remuneration and conditions of employment of its members.
>
> The first question which occurs to us is whether its formation would not be a departure from the conditions hitherto laid down for the representation of the prison staff. Is it not the case ... that it is a condition of a prison officer's appointment that he should not become a member of any Union or Federation?

On a request by the CSCA leaders, Brown and White, that payment of subscriptions should be by deductions from salaries, he writes: 'I really doubt whether the C.S.C.A. intended that their request should be taken seriously. It seems very odd that they should expect the administration to go out of its way to assist an Association which in all probability will indulge in activities designed not to foster the smooth working of the administrative machine!'

In January 1939, much the same response was made to prison officers organising in Scotland. Waddams wrote to a T.M. Walker, possibly his Scottish counterpart, regarding the proposed Scottish Prison Officers' Association:

> I agree with Harvey that the proposed Association ... virtually constitutes a Staff association of the normal type ...
>
> The request for the official collection of subscriptions ... is a striking example of seeking the best of both worlds and its refusal does not, I think, call for any apologetic remark ....

However, his next comments do appear to lend weight to the notion that following the crucial concession on arbitration the Prison Service was becoming resigned to the idea of independent organisation: 'It appears that we have now reached a stage when the prison officers are to have the advantages of trade union organisation ... it is for consideration whether at this stage a frank recognition of a prison officers' Association within the Whitley Council orbit and consequentially the abolition of the board with its special privileges would not be the straightforward course.'

On 20 January 1939, Harvey reported on a meeting of the Prison Commissioners at the Home Office which had considered the position of prison staff 'as affected by the suggestion that a new Prison Officers' Association should be formed'. The conclusion appears to have been that 'there would be no objection to the introduction of the ordinary Whitley machinery' – bringing prison officers in line with standard Civil Service union representation – 'if the Home Office were satisfied that the change would not have any awkward repercussions on the Police Service'. The resistance appeared to be melting!

However, it remained as strong as ever to any sign that organisation was spreading. As a confidential note puts it:

> A proposal has been made by the Broadmoor staff that an Association should be formed on the same lines as the new Prison Officers' Association ... The new regime is not functioning fully at the moment and the Board of Control were rather anxious that Broadmoor should be kept out of any changes which might be agreed for the Prison Service ....[48]

As a 'Note' of the Conference held at the Home Office on 18 January 1939 put it, perhaps in explanation of the apparent change of heart regarding the POA, the promise originally granted to prison officers in 1919 that if they accepted the PORB system 'they would be allowed to bring any dispute as to conditions of service before the Civil Service Arbitration Board ... seems to have been overlooked'. This important admission, one apparently never made before, is offered here as an explanation of why 'the Home Office for some time took the view that Prison Officers were not entitled to take their claims to a Tribunal' – a position unchanged, as we have seen, until very recently.

The Note goes on:

> Last year, however, this view was modified and officers were given access to a Tribunal and, since they alleged they would be prejudiced in presenting their claims by their ignorance of conditions elsewhere in the Civil Service, they were allowed to have the assistance of Mr W.J. Brown and Mr L.C. White ... Subsequently it was agreed that they might continue to have the help of these two gentlemen ... in their negotiations with the Prison Commissioners on any matter on which their knowledge ... might be of value.[49]

Now that prison officers were 'seeking to obtain the advantages of a Trade Union organisation in addition to the privileges of the Board system', the Note goes on, 'In that event there would be no reason for the continuance of the Board system.' And this arrangement, it was now felt, would have positive merits; for example, 'the advantage that the distinction between Prison Officers and Police would be quite clear cut. Prison officers would be treated as civil servants, and the Police could be told if they asked for similar treatment that it could not be granted, since they were not civil servants and were subject to the restrictions of the Police Act, 1919.' So police officers' loss was prison officers' gain – though whether this was ever communicated to the police service is not recorded.

Further items within the correspondence deal with the extension of 'Whitley arrangements' to Broadmoor. A letter to Miss Curtis at the end of March 1939 notes that there had been 'some objections' to this, but 'It is clearly impossible to attempt to exclude Broadmoor from operation of the Home office proposals.' From April to September 1939, the correspondence confines itself to letters concerning the final arrangements for the introduction of 'Whitleyism' into the Prison Service.

These developments are reflected in exultant editorials within the *Prison Officers' Magazine* (now no longer 'published under private auspices' but 'acquire[d] as the official and authoritative organ' of the rapidly strengthening PORB). In its April 1939 editorial, the *Magazine* asked 'Is it Good-bye to the PORB?', and replied to its own question:

> There is every reason to believe that before long the Prison Officers' Representative Board will be no more ... Staffs in the prisons of Britain ... may regain the liberties of which they were deprived after the Police Strike of 1919. The Government may decide to return to those Services the right to form a Staff Association ....

A separate article in the same issue, headed 'The New Association', confirmed that 'the authorities are considering abolishing the Prison Officers' Representative Board. Discipline Staffs of the Service would then be given the same freedom to organise themselves in a Staff Association as has always been enjoyed by other sections of the Civil Service ....'

The article went on to set out the new arrangements, including branch committees in each establishment, 'some form of district machinery', and 'a National Executive Committee responsible among other things for negotiating with the Prison Commissioners'. As indicated in the Home Office correspondence, Whitley Machinery was also being set up. As the writer pointed out, 'The setting up of a Staff Association for Prison and Allied grades' would bring about a much closer connection with the National Whitley Council and thus Brown and White, who regularly sat as members on the Council.

These new negotiating structures would mean that:

> We should [now] achieve a position of freedom which has been denied to us for nearly twenty years. We should have broken with the weak tradition

> created by the Representative Board system of working ... We should go
> forward in an organisation that belonged to the members ....

The triumphant tone continued. By May, W.J. Brown could announce 'Freedom at Last':

> Wednesday, the 5th of April, 1939, should be treasured as a historic date
> in the long history of the Prison Service ... On that day the right of Prison
> Officers to have a Union of their own, democratically elected and controlled
> ... was won.[50]

It seemed that the Prison Commissioners had resigned themselves to the inevitable. And indeed, on 25 September 1939, the 'inevitable' took place.

As the October 1939 *Prison Officers' Magazine* announced on its front page, the Prison Officers' Association had been granted 'Official Approval by H.M. Government'. The Certificate of Approval issued under the 1927 Trades Disputes Act, itself depicted in the *Magazine*, was signed by 'Two of the Lords' Commissioners of His Majesty's Treasury', and was 'Granted this 25th day of September, nineteen hundred and thirty-nine.'

Interestingly, given its importance and the long period of preparation and argument running from May 1938, when prison officers took their first steps towards independent representation at the Arbitration Tribunal, the actual 'birth' of the POA almost 18 months later has received relatively little attention. Perhaps this was due to the almost simultaneous outbreak of the Second World War (see next chapter). But, in any event, the October 1939 issue of the *Magazine* carried a modest, but unmistakeably confident, advertisement:

> One stick can be easily broken.
> Several sticks are hard to break.
> *1 Prison Officer alone can't do much.*
> *3,500 Prison Officers acting together can do a lot.*

> JOIN THE 3,500 IN THE POA

Although its wording raised uncomfortable echoes of the 'bundle of sticks' image adopted by the Fascist ideology only too current in the period, the logic of the appeal clearly pointed in an entirely different direction – that of the unity, collectivism and solidarity which lies at the heart of all forms of trade union organisation.

2

1939–79: 'THE ORGANISATION WE HAVE CREATED ...'

'The Organisation We Have Created ...'

Set in motion by a strike at the end of the First World War, and finally recognised on the outbreak of the Second, the fortunes of the newly-born Prison Officers' Association mirrored the tempestuousness of both conflicts. As the *Prison Officers' Magazine* put it, 'On 13th and 14th May, 1941 ... just after the Battle of Britain had been fought, another – less important but nevertheless very significant – battle was brought to a successful conclusion.'[1] It was on those two days that the first meeting of the Prison Department Whitley Council was held at the wartime headquarters of the Prison Commission:

> The occasion was historic, for it heralded a new era of staff representation for Prison Officers, with the recently created Prison Officers' Association forming the Staff Side of the Council ... Thus ended the long years of futility and frustration under the aegis of the old Prison Officers' Representative Board, the 'House Union' which had provided the only possible method of expression for prison staffs during the period between the two world wars.[2]

May 1941? Surely the history of the POA goes back almost two years earlier, to the first major breach with the PORB in May 1939 and official government recognition of the POA as an independent trade union that September. However, the history of prison staffs' attempts to rally around their cause has always, it seems, been beset with delays and official indifference; and so it was even after the POA came into being. At this point, the authorities had the 'excuse' of the war to justify their snail-like pace in responding to the Association's demands. As Harley Cronin and 'Messrs Brown and White' wrote in the October 1939 edition of the *Magazine*:

> The outbreak of war makes it necessary that an authoritative statement should be issued to all members ... to assist them in understanding the effect of this unfortunate catastrophe upon their official position ....
>
> [We need] ... to impress upon all members ... the need for maintaining, and indeed strengthening, the organisation during the difficult period which confronts us. War conditions will create numerous problems ....

Such problems, including increases in the cost of living, extra duties and possible evacuation, were likely to create 'a state of affairs in which the machinery of the organisation we have created will have to work at full pressure'.

The statement made a plea for maintaining the precious gains made so far by the new Association:

> In the months preceding the outbreak of war, many important victories were won, and we were rapidly advancing to a new and better condition of affairs for [prison staff]. It would be an act of major stupidity if the occasion of a war to protect ... democratic rights ... were permitted to deprive us of what we have gained, or to obstruct us in ... further progress ....

In part this anxiety was related to the small number of prison officers who were still undermining the Association's aim of 100 per cent membership. The letters columns of the *Magazine* were full of complaints against such 'free riders', resented for receiving the benefits conferred by the new Association while refusing to contribute to it financially or organisationally. One member at Rampton special hospital put the point succinctly in poetic form:

> Some of the Staff showed unrest in their job
> They gathered together and formed quite a mob,
> They uttered their grievances and remedies to seek
> By the aid of three pennies, per person, per week ....
>
> ... But the POA has come on the job,
> For each calendar month we pay out two 'bob' ....

… We don't wish for anyone to lose his fair job,
But think of the help that is promised with our two 'bob.'

That 'something for nothing' has been their craze
But we look with a smile on their magic ways,
If they had foresight they'd join in our mob
And get better pay by the aid of 'two bob.'[3]

The 'Bolsheviks' of the POA …

'Free riders' or none, however, there were other forces working
against the union during this early period; and these, predictably,
stemmed from the powers-that-be. Some of the frustrations that
the would-be organisers experienced are summarised vividly in
correspondence from the Northern Ireland section of the POA.
After staff at Belfast Prison had voted to join the POA in 1939,
as General Secretary-to-be Fred Castell wrote, 'Liaison was being
maintained between myself … and Harley Cronin in London …
[whose] guidance and support was invaluable … more especially
as the hierarchy were making it quite plain that my "bolshevik"
activities were not particularly welcomed ….'[4]

The POA was successfully set up in Northern Ireland, with
about 97 per cent of staff in membership. However, Castell
continued to suffer harassment: 'I was told on one occasion … that
because of a certain article I had written for the Prison Officers'
Magazine … I was to be transferred to Armagh prison. A couple
of days later … I was told that the transfer … was "off" because
the Governor at Armagh (one Colonel Booth) would not accept
"that bloody Bolshevik" on his staff ….'

'Bolshevik' or no, the early activities of the Association were
opposed as strenuously as if its members had indeed belonged
to that openly revolutionary tendency, though less through
open warfare than in the form of endless procrastination and
bureaucratic requirements from the Northern Ireland Registrar
of Friendly Societies. Castell wrote to L.C. White as late as 31
July 1940,

to ask you if something cannot be done to expedite the issue of the above Certificate. We realise, of course, that there is a war on [but] it is very annoying to us to receive word from time to time of what the Association is doing for the benefit of its members in England and Scotland ... and know it doesn't refer to us – we still have to carry on in the old P.O.R.B. way ....

White replied, no doubt understating the issue, that 'we are finding some little difficulty with [the Certification Officer] who seems to be putting as many difficulties as he can in the way of issuing the certificate of approval'.[5]

We can only assume that the niceties were finally addressed by the ever-patient Castell and White, since the Northern Ireland POA was obviously 'in business' by the autumn of 1941. However, more broadly, confidential Home Office correspondence reveals continued hostility towards the Association, and particularly towards their most articulate supporters, Brown and White.

'Eliminating' Brown and White?

Home Office Minutes from November 1941, for example, note regretfully that 'there has been no improvement in the methods adopted by Brown and White'. One Home Office official remarks that

The P.O.A. have again been indulging in publicity of an objectionable type ... From the point of view of maintaining a proper discipline and sense of responsibility among Prison Officers, I believe that the influence of Brown and White has been wholly mischievous ... I am quite sure that our relations with the Staff would be much happier, and that Staff interests would not suffer, if Brown and White could be eliminated from our discussions ....

But Brown and White were far from being 'eliminated'. Throughout this early period, they fought stoically for improvements in the lot of prison officers despite the difficult wartime conditions. Barely had the Association been formed, for example, when Minutes from a meeting with the Home Office held on 9 October 1939 document that 'In view of the conditions prevailing during the [wartime blackout] ... Mr Brown suggested that the Bell Scale should be revised so as to provide for ... the main activities of the prison to be confined between the hours of 7 a.m. and 5 p.m.'

During the same meeting, 'Considerable discussion took place on the treatment of disciplinary questions', presaging the changes described below. More dramatically, 'Mr Brown represented that there was a serious state of unrest at many prisons ... It appeared that [they] have received numbers of prisoners from London prisons, and there was a tendency [for] these prisoners to [form] gangs.' Clearly as part of these developments, officers were being injured on duty: 'Mr Brown drew attention to the case of [a prison officer] who was assaulted at Feltham Borstal ....' Yet the Home Office was stony-faced: 'It was explained to him that as the officer had exhausted his sick leave, he could only be paid under the Workmen's Compensation Acts. Mr Brown protested at this, but it was pointed out that the Commissioners could only act under Treasury regulations, and that the matter was not one for departmental discretion.'

Later that week, during an extended discussion on the treatment of disciplinary questions, it was noted that 'Prison Commissioners were anxious, if possible, to avoid any ... discussion between Messrs Brown and White and Prison Governors on disciplinary cases.' The government officials discussed the possibility of extending existing discipline clauses 'so as to make clear the generally recognised fact that Whitley Councils are entitled to discuss general principles in disciplinary matters but are not entitled to discuss the merits of individual cases'. The purpose here was clearly to forestall the right to represent individual officers at tribunal, which Brown and White were rightly anxious to pursue, and which they won in 1943 (see below).

In late December 1939, C.D. Robinson of the Prison Commission wrote to Brown on the crucial question of representation of officers on disciplinary cases, repeating earlier refusals to allow the discussion of individual cases at Whitley Council meetings: 'In the Prison service where officers are specially liable to disciplinary reports, an impossible situation might arise if the merits of every such case were open to discussion.' And Brown and White were subtly, but categorically, excluded from representing such officers: 'in selecting a friend or colleague to [represent him or her] an officer is limited to a colleague in the Service'.

On 10 January 1940, Brown replied eloquently on that point and others:

> As regards ... the right of the Prison Officer to be represented by a friend or representative who may be an Association representative – I hope you will agree to the standard formula. [T]here is a very real fear of victimisation in the Prison Service, and ... so long as it exists the right referred to is regarded by the men as very important ....

While he was unlikely to be called on in this respect 'unless things were very badly agley, and I can't imagine myself going unless they were', the right was 'regarded as a very important stand by in cases where the Local Representative fears victimisation, and I hope you will agree to the standard phrase being used'.

Yet, despite Brown's moderate approach, wrath against himself and White continued unabated. In February 1940, a letter from one Kerswell at the Home Office confirmed his earlier view that 'there would be no harm in letting Prison officers form a Prison Officers' Association', but added: 'Unfortunately Brown and White have used and are using their position in a manner which is inconsistent with the maintenance of proper discipline. Brown in particular [is] stirring up an undisciplined spirit among prison officers ....'

The sins for which Brown was taken to task included his 'agitation for a large increase in the Prison staff'. Spelling out the current situation in which, 'while a large staff has to be on duty from unlocking time in the morning till [lockup] between 4 and 5 in the evening, there is a comparatively small staff on duty in the evenings ... [therefore] officers have to work long hours on one day and short hours on another day', Kerswell protested against Brown's demand for an increase in staff to enable them to work straight shifts: 'Apart from other considerations it is of course impossible to comply with this demand at present because the man power is not available.' Attempts by both Brown and Harley Cronin to get the issue of understaffing, with its attendant dangers of prisoners getting 'out of hand' taken up in the press, were condemned as 'a breach of a prison rule which prevents a serving officer from making public any information'. Despite this, 'Cronin, inspired by Brown, insists that he must have a right to present [information] to the Press and ... public.'

Puffed up with indignation, Kerswell trumpeted:

> As far as I can see there is no effective cure for this situation except either to abolish the Association or to threaten to abolish it and return to the Representative Organisation ... The first question is therefore ... what would be the formal steps necessary for this purpose?

Fortunately for the POA, other officials were more circumspect. His correspondent replied:

> I do not know how you abolish an Association ... you can refuse to recognise it, and possibly prevent people from joining it ... My immediate reactions are that although the conduct of Messrs Brown and White is discreditable any attempt to abolish the Assn. would be swamped by the cry of victimisation.

The debate continued, with much regret apparent between the lines at the various concessions which had enabled the Association to come into being, but, as one contribution put it:

> Any of these decisions can be reversed. The Association could be suppressed simply by restoring the old rule that Prison Officers, like Police, mustn't join an Assn ... even if this Association continues to exist, with a certificate of approval, the Dept can always refuse to treat with it ... [But] this of course would cause a great rumpus. Abolition of arbitration and Whitleyism would also cause a great rumpus, and isn't really what's wanted.

The threat of 'rumpus', as always and as with any other organisation of workers, constituted the new Association's strength. Thus, as one comment put it: 'abolish[ing] the Association ... would cause such an uproar that it should be contemplated only as a last resort'. A still more notable comment comes in handwritten and highly compressed notes from one Miss Curtis: 'You will notice that the case for suppression of the Assn ... bears a striking resemblance to the case for suppression of the Daily

Worker [the Communist Party's daily paper] ....' While difficult to interpret, the general sense of these notes is clear – that of the highly subversive implications of organisation and action between prison officers, particularly in wartime.

Given these dangers, correspondents confined themselves to possible threats to Brown and White: 'The best hope ... seems to be severance of their connection with the Association', but this, too, was seen as unrealistic: 'I agree generally, but I am not sure we can debag Messrs Brown and White.' In pursuit of such debagging, a letter in March 1941 asks for 'concrete examples' of 'offending articles' by Brown 'or any member of the prison service' in the *Prison Officers' Magazine*, 'and any written record of the trouble you have had with Cronin'.

The following month, in a letter to Clement Attlee who was now the Prime Minister, another Home Office official wrote: 'the effect of Brown's influence and methods of agitation has been to impair the spirit of co-operation which had previously existed between the superior officers of the Service and the staff and to introduce a serious risk that the discipline which is vitally important in ... the Prison Service may be undermined'.

The matter was duly discussed by government worthies including Attlee, Home Secretary Herbert Morrison and none other than Aneurin Bevan in April 1941. Minutes of the discussion concluded:

> It is clear that Mr W.J. Brown and Mr L.C. White are making themselves a nuisance to the Prison Commission, who are admittedly infants in arms when it comes to discussion with Mr Brown.
>
> ... On the other hand, there was no very specific accusation which could be brought against him.

Continued complaints about 'Messrs Brown and White' recurred in correspondence and Minutes regarding the establishment of the Association in Scotland. Home Office correspondence on the issue notes that 'Now Messrs Brown and White are turning their eyes towards the Scottish Prison Officers Departmental Whitley Council', and any notion that their 'special position' could be replicated in Scotland was sternly resisted: 'I can see no reason why the Scottish Home Department should give these two gentlemen any more rope for making mischief in the Scottish Prisons Service than they already possess.'

Finally, however, a letter from W. Wilson of the Home Office to Miss Hackett of the Treasury on 15 December 1943 officially conceded defeat. Regarding 'the attendance, as advisors, of Messrs W.J. Brown and L.C. White on the Prison Department Whitley Council ... I am ... enclosing a copy of the Prison Commissioner's letter of the 6th December, from which you will see that the Commissioners are prepared to acquiesce for the present, on the understanding that its exceptional character is recognised ....' The magnitude of the concession can be judged from the fact that only a week earlier, Harley Cronin, POA General Secretary, had received a letter from Waddams of the Prison Commission categorically stating that 'the Commissioners reaffirm ... their view that the present arrangement is extra-constitutional'.

The 'Officer's Friend'

In addition to these constant battles with the authorities, the war years saw extra strains on Prison Service staff. As J.E. Thomas relates: 'The effect of the emergency on the prison service was disastrous.'[6] Prisons had to deal with new problems such as 'London recidivists' – prisoners evacuated when the London jails closed down for the Blitz – and imprisoned conscientious objectors whose behaviour was notoriously 'difficult'. Harley Cronin's memoirs give some flavour to the account of these years:

> Prisoners in London jails ... were evacuated to prisons in the provinces. Exeter and Bristol got the hard cases from Wandsworth and Pentonville ... They were the big-time boys from the Smoke who would show the country bumpkins, staff and prisoners, a thing or two. They refused to obey orders, staged riots and strikes ....[7]

Prison staff, though greatly reduced in numbers by conscription to the armed forces, were forced to cope with these problems at the same time as enduring wartime ordeals such as heavy bombing raids. Prisoner reforms introduced by the Prison Commission added to the strain. In 1942 the ban on talking during exercise was lifted, and some privileges were allowed at an earlier stage of sentences. While seemingly trivial, these concessions were given at a time when the staff situation was becoming desperate; even the Prison Commission feared that there might be a 'serious breakdown of the machine'. The autumn of 1945 'saw the staffing position reach its nadir'.[8] As an indication of the Commission's concern, its Report for 1945 devoted four and a half pages to staff matters, the first time for many years that they had been discussed at such length.

In April 1945, as the war drew closer to its end, the POA had raised the question of the low salaries proposed for new entrants to the service, most of whom would be returning from the conflict:

> These recruits would in normal times be young men of 20, but in view of the undertaking which had been given by the Government to accept ex-Servicemen for the majority of vacancies in Government Departments after the war, it was quite clear that for a long time to come candidates would be from 25-30 ages on joining, and many of them would be married men with children, for whom the proposed rates of pay would be quite inadequate.[9]

Representatives from the Whitley Council Official Side at first expressed the hope that a special concession would be made; however, the next month's Minutes record the Official Side insisting that 'the pay position of older ex-Service men and women ... must wait for the promulgation of Treasury policy with regard to the Civil Service generally'.[10]

Such problems, in addition to the constant stalling of the authorities in dealing with the POA, must have taken a severe toll on the energies of the Association's early supporters; yet progress was made in these years. A POA *Short History*[11] reports that 'Between 1939 and 1945 the Association was able to obtain precisely the same Cost of Living bonuses as were granted to Civil Servants elsewhere. These bonuses were, in 1946, consolidated into basic pay ....' And, in 1943, the much-contested right of representation of individual officers faced with disciplinary action was introduced in a new Discipline Code.

As the *Short History* confirms:

> Efforts to amend the disciplinary procedure in the Service [had been] frustrated with all the vigour that the Official Side could command ... Prior to 1943, there were no set rules governing the conditions under which officers charged with disciplinary offences could defend themselves ... very frequently, the wording of the charge was chosen to 'colour' the case against ... The officer saw no statement except the bare charge until he was actually being adjudicated upon.

By contrast, now 'The draft of the new Code allowed a serving officer at any establishment to act as a "friend" to an officer accused of a serious offence.'[12] This was a significant step forward, although the right of POA full-timers to undertake such defences was not granted until 1952.

For this and other reasons, during the war years 'the scope and work of the Association ... tremendously increased'.[13] Part of this was related to the increase in the prison population. Whereas during the 1914–18 war the number of prisoners had gone down, alleviating the situation created by the call-up of prison staff, during the Second World War the average prison population increased due to longer sentences. Adding to the problems of the Association was its falling income, attributed in the *Prison Officers' Magazine* to 'The reduced subscriptions from Forces members and temporary officers, and the diminishing number of established staff.' Although 'it was felt that there was no immediate need for anxiety ... The Secretary was directed to contact all branches with a view to bringing all the forces ex-members back into the Association.'[14] The accumulation of work which resulted from all these pressures meant that in 1943 'it was necessary to appoint a full-time General Secretary to carry on the day-to-day duties'.[15] That General Secretary was, of course, Harley Cronin, who was to remain at the head of the Association for the next 18 years.[16]

In the early 1950s, membership of the POA could still cause prison officers difficulties. As one activist recalled: '[My father] arrived at the Scrubs '52–53. The POA had only been in existence 13 years. It was never something you mentioned, it was all secret ....'[17] Yet from that time on, progress for the POA in terms of membership, growth and influence continued almost uninterrupted. By 1960, membership numbered 7,838 – 'about 98% of the potential', according to the POA Annual Report; and in 1964 the Association could claim 'some 9,000 members in the uniformed grades ... virtually 100 per cent'.[18] In 1959, the POA began work on transferring its headquarters, previously housed in cramped offices near Holloway and Pentonville, to its current, much more spacious head office in Edmonton. The 1960 Annual Report noted that 'The Association now has a Headquarters' building of which it can be proud and the centralisation of the office accommodation has made for more efficient administration of the Association's affairs.'

By 1963, the Association was beginning to reach out to the wider trade union movement. An article in the May issue of the *Prison Officers' Magazine*, headed 'What is the TUC?', noted that 'In the last hundred and fifty years there has gradually grown up in Britain an increasingly strong and effective trade union movement ....' While at this stage the Association made no direct recommendation to affiliate to the Trades Union Congress, the 1966 POA Conference eventually agreed to affiliation, despite some rumblings from members as to the over-'political' nature of the TUC.

Much sadder events befell the Association in those years, with the deaths of W.J. Brown in 1960 and of E.R. Ramsay the following year. The 1960 Report mourned 'The late W.J. Brown', its stalwart friend: 'On the 4th October, W.J. Brown passed from this earth ... Throughout the whole of his life [he] moved from one controversy to another but he was ever prepared to do battle for the "under-dog" ....' And as an Appreciation in the May 1961 *Prison Officers' Magazine* reminisced: '"E.R. Ramsay" ... was known throughout the length and breadth of the British Isles wherever Prison Officers congregated over a period of years stretching from 1915 to 1949.'

'Trouble and Concern ... '

The wartime period also saw a significant extension of the POA's jurisdiction with the setting up of Whitley Machinery for Broadmoor and the other special hospitals. Just as with the more mainstream Prison Service, the redoubtable Brown and White were persistent in pressing for their right to represent special hospital prison staff, initially at Broadmoor.

Whitley Committee Minutes from late 1942 demonstrate that this battle was in fact won relatively quickly. While in late October the Home Office was still insisting that only POA members could represent the Association, as early as mid November a letter to White informed him that although 'you do not fall within that description', he would be permitted to attend Broadmoor Whitley Council meetings as an adviser. While the letter added that 'This concession should be regarded as personal to yourself', White, ever loyal to his colleague, replied: 'This is all right so far as it goes – but what about W.J.B.?' He was duly informed that 'With reference to your note of the 13th instant ... It is agreed that the same concession should be extended to W.J. Brown.'

Once thus conceded to, Brown, White and Cronin lost no time in moving to improve the conditions of Broadmoor staff. On 4 March 1943, at the first meeting of Broadmoor Asylum Departmental Whitley Council, White 'asked that the four days' extra annual leave enjoyed by the Prison Service should be made applicable to the Broadmoor staffs and that ... time off in lieu should be given [for Bank/Public holiday working] or overtime payment made, as in the Prison Service'.

'The Official Side Agreed to this Request ...'

Further meetings demonstrated the increasing confidence of the Staff Side in raising a widening range of issues. In mid December they argued that 'a complete revision of the allowances paid to the Attendant Instructors might be made ... Further, that an avenue of promotion might be created ....' It was also reported that 'The Female Staff wish to register a protest against a recent order regulating the wearing and the period of wear of uniform before it is washed ....'[19]

During the war, the situation of these part-prison, part-hospitals was further complicated in that their daily administration was transferred to the Ministry of Health (later the National Health Service). As Cronin records in his usual acerbic tones: 'The sort of thinking which, in my view, produced the present flaws in the Broadmoor system, goes back to 1938. In a Criminal Justice Bill then proposed the plan was to shift control of Broadmoor from the Home Office to the Ministry of Health ....' Broadmoor, set up in 1863 as an alternative to prison or 'ordinary asylums' for the criminally insane, is characterised by Cronin as 'an establishment ... rivalled only by Dartmoor in the trouble and concern which its organisation and methods have caused to the Prison Officers Association'. Nevertheless, Cronin, his bark worse than his bite, was clearly supportive of the aims of special hospitals. The problem with transferring control to the Ministry of Health was that 'the measure, and the thinking behind it, [might] blur the very real distinction between Broadmoor and an ordinary lunatic asylum'.[20]

In fact, the 1938 bill was postponed 'owing to the international crisis which led to the outbreak of war', and the change of control to the Ministry of Health was not introduced until 1949 (see below), as part of the recommendations of the 1941 Rushcliffe Committee, which drew up agreed salary scales for State Registered Nurses in England and Wales which for many years were used as the basis of pay awards for prison officers in the special hospitals. A Minute from the Whitley Council for 22 January 1946 expressed the POA's concerns over the relatively low rates of these 'Rushcliffe scales' with submissions from Staff Side, noting that 'Ex-Service men and women ... recruited to the permanent staff ... should commence at a much higher rate of salary than stated in the Rushcliffe Report.' In August that year, when the 'proposed revised Rushcliffe scales' were 'to be applied to the Broadmoor side, Mr White ... criticised the date of operation and the method of application in giving only half of the difference in the initial stage ... further, the Staff were not as well off as they would have been with Civil Service bonus ....'

Interestingly, the (predictable) refusal of the Official Side to reconsider the application of the Rushcliffe scales to Broadmoor staff was in part justified by 'the policy of H.M. Government as outlined in the White Paper on Personal Incomes Costs and Prices [which means] it is not possible at the present time to agree to salary increases'. As had happened under the National Government of the 1930s under the Labour Party's Ramsay MacDonald, as was to happen so much in subsequent decades, and as was now happening under the postwar Labour government of which many had hoped for so much, the fortunes of prison officers, like those of working people in general, were being held back not only by their immediate employers but also by their overall paymasters – the government.

Threeing Up ...

By this time, of course, the war was long over. As the Birmingham POA branch had announced in the 'News and Jottings' of the *Prison Officers' Magazine* for July 1945, 'Now that hostilities in Europe have ceased we are hoping to see the early return of our brother officers from the Forces. In the meantime, our best wishes to them all ....' Children of prison staff at Borstal celebrated with the rest: 'Our children had their V.E. Day celebrations on 18th May; a huge programme was arranged ... The first item of the day was a fancy dress parade ....'

Not everything about the postwar period, however, was as festive. In 1946, a radical change in the structure of the Prison Commission was announced which added to the creeping bureaucratisation of the Prison Service by introducing civil servants at the highest levels and developing staff hierarchies in the clerical and administrative functions. As a result, 'the prison staff was increasingly fractured into separate compartments with officers categorised as the punitive force within the progressively open conditions of the prisons'.[21]

These 'progressively open conditions' developed during a period when the prison population continued to increase relentlessly: In 1945 the daily average population was 12,910; by 1950 this had risen to 20,474, and '1951 saw the highest numbers of prisoners since just after 1877'.[22] As early as 1949, the contradiction between these pressures and the increasingly reformative policy of the Prison Service had led to a 'mounting crisis' in which 'confusion about the task of the prison service reached its zenith'. This 'task', which was, of course, primarily carried out by prison officers, varied between rehabilitation and control in a continual and confusing manner. The Prison Rules of 1949 set out 'The purposes of ... treatment of convicted prisoners' as 'to establish in them the will to lead a good and useful life on discharge, and to fit them to do so'; yet the courts continued to issue sentences 'which in various ways instructed the staff to secure the prisoners, making no reference to reform'.[23]

Meanwhile, the 'remedies' for overcrowding applied by the Prison Commissioners were hardly calculated to relieve pressure on staff. A major programme of building open and medium-security prisons and borstals was undertaken in line with the 'reformative' approach, and by 1952, 17 such establishments had been opened. However, even this expansion failed to cope with the numbers, and the department introduced 'a new device ... into English prison administration – "threeing up"'.[24] By 1948, an average of 2,000 prisoners were sleeping three to a cell, and by 1958 the numbers of 'three-up' prisoners had risen to 6,000, all of them in local prisons.

Not surprisingly, the number of complaints received from prison officers about the stresses of work was increasing, particularly 'when new duties were thrust upon them in order to still further extend activities for prisoners'.[25] At the November 1960 Whitley Council, the Staff Side argued that 'much greater consideration should be given to the needs of the staff, most of whom were already working excessive hours of overtime'. Meanwhile, a greater crisis was emerging in the form of what was, perhaps predictably, a growing number of prison escapes. Since 1946, the total number of actual and attempted escapes at prisons and borstals had risen steadily from 864 to almost 1,300 in 1958. While the Prison Commissioners tried to argue that 'changes in the method of treatment' of prisoners were not a cause of the increase, 'the Prison Officers' Association was certain of the opposite'.[26]

Clearly, some escapes were more dangerous than others, both to prison staff and to the wider public; for example, the notorious John Straffen, committed to Broadmoor after murdering one child, murdered another when he escaped in 1951. In response to this episode, Cronin writes: 'It is the staff at Broadmoor that incurs the blast of public indignation if there is an escape [yet] ... The opinions of uniformed staff, whose job is security and who have years of experience in enforcing it, are ignored.'[27]

'Psycho-Witch Doctors'

In 1951, an inquiry carried out by the Franklin Committee was prompted almost entirely by the concerns of prison officers, who made serious allegations over the deterioration of discipline since the war. At roughly the same time, the Seventh Report of the Select Committee on Estimates, an ongoing House of Commons budget monitoring body, reported officers' allegations that at Portland borstal 'the boys were in charge' and that 'an appeasement policy' had developed at the institution since the late 1930s. Part of the problem, according to the repressive morality of the period, was the increasing reported incidence of homosexuality: in 1954, eleven borstal boys were sent to prison and two to further borstal training for 'indecent offences' committed at Usk.

Yet it was during this period that many more moves – praiseworthy in principle but difficult in practice – were put in place which leaned still more heavily towards the rehabilitation of prisoners rather than a concern with the responsibilities of staff. These included the increasing proliferation of specialists such as psychiatrists (decried by Cronin as 'psycho-witch doctors'[28]) and the development of the 'Norwich system', named after the prison of that locality, which introduced group psychotherapy into the treatment of prisoners. This system, described in the Prison Commission Report for 1956, was the beginning of a process in which the skills of groupwork and casework developed during the period were increasingly introduced into the Prison Service.

Healthy though these moves were in many ways, they again conflicted with the basic role of the prison officer in terms of discipline and control. The practical implications of the process of reformation increasingly robbed officers of control over inmates, with only too brutal consequences: 'the possibility of being physically assaulted ... would appear [to be] more likely than at any time since 1877'.[29] As a result, the issue of assaults on staff was constantly raised by the POA, whose 1954 Conference passed a number of resolutions urging the Prison Commissioners to do something about increasing violence against staff.

There was a widespread feeling amongst prison officers that prisoners were not punished severely enough for such attacks. As one delegate to the 1958 POA Conference put it, 'In some cases they get awards tantamount to being deprived of their boot-laces for a fortnight.'[30] In addition to the rising incidence of assaults on staff, the period saw an increase in prisoner uprisings – in 1959, prisoners at Cardiff and Birmingham staged sit-down strikes, presaging the serious riots of the later 1960s and 1970s.

The increasingly corrupt and violent behaviour of some prisoners towards others was part of the problem. At Parkhurst, for example, between 400 and 500 men were allowed 'compound association' outside their cells, and a Prison Commission Report admitted that 'this ... association time is used by prisoners for the passing of contraband goods, the indulgence of gambling, and for the various activities of the barons'.[31] Such 'barons' were, at the time, reaching 'the height of [their] power', allowing for the terrorising of weaker prisoners and an increasing normalisation of violence inside prison walls. Thus, ironically, the general loosening of control under the reformative regime had contributed to a 'malign ... [and] elaborate inmate sub-culture'.[32] In response to the domination of the 'barons', the POA, as Cronin recounts, 'had been agitating for years in favour of the segregation of troublemakers in a small prison on their own'.[33]

The Wynn Parry Report – A Move Forward?

In the meantime, however, there had been movement on another issue of major concern to prison officers – their pay. The 1958 Wynn Parry Committee, initially convened in order to consider the vexed questions of promotion and direct entry to governor grades, was also charged with reporting on the pay and conditions of prison officers – an investigation last staged in 1923 with the disastrous Stanhope Report.

As the POA argued in evidence to the Committee: 'Prison officers have had to fight every step of the way for improvements in their conditions ... under the disadvantage that crucial decisions over their conditions are in effect taken by the Treasury, which is remote from their problems, and ... liable to be influenced by political considerations such as the pay pause' (see below).[34]

Perhaps in response to the POA's evidence, paragraph 98 of the Committee's Report made two major recommendations: firstly, that central pay settlements agreed by the national Whitley Council should apply to prison officers and, secondly, that prison officer remuneration should be linked to the movements of pay of civil servants in similar pay ranges. In relation to the status quo, this appeared as a significant step forward. Certainly, the POA reacted positively, commenting in its 1959 *Short History* that 'The difference between the "Stanhope" and "Wynn Parry" Reports is very remarkable ....'

The linkage to Civil Service pay was a particularly welcome aspect of Wynn Parry. In Whitley Committee documents from the mid 1950s, the point is made over and over again that 'there has been no consistent historical relationship with outside [pay] movements'. Nevertheless, as so often, the Wynn Parry Committee appeared slow to make good its promises. As the *Short History* reports, 'The Government of the day did not automatically accept all of the Recommendations, and protracted negotiations took place ... before the great majority of the proposals were put into effect.'[35] In particular, the Association was forced to go to arbitration in 1959 in order to give effect to the recommendation that 'where the pay of civil servants ... is varied by a central pay settlement', prison officers' wages should be 'varied' similarly. The Arbitration Tribunal ruled for the POA, and the 3.5 per cent increase agreed by the national Whitley Council was accordingly applied to prison officers as well as the civil servants covered by the Council.

Despite this, the 1960 POA Annual Report notes that since acceptance of Wynn Parry, 'the Prison Officer class was beginning to lag behind other grades in comparable pay ranges'. The Report also noted a lack of movement in putting into effect new shift patterns relating to the eleven-day fortnight, which had also been recommended by the Committee. At a meeting held at the Prison Commission on 22 July, difficulties mentioned in putting the scheme into effect included in particular those experienced by prisons operating three-shift working. The POA urged local committees 'to draw up their schedules of attendance, get them agreed with their members, and then enter into discussions with their local Official Sides'. Yet the July 1961 issue of the *Prison Officers' Magazine* noted that the 'Wynn Parry recommendation of an 11- rather than 12-day fortnight' had still not been implemented.

Closing the Ranks

As late as December 1962, a letter to the *Prison Officers' Magazine* from Barlinnie Prison in Scotland complained that 'we, like many other establishments in Scotland, are as far away as ever in obtaining that extra day off'. In a reflection of the increasing industrial unrest of the time, the writer added: 'One hears of proposed strike action by the railways, buses, etc., to obtain better conditions. We fully realise we are not able to do likewise, but what is wrong with our Executive Committee that we should be messed about for four years and nothing further gained?'

This letter marks the beginning of an era of greater dissension within the Association which, while clearly troublesome for the leadership, also indicates the greater maturity of an organisation then approaching its quarter-century. In June 1964, the *Prison Officers' Magazine* carried an editorial noting that 'The past twelve months have not altogether demonstrated the desire for unity ... Great things have been achieved ... but there remains a great deal to do and the only way to achieve success is to close the ranks and face the future with a united membership.'

In the same issue, the General Secretary's column addressed the question of Schedules of Attendances which had, as signalled in the letter, caused much of the dissension: 'Nothing has caused more heartburning, dissension and ill-feeling throughout the Service than the almost intractable problem of devising a system ... which would be acceptable to all types of establishments.' Nevertheless, faced with this 'heartburning', the Association was doing what a union should – responding to its membership. In July 1964, the General Secretary's column in the *Prison Officers' Magazine* reported the decision of that year's Conference that the POA should pursue a claim for a working week of 40 hours, with weekend working paid for at overtime rates. And, perhaps in response to these healthy signs of internal democracy, membership was reported to be 'rapidly approaching the 10,000 mark' with more than 100 branches.

In fact, during the intervening years, the Association had continued to press for full implementation of the Wynn Parry proposals. On 18 July 1960, the General Secretary informed the Prison Commission that the POA had 'noted particularly' movements of pay among other 'classes' of Civil Service workers: 'It appears to the Staff that the evidence very fully justifies an enhancement by 10 per cent of the scales laid down by the Wynn Parry Committee ....'[36]

On this basis, the POA put in a claim of 6.5 per cent. However, 'There was a considerable delay before a reply was received', and this eventually consisted of an offer from the Prison Commission of only 3 per cent, while at the same time they proposed to 'discontinue ... free quarters or rent allowances ... and to substitute ... a consolidated pay scale incorporating the value of quarters and rent allowances'. Finally, in December 1960, the POA won 4 per cent as part of the Central Pay Agreement for Civil Service grades.

Yet better news was on the way. Commenting on the Central Pay Settlement and an overarching new agreement on future pay determination on the basis of research, the Whitley Council Bulletin promised that:

> In future there will be controlled use of the Pay Research Unit. Surveys will be … [of] one class every five years … The wages rates index will be the barometer by which we shall judge the … pay levels prevailing in industry. The barometer will be regularly inspected and if in November of any year it has risen by five points or more over the index figure which led to the last Central Pay Settlement … this will be the signal for a Central Pay Review. The operative date for any resulting Central Pay Settlement will be 1st January.[37]

Some of this promise appeared to be realised with the 1960 pay settlement for special hospitals. Staff claims for increased pay, shorter hours and new overtime arrangements were taken before the Civil Service Arbitration Tribunal, where the Staff Side case was 'brilliantly handled' by yet another Civil Service trade union ally of the POA, Charles Smith, whose name was added to those of Brown and White after the retirement of the former and the death of the latter in the 1950s. Perhaps thanks to Smith, the claim was largely upheld; the POA Report commented that 'in some respects, the award represented the first major breakaway from National Health conditions'[38] for special hospitals staff, a much-desired outcome.

'The Pay Pause is Dead …'

Yet in 1961, dissatisfaction with pay was massively increased by the government's 'pay pause' – in reality, freeze – and ban on arbitration. In August 1961, the *Prison Officers' Magazine* reported 'a packed protest meeting … with overflow meetings taking place' at the Central Hall, Westminster. The meeting unanimously passed a motion condemning the government for 'interfering with the system of free wage and salary negotiation … In particular, it objects to the withdrawal from the scope of the Civil Service Arbitration Tribunal.' That October, the *Magazine* reported that 'Many members of the Prison Service have attended the mass demonstrations that have taken place in London.'

In November, the *Magazine* drew attention to the protracted length of the pay pause, creating

> the general impression that the Government is deliberately seeking a showdown with the trades unions ... It looks as though the Government is deliberately fostering a situation in which civil servants must take industrial action in order to secure their just demands ... Prison officers, as civil servants, will be no less affected than their colleagues in other government departments.

In December, a mass meeting was held in the Prison Officers' Club at Pentonville, to protest against the pay pause and 'Government interference in the Civil Service Arbitration Agreement'. Speakers included Harley Cronin.

Perhaps the only good news in that year was the introduction of equal pay for women in the Civil Service, years before the 1970 Equal Pay Act brought it to women workers across the board. As the February 1961 *Prison Officers' Magazine* proudly trumpeted: 'Within the Civil Service, 1st January, 1961, marks the end of an era; the era of unequal pay for women. On that day equal pay for women civil servants will be fully and finally achieved ....' Whether the POA could be so sanguine about the conditions of women prison officers in general is examined more fully in the next chapter.

It was not until April 1962 that the *Magazine* could satirically declare: 'The pay pause is dead – long live the pay pause', and even then, the freeze was replaced by a new phase restricting pay to 'strictly limited increases'. The new policy barred arguments based on cost of living or, as in Wynn Parry, comparability, as the basis for increases. In February 1963, the *Magazine* reported that prison officers had fallen behind overall Civil Service pay rates by more than 2 per cent since the last pay review; the POA was now demanding a 5 per cent increase, to be remitted to the CSAT if the Treasury was unwilling to make an offer.

'The Role of the Modern Prison Officer'

Both before and after these dramatic events, however, disappointment would continually be expressed in the *Prison Officers'*

Magazine and at POA Conferences over the vexed question of direct entry, rather than prison officer promotion, into governor grades. In its evidence to Wynn Parry, the POA had argued that 'The Association has for many years advocated the principle of a unified service, ie one in which recruitment takes place only at the basic Officer level and in which the Governor and Assistant Governor posts are filled exclusively from within the Service.' Yet, while allegedly giving 'considerable attention to the views put forward', the Committee nevertheless concluded that 'at present, at any rate, insufficient suitable candidates are available from officer grades for promotion to the governor grades'.[39]

The POA evidence had also referred to 'a great change in the accepted view of the functions of prison officers', originating with a description of prison officers by the then Home Secretary, J. Chuter Ede, in 1946, as 'masters who will control men by force of personality and leadership, who will by example and influence train them into decent habits of self-control and industry. The ideal prison officer … is an exceptional man ….' By contrast, Wynn Parry's pragmatic advice to the POA to 'take the realistic view of the hard facts' conveyed its largely unsympathetic perception of the average prison officer as little more than the traditional 'turnkey'.

This was unacceptable to the POA. Despite prison staff's resentment at the lack of sympathy for their needs versus those of prisoners, an important area of concern increasingly emphasised by the Association was the actual potential role of staff in the much-vaunted rehabilitation of the prisoner. As J.E. Thomas reports, 'at the same time as [staff] were protesting about the ill effects of reformation, they were demanding that they be involved in it'.[40] For example, in 1957, officers expressed a wish to become involved in group psychotherapy[41] as part of the 'Norwich system' described above.

Some of this concern was expressed in the POA evidence in terms of how standards of education expected of prison officers had deteriorated: 'The present practice of the Prison Commission does not … set a sufficiently high standard of education … The whole approach to educational standards is, in the Association's view, not good enough. The standards now accepted are markedly below prewar ....' In further evidence to a Labour Party inquiry in 1964, the POA again commented on 'the educational standard of recruits to the Service ... the POA views this standard [as] quite inadequate if there is to be an expansion of the constructive role of the officer'.[42] Clearly, the implication was that ill-educated officers were more likely to adopt a repressive and punitive approach towards inmates rather than an emphasis on their rehabilitation through education, again confirming the Association's enlightened attitude to prison reform.

When a 1953 government committee headed by A. Maxwell, a former Prison Commission chair, recommended the establishment of the post of Prison Welfare Officer, prison officers saw the post as one for which they were 'admirably suited',[43] although the committee specifically precluded prison staff from the role. In November 1963, the *Prison Officers' Magazine* argued that welfare officers 'should, in future, come from the ranks of Prison Officers' who had 'obvious, almost overwhelming advantages ... to offer' in the post. But Maxwell and the Advisory Council on the Treatment of Offenders (ACTO) were determined that only 'qualified', 'professional' staff should fill the position, envisaging mainly social work graduates.

In response, the POA published a three-page document on 'The Role of the Modern Prison Officer' which was unanimously adopted at the Association's 1963 Conference. As well as setting out the monotonous nature of a prison officer's daily routine – 'A day's duty for an officer usually comprises nothing more or less than unlocking the men and locking them up again' – it proposed a new five-grade staffing structure reflecting the different aspects of what could, or should, be a more widely varied role for prison staff.

The document failed to move the authorities, but the POA was far from giving up hope; in its Memorandum to the 1964 Labour Party Study Group on Crime Prevention and Penal Reform, it reported that 'The Association envisages as an ideal the future creation of a completely unified correctional service in which prison officers would be integrated with the social workers (welfare officers) and the After-Care authorities ....' When a Labour government was elected in October 1964, the *Prison Officers' Magazine*, with the headline 'New Fields to Conquer', expressed the hope that the new government might take the 'rehabilitative' role of prison officers more seriously.

However, despite these important moves, which belie so strongly the repressive stereotype of the prison officer, two major developments were soon to take place which would sweep the issue of welfare from the top of the POA's agenda. These were, firstly, the abolition of capital punishment and, secondly, the report of the Mountbatten inquiry, which in many ways was set up in order to deal with the ramifications of that decision.

A Misnamed Age of Enlightenment?

The use of traditional corporal punishments such as 'the cat' (cat o'nine tails – a multi-tailed whip) had already been severely restricted in prisons, with ten episodes recorded in 1960, down to two in 1963 and only one during the following three years. It was during this period, in 1965, that the decision was made to 'suspend' capital punishment of criminal murderers, leading to total abolition soon afterwards.

The response to this by prison officers was perhaps partly shaped by a general tendency towards the punitive treatment of serious criminals. An article in the January 1965 edition of the *Prison Officers' Magazine*, responding to widespread rumours of the abolition, argued fiercely, under the heading 'The Devil Watches Over His Own', against 'this misnamed age of enlightenment'. At the 1966 POA Conference, a delegate defended capital punishment as 'the only line of defence against the murderer, the rapist, the sadist and the pampered scum that are in our prisons today'.

Yet this comment was made in the context of a resolution calling for a lump sum of £10,000 to be paid to the family of any murdered prison officer – a major factor in the chorus of condemnation which followed the vote for abolition. The 1957 Homicide Act had specifically included murder of a prison officer in its category of 'capital offences', and the 1965 reduction of this offence to the status of a 'non-capital' crime was seen as a betrayal of officers who often risked, and lost, their lives in dealing with violent prisoners. The resentment came to a head towards the end of 1965, when a prison officer was killed at Portland borstal. Spluttering with anger, the December 1965 *Prison Officers' Magazine* editorial, under the heading 'But for the Grace of God …!', spoke of the 'Tragic death of Officer Derek Lambert at Portland Borstal [which] has sent wave of shock and anger throughout the prison service.'

A second, more pragmatic objection to abolition arose from the fact that the end of capital punishment meant the beginning of decades-long sentences, usually life, for convicted murderers. This inevitably led to enormously increased problems of security and of violent unrest by long-term prisoners with nothing to lose, with an ever greater number of prison escapes, many of them featuring highly dangerous and notorious criminals, ensuing during the early to mid-1960s, too.

A fascinating glimpse into the period is provided by an interview with Harley Cronin for the *Yorkshire Post* in June 1961:

> Every few minutes, the conversation was interrupted by the phone. Always the same subject – gaolbreaks … We were talking against a background of violence and gaolbreaks. Why the sudden outbreak of violence? Cronin's answer is simple. 'Too many inmates, not enough officers,' he says tersely. 'Since 1939, the prison population … has trebled. The number of prison officers has not even doubled.'
>
> If Cronin has an ideal, it is to see the Prison Service a respected, reasonably well-paid job, carried out under conditions which encourage self-respect and a proper use of leisure. If he believes in a devil, it is 'the dead hand of the Treasury', which he blames for the fact that none of these dreams is true.

In fact, not only growing anger against decisions like the abolition of capital punishment, but an increasing industrial militancy was to characterise the actions of prison officers over the coming years.

'They Murdered Us ...'

In August 1961, Cronin finally took up a well-deserved retirement, and was succeeded by F.G. ('Fred') Castell, who had so heroically defended early POA organisation in Northern Ireland during the war. For the Association, the mid to late 1960s were a turbulent time. One former prison governor has linked the heightened level of unrest to the more militant trade unionism of sectors from which prison officers were now recruited:

> During the sixties, the mines started to close; steel workers started to be thrown out of work ... the building industry started to decline. And what did the Prison Service do? We rushed into those areas and we recruited like mad ... But – what [the new recruits] brought with them were very different trade union attitudes that prevailed in the industries they came from. And they murdered us, for about seven years ....[44]

At the same time, the heightened unrest of the period was conveying itself to the prison population. As the then POA General Secretary recalled in the *Prison Officers' Magazine*: 'With the growth in the late sixties of outside pressure groups it was inevitable that [this would] reflect itself in penal institutions. [Many] acts of indiscipline and violence occurred.' And these in their turn were reflected in an increasing incidence of local action by prison officers:

> While all these changes were taking place in the late sixties, Prison Officers found themselves foisted by decisions which they were never consulted about ... There existed no effective national strategy and local autonomy was the order of the day.
>
> Consequently, the POA centred its arguments and authority at a local level ... There followed a number of local actions to resolve local issues ....[45]

Mountbatten

It was, then, a period of considerable chaos, unrest and near-crisis, symbolised by the growing distance between managers and staff on the ground, and the increasing prison officer 'militancy', signalled above; and by prisoners themselves, in rooftop protests, riots, and the growth of prisoners' rights organisations (see below) – and most of all, for an alarmed Home Office, an increase in prisoner escapes. John Boddington, a member of the POA National Executive Committee (NEC), summed up the many strands of conflict leading to the setting up of the Mountbatten inquiry:

> Capital punishment ended in 1965, around the time of the Great Train Robbery and gangsters like the Kray Brothers, and that was the start of when much longer sentences started to be put out by the courts ... from 1966 onwards sentences started to become a lot longer. The train robbers got 30 years, the Krays and the Richardson brothers got a long time ... That in itself created a problem for the prison service inasmuch as we had in 1966 a number of very high profile escapes. George Blake, who was doing 42 years for spying, a number of the train robbers ... high profile prisoners serving very long sentences.[46]

Probably all of these incidents contributed to the calling of yet another major inquiry into the Prison Service; but most of all, it was the escape in October 1966 of the notorious spy George Blake which precipitated the 'Inquiry into Prison Escapes and Security' begun under Lord Mountbatten that year. In this sense the inquiry was concerned less with the situation of prison staff than with prison security, and its main recommendation was that prisoners should be divided into four categories, A to D, of which Category A were the most 'highly dangerous'. Mountbatten recommended that an entirely new maximum security prison should be built for such criminals, 'which really should be escape proof', and should house no more than 120 prisoners.[47]

The suggestion was that the new prison, to be known as 'Vectis', should be located on the Isle of Wight, though in the event it was never built.

These were the issues with which Mountbatten was mainly concerned, and he added a number of comments on developments which had worsened the security situation, such as the new situation brought about by the suspension of the death penalty and the consequent lengthy sentences – 'The prison system had no plans for a prisoner like Blake.' Prison reforms such as association, recreation and paid work, while welcomed, increased the risks to security: 'Treating prisoners by modern methods ... inevitably means that some of them escape.' Moreover, this was taking place in a situation of enormous overcrowding; although millions had been spent on new prison buildings since the mid 1950s, 'the prison population has increased by about 50 per cent in this decade', from just under 15,000 to well over 22,500.[48]

In the light of all these pressures, Mountbatten was sympathetic towards staff, making a number of comments and recommendations which contrasted sharply with previous inquiries. For example, noting the high levels of prison overcrowding, he commented that 'the pressure on prison staffs is considerably greater now than it was ten years ago ... In my view some increase [in prison staff] is necessary ....' As part of this, pay and conditions of service should be 'adequate to attract sufficient men and women of good quality'.

In addition, 'several things ... could be done, apart from questions of pay to increase the number of recruits ... and retain [them]'. For example, improved promotion procedures. 'Prison Officers have to wait 16 years for their first promotion and this is based entirely on seniority, so that no amount of merit ... will enable a man to achieve earlier promotion ....' On this basis, he recommended an additional rank of 'senior prison officer' at an improved rate of pay.

Finally, Mountbatten paid tribute to the POA's initiatives in promoting the 'welfare role' of staff: 'I am glad to hear that on the initiative of the Prison Officers' Association the future role of the prison officer ... is being studied jointly by the Prison Department Whitley Council.'

All of this was highly welcome to the Association, which referred repeatedly and approvingly to the Mountbatten Report in the aftermath of its publication. But, whatever the rights and wrongs of the report, the problem as usual lay in its implementation – or lack of it. By November 1967, a *Prison Officers' Magazine* editorial was asking plaintively: 'What About Mountbatten?' The article reported that although Home Secretary Roy Jenkins had made it clear that he accepted the inquiry's recommendations on the Senior Prison Officer grade, he had also referred to 'his position [being] governed by [Labour's] Prices and Incomes Policy'.

As the editorial commented angrily, 'Money in abundance has been forthcoming to provide advanced and complex security techniques ... But when it comes to spending a little on improving career prospects for the prison staffs ... the Government invokes some obscure clause of its rigid and unbending Prices and Incomes Policy.' By January 1968, a *Prison Officers' Magazine* editorial, headed 'Hail and Farewell!', concluded gloomily that 'the main hopes of the prison officers to which the Mountbatten Report gave rise remain unrealised'.

However, the government was prepared to spend money on some of the Mountbatten recommendations. The immediate result of the inquiry was a massive effort to tighten up prison security, at enormous cost. The conversion of even one prison, Hull, cost £1 million, a huge sum in the late 1960s. The effect on staff of this emphasis on security was no less drastic, with a sharp reversal of the emphasis on rehabilitation to an overwhelming need to concentrate on security.

Yet despite this renewed emphasis on control and security, itself welcomed by many prison staff, the record on prison escapes and inmate unrest was not significantly improved in the years following the Mountbatten inquiry. Although the number of prison escapes fell between 1967 and 1968, those from borstal actually rose, meaning total escapes rose between the two years, from 1,352 to 1,566; and by the late 1960s serious disturbances had already taken place at Durham and Parkhurst, with much worse to come. Mountbatten's recommendation of a new 'super-security' prison was in fact never carried out, and in 1968 another report, this time from a Professor Radzinowicz, resulted in a policy of dispersal of the most dangerous (Category A) prisoners across several jails. While Radzinowicz recognised the possible consequences of placing unnecessary restrictions on large numbers of less dangerous prisoners in these institutions, the strategy nevertheless went ahead, with what appeared to be inevitable consequences in terms of deteriorating conditions and thus an increased likelihood of disturbances.

As one prison history puts it: 'It is impossible to avoid the conclusion that the dispersal policy was responsible for the massive deterioration in the quality of [prison] life between 1969 and 1972.'[49] And so indeed it turned out. As the POA NEC member, John Boddington, continues his story:

> There was a percentage of Category A prisoners in each of the dispersal prisons – very high profile people like Ian Brady, child murderers ... With these high profile sentences we had a big period of unrest in prisons. It started in 1969 with the Parkhurst riot – that was where you had some of the Richardson gang and some of the Kray gang incarcerated – that was a major riot. Then in the 70s we had a period of riots in the high security estate ... right up till about 1975 – there was a major riot in Hull in about 1975 or 1976, the same time as Gartree ... Albany rioted ... The only one that didn't have a major riot was Long Lartin. Everyone in the dispersal system at the time was keeping a watch waiting for Long Lartin to go ...
>
> But there were major riots, and that was what eventually led to the high security estate and the dispersals coming to an end – that and the cost of keeping them up.

Nevertheless, in this officer's view, these events had some positive implications for the union:

> All these things, all these significant events, had a tremendous effect on the POA. Certainly with all the unrest of the early 70s within the dispersal system, I think the POA then very much came into prominence and I think that was possibly when it started to gain its political voice. There was a lot going on, all these riots, and the media ... started to want to talk to local POA representatives ... there was a great deal of media interest and I think possibly prison officers were encouraged from Cronin House to talk to the press and actually give quotes in the press, and I think that's when we started to get our political voice as it were. That was a bit of a sea change ... when you look at the amount of media coverage and the political voice of the POA now, I think that was the start of it.[50]

'That Healthy Babe ...'

Nevertheless, prison rioting and other pressures were to lead to unprecedented conflict among prison officers in the late 1960s and early 1970s – generally a highly turbulent time within the labour and trade union movement. During this period, 'With ... the refusal of the Home Office to provide the prison officers with what they considered to be an adequate wage the officers were to increasingly use the weapon of industrial action to put their views forward in a more militant fashion.'[51] By 1968, the POA General Secretary was expressing fury over the pay question: when part of an increase was postponed until January 1969, without retrospection, he wrote: 'It cannot be denied that this represented active discrimination by the Government against its own employees ... Civil servants are as loyal a body of men and women as can be found anywhere but there is a limit beyond which even they cannot be pushed. In my view THIS IS IT ....'[52]

Perhaps as a result of this understandable indignation, the fortunes of the Association at least seemed to be thriving. In a celebration of the Golden Jubilee of the Civil Service National Whitley Committee, the October 1969 *Prison Officers' Magazine* could claim that it was now 'a far cry from those days ... when ... the shackles of the ineffective House Union, the Prison Officers' Representative Board were being cast off and that healthy babe, the P.O.A., was being born'. Membership then had been fewer than 3,000; it was now more than 11,000 (excluding Scotland). Nor was the POA alone in its increased numbers: the General Secretary's column for the November 1968 *Prison Officers' Magazine*, under the headline 'Nearly Nine Million in TUC', described huge increases in trade union membership, with 'women leading the way'.

From 'Vee' schemes to 'CDCs'

Pay was not the only factor contributing to prison officer discontent. The ongoing struggle for a five-day week (or eleven-day fortnight) had, by the mid 1960s, resulted in the introduction of complex new scheduling systems. By July 1965, it could be reported that these 'schedules of attendances ... might be put into effect experimentally at a few "pilot" establishments',[53] and in

September 1965, pilot schemes were in place at Ashwell, Bedford, Hull, Lincoln and Manchester.

This marked the beginning of a long period in which the schedules, known as the 'Vee' and Functional Group Systems (FGS) schemes, were eventually introduced across the country, with the Vee scheme installed mainly at larger urban prisons and the FGS system at open establishments or young offenders' institutions. The new structures were initially seen as a positive move towards shorter working hours. When their introduction was delayed, the General Secretary's column in the November 1966 *Prison Officers' Magazine* commented regretfully: 'The blow fell and the Association was informed that the scheme would have to be deferred for six months.' However, when the schemes did eventually come into operation a year later, the General Secretary was forced to report that staffing shortages would still mean 'very considerable overtime working will have to continue for some time to come', and in general, though still welcomed in principle, the new schemes appeared to make little practical difference to prison officers' working conditions.

'You Become a Complex Person ...'

One NEC member linked this to the impact of Prison Service on the individual officer:

> Prison officers are complex ... Prison officers are ordinary people. They join the Prison Service and they move into a whole new world of working in an institution which is possibly like no other – an institution where none of the people within it are volunteers – they're all there because their liberty has been taken away – and you have to try and divorce yourself from what each prisoner is actually in for because that's immaterial – even the most heinous crimes – you have to know what it is but you have to divorce yourself from that because you have to treat them all the same. That's what makes you a bit complex – you have loads of rules and regulations; on the one hand, you have to keep control, you can't let people escape, you have to keep discipline because you can't let the place become anarchistic ... but on the other hand, you have to show compassion – you also have to deal

with the families who suffer greatly – and I think that's what makes you become … You may not have been a complex person before you went in, you only become a complex person through working in that environment because you spend so much time in there … Certainly in the 70s and 80s when you had to do overtime you spent virtually all your life in there. You start at 6.30 in the morning, probably don't finish till 9.30 at night, six days a week. When I joined it was a six-day week, it wasn't a five-day week – we used to work a twelve-day fortnight. So I think you actually become a complex person ….[54]

Another POA activist confirmed that 'You worked a lot of hours – you could work as much as 80, 90 hours a week if not up to 120 … What you'd be complaining about at that time from the 70s [was] the two main systems of work … the Vee scheme and the FGS ….' Another commented that:

One of the problems with the Vee scheme … [was that] managers were bastardising them … At the weekend we used to get an hour and a quarter for lunch … I said 'Why are we having an hour and a quarter for lunch when the men are only having an hour [giving women less opportunity for overtime pay]? … We're both Vee scheme, we're both working the same.' So we went on the seven-hour 45-minute day.

The other thing was evening duties … I'm asked if I'll do an evening and I say 'Hang on a minute, why are you asking me? You haven't before' And they've been doing this to a lot of people, because nobody knew what their working system was. And that wasn't just happening in my establishment, that was happening up and down the country ….

According to the other activist interviewed:

The local policy was … you came in on Thursday, worked Thursday lunchtime till half past nine, worked from half past six to half past nine Friday, and you either did Saturday or Sunday, those same hours, then you did Monday and then you finished Tuesday lunchtime … So then they said to me for the princely sum of £2.46 you're going to have to go home at eight on one of these nights, be back at nine, and then you'll lock the prison up at ten, and you'll get into a cast-iron bed with freezing cold sheets … and they called it 'sleep-in'. It was a different system of working then, there wasn't many of you ….[55]

An account by Northern Ireland POA Area Chairman Finlay Spratt confirms this picture: 'In 1976, when you came to work, you didn't know when you would be coming home – could work 9am–7pm, come back at 10pm. In those days to get a decent wage you had to work round the clock.'[56]

By 1971, the *Prison Officers' Magazine* was beginning to reflect widespread dissension over the new schedule, and in January 1972 an editorial reported ruefully that 'For the sake of clarity it is necessary to establish that the FGS is unpopular.' Both the FGS and Vee schemes had been voted in on a 4–1 majority on the basis of pilot schemes run by 'manpower project teams', but whereas the joint working party setting up the pilots 'adapted the scheme to fit local requirements ... the M.P.T. [Manpower Project Team] adapts local requirements to fit the scheme'. Scheme Vee itself was 'start[ed] in a kick and rush manner and has produced a situation where hardly any two places work the same type of Scheme "Vee"'. Letters to the *Magazine* argued that FGS schemes interfered with staff involvement and stability at high-security prisons, and in 1973 a poetic 'Rookie's Lament' summed up the problems:

> Join the Prison Service
> If you wish to lose your friends,
> For this you surely will do
> By working at weekends.
> You work ungodly hours
> To which you have no say;
> Then comes the Golden Eagle
> Bringing peanuts instead of pay.[57]

No Provision for Breakfast ...

As many of the above accounts indicate, working schedules were also affected by a still more complex system known as 'Continuous Duty Credits' (CDCs). This system was based on national agreements for 'net hours', meaning that prison officers received pay only for hours actually worked and not for meal breaks falling within the span of their normal working day. The unclear definition of such shifts, and of 'on-call' and 'standby' duties, led to an increasing number of disputes, including action at Liverpool and Leeds which led to questions in Parliament in early 1979.

As the 1979 May Report (see also below) commented: 'One of the main features that characterised the period of industrial unrest immediately prior to [this Report] was a series of claims by prison officers for payment of what have become known as "continuous duty credits" ....' The first of these occurred in 1973, when a number of establishments assumed that staff beginning work at 7.45 a.m. would have had breakfast before starting work. '[T]he attendance system accordingly made no provision for a breakfast break ... it proved necessary to detail a number of such staff to commence work at 7.00 am, and they were assumed not to have had breakfast before starting work. Consequently, they were sent off work for a 45 minute break at about 7.45 am and received no payment for that break.'[58] Not surprisingly, such 'assumptions' caused considerable dissension amongst prison staff.

Disputes over CDCs continued to surface throughout the mid to late 1970s; for example, 'Duty Credit Disputes' led to industrial action, supported by the NEC, at both Birmingham and Wandsworth in late 1978. While the Home Office had insisted that 'compensation for CDC would be paid at time rate', the Association argued that this interpretation was incorrect. Following deadlock on this dispute, the TUC intervened and the issue was referred to an independent investigator, with the industrial action called off as a result. However, the general level of unrest over such 'Duty Credit' issues was such as to persuade the government to include the CDC issue in the terms of reference of the forthcoming May Inquiry.

The impact of 'Vee', FGS and CDC schemes in terms of local conflict was matched by a general increase in the willingness of prison officers to take industrial action over a range of issues. An article on prison industrial relations reports that 'Industrial action in the prison service was virtually unknown until the early 1970s. During the 1970s, however, public service trade unions and their members banished their traditionally moderate image ... The POA was no exception.' This analysis emphasises that '[T]he steady deterioration in the industrial relations climate in prisons owes much to the rise in the prisoner population without corresponding increases in prison staff. This led to disputes about staff and a number of incidents of local industrial action ....'[59] Another comment on this rise in 'agitation' among prison officers in the early 1970s describes it as 'a manifestation of the militancy of industrial relations in general' during the period. Like the analysis cited above, this argument emphasises the role of new recruits from 'the industrial sphere' whose more confrontational traditions meant 'militancy became increasingly used as a weapon against the Home Office'.[60]

A former POA full-time official, recalling the period, also invokes the 'inexorable' rise in the prison population, alongside continued staff shortages, which meant that by 1973, POA members were working unacceptable levels of overtime:

> However, the Home Office insisted that overtime was not excessive ... So we invoked the 54-hour agreement [as a form of 'go-slow'] for a four-week period at the end of the summer. This produced an immediate effect and proved conclusively that the Prison Service could not operate at all effectively within the 54-hour limit.

In fact, 'Excessive overtime [had been] disguising the extent of manpower shortage. Combined with an increasing prisoner population, the situation meant that the Prison Service was moving towards a major crisis.' 1973–75 was 'a period where overcrowding and staff shortages were at the heart of industrial relations', worsened by the fact that in 1973, while prices soared, the government had declared a total wage freeze: 'The value of two pay awards was wiped out by unprecedented price inflation.'[61]

Prisoner Power?

During these turbulent years, when Britain as a whole was swept by an almost unprecedented wave of strike action, prisoners themselves caught the protest 'bug' with a wave of rooftop demonstrations and other actions in 1972–73. As the POA full-timer takes up the tale: 'There was a spate of inmate demonstrations by a prisoner organization called PROP – Preservation of the Rights Of Prisoners. Governors, with no inkling of what to do, met with prisoner deputations who gained in importance, thereby undermining the authority of staff ....'[62]

The *Prison Officers' Magazine* for 1972 gives a vivid picture of the mayhem. Its September editorial, headed 'Prisoner Power?', refers to 'The recent spate of demonstrations by prisoners, ranging from sit-down in the exercise yard, refusal to return to cells, squatting on roofs and refusing labour, to all-out strike action ....' It was not only the prisoners who were adopting these 'direct action' tactics. As Steven Thomas notes, 'With the formation of PROP in 1972 the unique situation occurred when demonstrations of staff were matched by those of the inmates creating an atmosphere of uncertainty throughout the service ....'[63]

This accord with the militant mood of the period was also shown in prison officers' sympathy with groups of strikers imprisoned under the Conservatives' Industrial Relations Act and other anti-strike laws. Referring to the famous 'Pentonville Five' episode of 1972, a retired senior prison officer recalled: 'During my last years at Pentonville we had the dockers' strike and they were locked up in Pentonville ... and as best we could we looked after them as trade unionists, leaving their cell doors open most of the day ... and we tried to be as accommodating and as friendly as we could.'[64] While prison officers have been criticised by the two most prominent strikers from the 1973 building workers' strike, Des Warren and Rocky Tomlinson (the 'Shrewsbury Two'), one POA NEC member put some of this down to the deliberate 'localisation' of the Shrewsbury prosecution, and expressed his sympathy for the strikers: 'As a young activist I put a motion to conference in support of the Shrewsbury Two – well, they were trade unionists.'[65]

A Climate of Unreason ...

Prison officers themselves were involved in intermittent strike action in 1972, mainly over the chaotic situation within the prisons. As the retired senior officer recalls:

It was essentially about the inability of the Prison Service to resolve the PROP riots – there was a massive influx of prisoners then, overcrowding was rife, slopping out was a national disgrace ... and the general condition of the prisons themselves were atrocious ... So it was a climate of unreason at that time and we just tried to defend what we had because we felt vulnerable due to the lack of perception and direction from those who employed us.[66]

However, not all POA officials were sympathetic to the general climate of subversion. The then General Secretary, Fred Castell, drew a parallel between the PROP 'strikes' and a recent demonstration by officers' wives at Verne prison: 'The action of the wives seems to indicate that they believe that anarchy pays for prisoners, and may well pay for themselves also.'[67]

Yet the 'anarchy' continued; prisoners on 'strike' at Albany and other prisons refused to return to their cells throughout the day and night over the weekend of 19–20 August 1972, and at Albany and Gartree Prisons, protests reached such a pitch that it was necessary for the Home Secretary to return from holiday in order to take personal charge of the situation. In a statement he subsequently 'fully vindicated the stance taken by the Association', which had by now issued a formal protest and, in the absence of any action by the Home Office, instructed branches to take action. Yet this verbal support had few practical implications. As the POA full-timer put it, 'The whole episode proved to the POA that to rely on the Home Office for support was futile, and the Association resolved to look to their own endeavours to deal with matters.'[68]

As suggested above, the new 'high security' policies and dispersal of Category A prisoners resulting from the Mountbatten and Radzinowicz recommendations were implicated in many of these difficulties. Albany, one of the prisons involved in serious riots, had been allocated a group of Category A prisoners who arrived in September 1970, instigating a 'series of incidents until the prison was seriously damaged by destruction of cells in 1973'.[69] These were immensely stressful experiences for prison officers. As staff at Albany told the POA Executive in August 1972, 'We just cannot stomach any more abuse from the prisoners. We are as anxious as the Home Office to help in rehabilitating these men, but they do not play by the same rules as us.'[70]

In 1976, the massive riot at Hull Prison, which caused £2 million worth of damage, drew the comment from John Prescott, MP for Hull East, that the 'swing away from informal contact to the more rigid use of formal procedures' observed at the prison had led to 'increased tension which ... [was] a significant factor in the occurrence and nature of the ... riot'.[71] Not long afterwards, a prisoner called Hughes who had escaped from Leicester Prison took hostage and murdered four people; he had also stabbed the two prison officers who were escorting him at the time. The POA blamed new, more stringent budgets in part for these problems: 'The Association had constantly drawn to the attention of management that artificially contrived budgetary limits would undermine general security and control.'[72] Yet still the Home Office refused to reconsider these policies.

In a 1977 report on the Hull riot, presented in the October issue of the *Prison Officers' Magazine*, Home Secretary Merlyn Rees commented: 'I believe that there can be no doubt that the nature and temper of the prison population has changed significantly since the Radzinowicz Committee reported in 1968.' The intimate knowledge by prison officers of such 'significant change' is captured in a lengthy letter to his MP by a Lincoln prison officer, J. Kay, which graphically conveys the major issues contributing to the explosion of industrial action by the Association's members in the 1970s. For example:

> At present we still uphold an agreement with the Home Office that we will work a maximum of 10 hours overtime per week whenever the Department so wishes us to do. In reality, however, most Officers given the chance will work well in excess of this figure willingly simply because they cannot afford to bring up a family and save for retirement on basic pay which is approximately 18% below the national average for industries.

Kay continued with a bitter attack on the government's determination to cut public spending, high on its agenda since 1976:

> Hopefully the truth will eventually dawn on the Labour Government that we are dealing with Human beings housed in a most unnatural environment … [within which] there exists a hard core of violent, professional criminals who are an absolute menace to society. The fact that this latter category … is increasing at an alarming rate … emphasise[s] the volatile situation in the Dispersal Prisons. If we consider that point alone, how can the Government talk of saving money and protecting the Public in one and the same breath?[73]

Perhaps it was views like these, or at least their expression in the spate of local disputes during those years, that lay behind the POA General Secretary's comment to the 1985 Conference that 'when the [Prison] Department decided to curtail regimes for budget reasons in the late seventies, it was locally based action and argument which changed Departmental thinking'.

'As Ye Sow …'

In fact, during this period, the tendency among POA members towards local action became increasingly apparent; and such establishment-based action was often unofficial, a break away from POA discipline the leadership found hard to accept. Contributions to the 1971 *Prison Officers' Magazine* had already indicated some internal unrest: the General Secretary wrote in February of 'internal criticisms' within the POA, with pressure for more regional forms of organisation and 'taking the power out of the hands of an elected Executive Committee.' In the February issue, Under the heading 'As Ye Sow …!', the POA National Chair referred to Circulars seeking action against the Executive, and also to the expulsion from the POA of two local officials in the Dartmoor branch for withholding of union subscriptions: 'This type of so-called militant action is born of ignorance out of inexperience … The whole of the dissatisfaction appears to be based on the feelings of some branches that the leadership of the Association is not militant enough for them.' A 'Feltham meeting' of disaffected local activists was also criticised as unconstitutional and 'morally wrong'.

In March 1971, an article titled 'The Harvest', described by its author as 'an answer by one of those "militants"', said of the Feltham meeting:

Present were a lot of people who have an avid interest in POA affairs. For some time there had been a growing unease among the membership. They felt they had not been getting the best representation possible ... It seemed that all those present were searching for some formula to revitalise the P.O.A. ....

The tensions were illustrated in 'spontaneous strikes without reference to the POA' by staff at Albany. In 1972, as a result of the increased tension within the prison cited above, prison officers demanded extra staff; when the Home Office refused to grant the request, 'the staff decided to take industrial action which was only prevented by the intervention of three members of the POA's executive'.[74]

Such pressures eventually resulted, by 1975, in a POA decision to grant regions the right to take independent action 'without reference to central HQ'. Once again, the leadership had responded readily to 'the pressure of their local organisations' and to principles of internal trade union democracy. Perhaps inevitably, the decision 'resulted in a major escalation of disputes': between 1975 and 1978, the number of times branches took industrial action rose from 19 to 119.

By no means all disputes were 'wildcat' strikes. In March 1975, official one-day protest action was taken by all branches in the London area in protest over a 'totally inadequate' offer on London Weighting:[75] 'At the end of 1974 there had been no response to the claim submitted by the Association regarding the London Weighting allowance. This situation continued until March 1975, when an offer was received and rejected ... Prior to this certain London branches had taken local industrial action in protest against the amount offered' according to the senior full-timer quoted above.

In March 1976, in response to a Prison Service Circular authorising a £2 million reduction in manpower resources 'throughout the prison officer class as a whole', and the subsequent 'surprising degree' of mismanagement of the policy's practical application, direct action broke out at a number of penal establishments. In the same year, 'there were local disputes resulting not only from undermanning but also from the Government's insistence that the Association should accept pay abatement'. This was required 'as a pre-condition for payment of an interim award and further negotiation regarding transition to differentiated rates of pay', according to the senior full-timer quoted above. Yet the reality of low pay for prison staff at the time is borne out by a letter to the *Prison Officers' Magazine* in March 1977 supporting the need for industrial action on the grounds that teachers, at £3 an hour, were paid twice as much as prison officers.

In 1977, the Association began indicating increasing opposition, allied to a policy of non-cooperation, over a new government policy of 'budgetary controls'; branches were directed to inform governors that the NEC had issued instructions to no longer cooperate with the policy. Manning level disputes broke out at Bedford and Sudbury in the same year, with official support for the action resulting in agreement to 'interim manning levels ... which satisfy the main objections of the Bedford branch',[76] as well as favourable concessions at Sudbury.

However, the problem of unofficial action resurfaced. In late 1978, a POA Circular referred to a meeting at Pentonville 'not arranged by the NEC', at which a motion was adopted 'to take unspecified industrial action' over pay, unscheduled meal breaks and Pensionable Value of Quarters. This proposal was seen as 'represent[ing] a splinter movement ... at odds with ... the elected national body'.[77] In a further Circular, the NEC announced that branches should adhere to the terms of the Industrial Action document published in the September 1977 *Prison Officers' Magazine*:

> Branches which undertake industrial action on a unilateral basis without reference to the NEC should note that the NEC will not subsequently support such action ... The National Executive Committee feels there is a need to stress that adherence to POA policies and to NEC directives

to branches is essential. Otherwise anarchy will be the result, which will inevitably weaken the POA both from within and from without ....

Nevertheless, the Association continued to support a militant stance, particularly on pay. After the Civil Service Pay Agreement was suspended by the government as part of its Stage 1 incomes policy in July 1975, restoration of the agreement became a major priority. In late 1977, a POA Circular reported on a Special Meeting of the Staff Side which had agreed that all constituent unions should engage in various forms of protest during the week beginning 28 November. There was now no system in existence for dealing with Civil Service pay reviews due on 1 April, 1978, which, in the words of the Circular,

> means that the TUC/Government agreement for an 'orderly return' to free collective bargaining will not operate in the Civil Service. In fact a highly disorderly situation is likely to prevail between now and 1 April 1978 when a settlement is due. This situation has provoked a wave of bitter anger and disappointment throughout the Service.[78]

By October 1978, the Association was warning of possible 'direct conflict with the Government' over the recently announced 5 per cent pay limit.

> One naturally hopes that persuasive argument will prevail and confrontation be avoided. However, should this not be the case then we shall need to close ranks and be united as never before. For the resultant struggle could be both a bitter and enduring one.[79]

In March 1979, the government's latest pay offer was rejected and 'the need for direct action of an industrial nature ... considered necessary'. The decision to limit overtime along with other sanctions was 'communicated to all branches by telephone on Thursday, 29th March due to postal delay caused by industrial action by the Post Office' – a comment indicating the widespread extent of strike action during that year's notorious 'Winter of Discontent'.

Yet again, in the face of mounting crisis over both pay and resources for the Prison Service, the government dealt with the rising tide of prison officer unrest with a Committee of Inquiry into the United Kingdom Prison Services, on this occasion led by Justice May, which it was hoped would 'bring order out of the industrial relations chaos within the Service'. Given that a central objective of this inquiry was to investigate claims over both terms and conditions and prison management put forward by the POA, the Association, perhaps overconfidently, suspended the forms of industrial action then taking place until its Report should be published.

The POA terms of reference to the May inquiry were very strongly worded:

> Total breakdown is imminent in the prison system ... a series of developments [includes] the inmate disorders of 1972 followed by the emergence of staff unrest in 1973 ... Prison Officers are resorting to industrial action on an increasing scale ... Prison Officers' industrial action is partly the result of an outdated and unworkable industrial relations structure. There are also many genuine grievances. These include the continuing existence of high overtime ....

After the Home Office rejection of their claim, the Liverpool dispute over CDCs was to be referred to the inquiry, whose conclusions are examined below. According to an academic account, 'the most serious incident [of CDC industrial action] occurred at HMP Prison Walton, Liverpool, during February and March 1979 when the local POA branch refused to admit new prisoners over the certified normal accommodation (CNA) figure'.[80]

A Social Con-Trick?

By the mid 1970s, though the ongoing pay limits imposed by the Labour government under its 'Social Contract' (widely mocked in the labour movement as the 'Social Con-Trick') were causing the Association increasing irritation, POA organisation could benefit internally from legislation which introduced 'Facilities for Non-Industrial Trade Union Representatives', as noted in a POA Circular of May 1976, and, in August of that year, a Certificate of Independence for the POA under the Employment Protection Act

1975. As the Circular joked somewhat defensively, the Certificate might 'dispel ... doubts voiced by some of our members on the status of the POA as an independent trade union ... the POA now has a certificate to prove it!' The extra facilities granted to POA representatives under the Trade Union and Labour Relations Act 1974 were perhaps of more immediate practical use; it was agreed with the National Whitley Council that for each POA branch there would be five accredited representatives, who would receive 'Time off for industrial relations duties' of up to eight hours per week. The new regulations also encouraged the provision of furnished office accommodation, phones, notice boards, deduction of subs from pay, notification of new entrants, election of reps in official time and paid special leave for recognised POA activities – a cornucopia of new trade union rights many of which still exist and are in daily use, although they have been criticised for contributing to the 'bureaucratisation' of workplace trade unionism.

'Society's Forgotten Men'? Prison Officers in Scotland

The account of these years will not be complete without some reference to the specific issues and problems surfacing in Scotland and Northern Ireland (see below). In Scotland, prison officers broke away from the POA in the early 1970s and maintained a separate organisation, the Scottish Prison Officers' Association (SPOA), for almost 30 years. John Renton, the General Secretary of the SPOA from 1971, became involved with the Association, 'which at that time was regarded as the Scottish area of the POA', when he joined the Prison Service in 1959. By 1969, he had become Area Treasurer, a post which shed light on many of the connections with the POA nationally. For example, the Scottish section held a seat on the Council of Civil Service Unions (CCSU), paid a proportion of fees for membership of the TUC, and obtained the attendance of a POA full-time official at their own Annual Conference, with advice given both on that occasion and at the Annual Meeting of the Scottish Whitley Council. Thus, 'In many respects the Scottish area was treated as a rather large branch ... but with no opportunity of shaping opinion, because although we could attend Annual Conference, we had no voice and no vote there', given their own separate Conference in Scotland.[81]

The situation meant, amongst other things, that the Scottish section had no full-time official devoted to its concerns, and given the 'minimal amount of facility time' available for union representatives, 'anything we could do, had to be in our own time'. Full-time POA staff were extremely helpful, but had a heavy workload with their own membership and 'no time to consider the different circumstances of the problems presented by the different law in Scotland, or the different negotiating procedures ... There was nothing wrong with the people involved ... What was wrong was the structure.'

In late 1970 and early 1971, Scottish representatives began to look closely into the question of employing their own full-time official. Renton's calculations as Treasurer suggested that 'we could go it alone with a modest increase in subscriptions', but only as long as the payments to the POA nationally for pay negotiations, TUC membership and services provided by POA headquarters were dropped. 'The strong view was that it would be better to stay within the POA, but ... we should consider going it alone ....' In the event, the proposal to form an independent SPOA was put to the Scottish Annual Conference for discussion and approved by delegates. Renton comments that:

> although the POA did not approve of the action we were taking, they put no obstacles in our way, and indeed were most helpful in the advice they gave ... I will always be grateful for the support I was given. It would have been quite easy for our colleagues in England to put obstacles in our way, but they did not do so.[82]

From the beginning, the SPOA had to address problems of prisoner violence and brutality which in many ways exceeded those in even the worst English prisons. The circumstances are vividly recounted in the memoirs of Jimmy Boyle, once labelled 'Scotland's most violent man' but later to become a successful sculptor through rehabilitation in Barlinnie's 'special unit'. As Boyle recounts:

In 1967 I was one of a group of young men sentenced to long prison sentences in the wake of the abolition of capital punishment … I had nothing to lose. I found myself connecting with other prisoners who were in the same boat … After a succession of fights, riots and demonstrations five of us found ourselves held in the Cages in Inverness prison. These were iron-barred cages that sub-divided a prison cell … The climax of this downward spiral took the form of a bloody riot in the Cages. Many prison officers and prisoners were injured … Four of us were eventually charged with the attempted murder of six prison officers … Behind the scenes … the authorities were stretched to the limit. A number of prison officers in Inverness resigned from the service in the aftermath of the riot.[83]

Ironically, the outcome of this riot was that Boyle was removed to the much more liberal 'special unit' at Barlinnie Prison, itself set up largely as a response to the riots when prison staff 'refused to have the hard core of us back'. The unit, based on a prisoner-centred, therapeutic approach, was perennially controversial, amongst prison staff as well as politicians. As one account puts it, while 'the experiment of the … Special Unit … has created world-wide interest … One often-heard criticism is that the really "bad boys" are being given all the advantages of special treatment ….'[84] Such criticism was heard amongst prison staff as much as others (see below), yet Boyle pays generous tribute to those prison officers who did support the project. Initially himself sceptical, he recounts that, 'Ironically, it was a group of prison officers who helped dispel my doubts about the place. It was impressive to see them push forward radical steps for the development of a more humanitarian regime ….' As Boyle notes later: 'Within the Unit … the morale of the staff was very high as they felt the work they were doing had some purpose, they were seeing an end product. This was very rare within the penal service … .'[85]

The 'cages' at Inverness Prison had played a key role in the riot Boyle describes and in the attacks on prison officers; their reintro-duction some years after the riot led to further horrific violence against staff, conveyed in the following account:

The controversial five segregation cells known as the 'cages' at Inverness Prison … were intended for occupation by very violent prisoners … guilty of grievous bodily harm to prison officers. They were not used from March 1973 until 1978 when an inmate who attacked a prison officer with a razor and inflicted serious injury was sent there ....[86]

In late 1978, staff at Inverness began industrial action in opposition to the removal of the 'cages' after several prison officers had been attacked by inmates.

In November 1978, a Special Delegate Conference was held to examine the question of the Inverness Segregation Unit. Here, it was reported that the Secretary of State had now made recommendations which had 'changed the position significantly, although they did not meet all that had been sought', and the Executive therefore recommended that the Conference should postpone industrial action. However, in direct contrast, delegates amended this motion to decide that industrial action should begin on 20 November 1978 rather than 31 January 1979.

Delegates to the Conference severely criticised the SPOA Executive for ignoring decisions of previous Special Delegate Conferences on Inverness, and in particular for declaring the industrial action agreed at that Conference 'unofficial'.

One resolution described the aftermath of industrial action over the cages as a 'fiasco', adding: 'This was the first time Industrial Action on a national scale had been attempted by the SPOA ... we were not sufficiently prepared.' Additional criticism was contained in a further resolution which argued that:

> Branches which failed to take industrial Action [should] be severely censured ... the Resolution speaks for itself. Why send Delegates to a Conference if they are not going to support the decision taken. If we are to be strong, we must be a united Association.

The SPOA had by no means been unaware of the growing crisis. In January 1978, a Memorandum it submitted on 'The Administration of the Prison Service' had expressed 'extreme concern' about overcrowding in Scottish prisons and advocated the use of suspended sentences as in England; in Scotland the courts tended to use deferred sentences, automatically resulting in a further court appearance. Recent cuts in government spending had halted any improvements in living and working conditions for staff and prisoners, as well as worsening an already difficult recruitment situation. General Secretary John Renton pointed out the difficulties in a system where the ratio of staff to inmates was 'about 1 to 20, or 1 to 40 in the more crowded prisons, [with] enormous mental and physical demands' on prison officers and 'insecurity in the face of increasing assaults in prison'.[87] Another problem was the continued obstinacy of the authorities over promotion. As Renton argued in 1978: 'Unless we start recruiting people who have the ... chance to become governors, we are never going to attract the right kind of person ... The prison officers have some justification when they claim that they, as much as their charges, are society's forgotten men.'[88]

In April 1979, the SPOA submitted a memo to the May inquiry into UK Prison Services which claimed that the Scottish service was being starved of resources, leading to lack of progress in modernisation at prisons like Barlinnie, Perth and Peterhead. The SPOA submission also contained proposals on the issue of CDCs – while shift systems in Scotland were different, it would not expect Scottish staff to be treated 'less favourably' regarding CDC payments – and argued, along general POA lines, for the end of open competition, or 'direct entry', for governor posts. On the effectiveness of the industrial relations machinery, they argued that 'There is a strong feeling within the SPOA that it should be possible to negotiate all conditions of service within Scotland', and called for the service 'to provide much more information to the staff. We seem to be very far behind our English colleagues in this regard.'[89]

By October, the General Secretary could refer in the SPOA's magazine, the *Link*, to 'recent events at Peterhead' which have 'again brought the Prison Service into the public eye ... We have those who cannot understand how a group of prisoners can get onto a roof and be allowed to cause so much damage.' As a full-time SPOA official graphically described this incident: 'At Peterhead the SAS had to break the riot up because we had an officer in chains by his neck being led across the rooftops threatening to kill him.' Less than a year later, however, three

POA members were on trial regarding the incidents at Peterhead. As Renton wrote: 'It seems quite remarkable that in an incident ... during which 25 Prison Officers were injured, one of them seriously ... the only people charged with a criminal offence were three Prison Officers.'[90] Although the Scottish Home Office had agreed that staff had acted with efficiency and restraint and had complimented them on those grounds, it had failed to take responsibility for their defence and had 'pass[ed] the buck' for this to the Association.

Peterhead, like too many other Scottish prisons, was particularly bleak in its atmosphere and environs:

> Peterhead has its own distinctive atmosphere ... The dreary environment and the grim climate have a bad effect on prisoners and officers alike ... 'Peterhead is a terrible place ...', is the comment one hears in every prison. Sufficient money has not been allocated for improvements ... There are no facilities for rehabilitation or recreation ... work facilities are inadequate ... So frustration, boredom and resentment are fostered and increase, a fact which unrest and many rooftop demonstrations illustrate all too clearly.[91]

In 1979, the May Report specifically recommended that Peterhead Prison, along with other of the 'worst prison building[s]', such as Dartmoor, should be 'substantially redeveloped'.

Horror ... and Comradeship

But it was in Northern Ireland that the violence and conflict of the period saw its most tragic expression, leading over the 1970s, 1980s and 1990s to a grim toll of 29 prison staff murdered in the course of their duty – a poignant reminder of earlier concerns over the abolition of capital punishment for murder of prison officers. The saga dates back to the late 1960s when civil rights protests among the Catholic communities in Northern Ireland led to a surge of support for the Provisional IRA ('Provos'), a paramilitary wing of the Irish Republican Army (IRA), which split off in 1970. This swiftly led to government retaliation, including, from August 1971, internment without trial for those accused of terrorist acts in both the Provisional IRA and the ultra-Loyalist UDR (Ulster Defence Regiment).

This inevitably led to a sharp escalation in the population of violent prisoners in the main Ulster jails, Belfast Prison and Long Kesh (opened in 1971). Many Republican prisoners were also interned on prison ships such as the *Maidstone*. IRA detainees burned down Long Kesh in 1974, and the prison was rebuilt in 1975 as 'the Maze', with purpose-built high-security 'H blocks' to house the paramilitary prisoners. Meanwhile, more conflict was generated inside the prisons by the removal of political status for these prisoners.

In the wake of a hunger strike by internees in 1972, the Conservative government had introduced 'special category' status for what were now regarded as political prisoners. However, in 1975 this political status was withdrawn by the Labour government, and prisoners, including women in Armagh prison, began a 'blanket protest' in which they refused to wear prison clothes or carry out normal inmate duties. This quickly escalated into the infamous 'dirty protest' in which the prisoners, clad only in blankets, also refused to wash or to clean out their cells.

However, internal conditions at prisons like the Maze were only part of the terrible experiences faced by prison officers during those years. Between 1974 and late 1979, 19 members of the prison staff in Northern Ireland, from clerks to governors, were murdered by members of the paramilitary organisations, while many more were seriously injured. A poignant letter from the widow of Albert Miles, a Deputy Governor at the Maze, to his murderer (who had escaped to the US) sums up the impact on the wives and families left behind:

Do you remember a cold dark night in November 1978 ...? My husband Bert had just come in ... when the front door was knocked. Thinking it was a neighbour I opened it ... but ... it was you ... Your two friends were shooting from the gate as well – three of you to murder one man ... At least six bullets went into my husband's body. He was a good man, a good husband and a good father ... I miss him so very much ....[92]

One of the few consolations in this horrific situation was the support of fellow-prison officers. As Finlay Spratt, National Area Chairman of the POA in Northern Ireland, recalled in an interview:

> Throughout the years of the Troubles there was wonderful comradeship [and] support … from the NEC and fellow-members right across the union … We were very grateful to the Prison Officers who came here from England and Scotland. The knowledge they imparted helped us build the Northern Ireland POA. When they came in the POA was just starting to get on its feet. With the increase in prison population, they couldn't get enough staff from Northern Ireland. The English and Scottish staff went through major skirmishes with us.[93]

With this last point, the POA Chairman (England and Wales) referred to what was described by the POA Chair at the 1972 Conference as an 'unprecedented step in the history of the Prison Service' – the transfer of officers from England, Wales and Scotland to Northern Ireland after the introduction of internment, which 'had a very profound effect upon our colleagues in Ulster and virtually doubled the inmate population by late autumn'. The opening of internment centres at Long Kesh, HMS Maidstone and Magilligan had 'produced such pressures that it became obvious … that Northern Ireland prison staffs would be unable to cope'. While a large intake of staff had been recruited in Ulster, this 'brought in its wake additional problems such as inexperience'. The Chair emphasised the increasingly dangerous character of prison life in Northern Ireland; for example, three guns had been found in the visiting area of Belfast Prison following an abortive escape attempt in early March. This incident 'serves as an additional reminder, if one were needed, of the hazardous nature of a prison officer's life in Northern Ireland at the present time'.

By October 1974, the *Prison Officers' Magazine* could report 'an appreciable dent' in numbers of prison officers on the mainland 'caused by volunteers going to Northern Ireland'. This situation was 'contingent upon internment remaining a permanent feature in Ulster', and the *Magazine* speculated that termination of the internment policy 'may be looked upon as a possibility'. In fact, internment *per se* was ended in December 1975. Nevertheless, paramilitary prisoners convicted of terrorist crimes were again denied political status in March 1976, leading by the late 1970s to a resumption of the hunger strikes which had won the prisoners Special Category status in 1972. These were now fought, literally, to the death, with all the traumatic consequences this brought for the prison staff most closely involved.

The impact on prison officers of such conditions – not only the hunger strikes but the continuing 'dirty protest' – was of course extreme. As the May Report put it, 'The most stressful present custodial work undoubtedly involves the staff responsible for the three H blocks in The Maze prison which house the non-conforming prisoners ... [T]he nature of these inmates' protests is bizarre in the extreme and the filth associated with it abhorrent and degrading'.[94]

'A Fractured and Militant Group ...'?

The experiences of prison officers on the mainland were of course less horrific. However, their conditions improved little during these years. As noted above, in 1978 a Committee of Inquiry, chaired by Justice May, had been appointed to look into issues like prisoner overpopulation and prison staffing, along with the questions of pay, working conditions and shift arrangements which had caused so much unrest amongst prison officers. However, once again the May Committee of Inquiry reported, in October 1979, less with a bang than a whimper. In what was by now a familiar pattern, the aftermath of the May Report saw hopes raised quickly dashed and recommendations only partially implemented.

Some of the most important aspects of the crisis in the system which had provoked the inquiry, like understaffing, were treated with complacent statements such as 'Prison service manpower has almost doubled in Great Britain in the last 15 years', while the POA's stand against excessive hours was met with the cool statement that 'The ... refusal of the POA ... to participate in the monitoring of overtime was an unnecessary impediment to the efficient allocation of public money'.[95] Nor should 'the present educational requirements' for recruitment of prison officers 'be altered', despite the POA's concerns (see pp. 68–9 above); and it was made clear, by implication, that the system of direct entry into governor grades would not be challenged.[96] On pay, the Committee commented disparagingly that 'Prison service grades are to some extent an isolated and inward looking group who may not always appreciate the true value of their pay and other benefits'.[97] Almost the only point to address prison officers' concerns was the recommendation that 'Urgent attention should be paid to improving the working conditions and facilities for all staff in penal establishments'.[98]

It was thus 'apparent to the officers that their demands had not been met'.[99] The May Committee had 'provided ... a factual analysis of the prison officers' dissatisfaction' through its 'graphic illustrations' of the decline in recruitment, as well as low pay; yet 'the Committee used this evidence in conjunction with an analysis of the prison officers as a fractured and militant group with a weak union unable to control its members'. Referring to the high level of industrial action which had in part sparked the inquiry, May argued once again in terms more apparently sympathetic to prisoners than to those employed to care for them: 'We believe that prisoners are among the most defenceless of any group within society affected by industrial action, and ... [their] conditions should not be made worse as a result of disputes to which they themselves are not a party'.[100] Given the violence towards prison officers which had contributed to the disputes, and the overcrowding and inadequate staffing which made it considerably more difficult to control frustrated and 'defenceless' prisoners, these comments must have been hard indeed for prison staff to swallow.

The attitude of the Committee was thus highly contradictory in responding to the crisis which had brought about its deliberations: 'The May Committee admitted to the justification of officers' demands and then justified their stand against giving concessions in terms of a struggle against militancy'. Placing this approach in the context of the then ongoing 'Winter of Discontent' and the current general mythology of 'trade union power', Steven Thomas comments that 'The industrial action taken by the prison officers was regarded as a manifestation of society's general problem of worker militancy and therefore their grievances were discussed in this light instead of as a specific result of the problems inherent in the prison system.'[101]

Not surprisingly, the POA was outraged. A Special Delegate Conference 'rejected the Report in its entirety', the recommended pay award of 6 per cent being described as 'derisory'.[102] In the light of the undoubted failure of the May Report to do more than comment on the systemic crisis which had brought it into being, while leaving the system itself 'fundamentally unaltered', the renewed militancy of the early 1980s was only too predictable.

However, by the time the May Report was published in October 1979, a yet more deeply-rooted disaster had hit prison officers and their organisation, just as it would workers across the board. This was the election in May 1979 of the Thatcher government, with consequences for social, economic and political policy which still reverberate today under 'New Labour'. As by now is well known, Thatcher and her Cabinet set out strategically to destroy the trade union movement, and used in that process methods far more sophisticated than the ill-fated 1971 Industrial Relations Act or Labour's abortive 1969 White Paper 'In Place of Strife'.

As Steven Thomas further notes in his account of the May Report, the Committee's condemnations of prison officer 'militancy' were:

> in accord with the political atmosphere of 1979 engendered by the return of a Conservative government coming to power on a 'law and order' ticket. This government did not just stand for the preservation of civil order but transcended this notion and entered the realms of industrial relations proposing to regulate them and reduce the influence of the Unions.[103]

This was to understate the case. Thatcher and her Cabinet were determined to crush so-called 'trade union power' and, as the years ahead were to show, would use any means, subtle or aggressive, to do so. Along with its passion for the 'free market' and the consequent drive towards cost-cutting and privatisation, the impact of this sea change in government on prison staff and the Prison Service was worse than anything that had been seen since the Gladstone Report of more than 100 years ago. These consequences are explored in full in the following chapters.

3

1980–87: THE IMPACT OF THATCHERISM: A 'FRESH START'?

Before the first anniversary of Thatcher's notably anti-union government, prison officers had signalled their disappointment and resentment at the non-event of the 1979 May Report in time-honoured fashion – by attempting to start a breakaway union. In 1980, prison officer J. Sutton proposed the creation of a 'Prison Force Federation' which, as a *Guardian* report put it, 'has grown out of prison officers' frustration at [the POA's] allegedly close identification with the management'.[1] POA Circulars for March 1980 quote correspondence from Sutton to the Certification Officer in which he writes: 'I have much faith in our ability to operate as a true Trade Union and certainly the P.F.F. [Prison Force Federation] will be no "Creature of Management".' Sutton's submission had argued that the POA was not independent because it included Chief Officers, described by Sutton as 'part of the policy-making senior management team'. The POA's reply noted that 'chief officers comprise less than 2 per cent of the membership [and] only one is a member of the NEC'.

Like most such initiatives, the 'Federation' lasted only a short time, but it was a warning signal on prison officers' continued frustration at any real lack of progress in advancing their conditions. In February 1980, a POA Circular expressed concern over the possible course of Civil Service pay settlements due on 1 April:

> Already, there are clearly visible indications that, once again, a great deal of storm and stress may have to be encountered before the 1980 pay settlement is finalised. This has been the pattern consistently over the past

decade, and the ominous signs are around that 1980 will be no different from recent previous years ....

From October of the same year, in fact, national industrial action took place as a direct result of the Prison Department refusing to extend the payments granted by the May Report to Functional Group System (FGS) workers to staff working at 'Vee' scheme establishments. Worse, this was followed by the refusal of the Home Secretary to allow the matter to go to arbitration, a move which 'saw the Association taking industrial action ... throughout the Service'[2] as mandated by a Special Delegate Conference on 6 October 1980. The action was described as 'unprecedented' by the POA Annual Report. However, in response the government successfully obtained the support of Parliament to extend the provisions of the Imprisonment Bill, which gave it unprecedented powers to combat the Association's industrial action. As Home Office minister Leon Brittan told Parliament on 27 November 1980: 'much as [the Home Secretary] regretted the necessity for the wide powers available under the Act, he would not hesitate to see their renewal should the prison officers' industrial action and its consequences persist'.[3]

This high-level statement in itself demonstrates the far-reaching impact the action had had. As POA General Secretary Ken Daniel put it in a speech to the 1981 Scottish POA Conference: 'This was the first time in contemporary industrial history that a government had passed special legislation to deal with an industrial dispute while it was still in progress ... indicat[ing] the measure of determination used to combat our action.' In response, 'inevitably, attitudes then hardened and the industrial action was to endure for more than three months'.[4]

'Bludgeoned by Legislation ...'

In fact, of course, 1980 saw the first in what became a notorious series of laws emanating from an aggressively anti-union government. The Employment Act of that year made trade unions liable to prosecution over 'secondary' or solidarity action, thus striking at the very heart of collective organisation. A resolution to the 1980 Scottish POA Conference, referring to 'current Government policy on Union reform' and calling on Conference to 'declare its opposition to any proposals that would remove the right of Prison Officers to take Industrial Action' was carried unanimously. A further Employment Act in 1982 removed trade unions' historic legal immunity from being sued for industrial action, narrowed the legal definition of 'trade dispute' and allowed employers to sack striking workers.

In 1984, the government's decision to ban trade unions at Government Communications Head Quarters (GCHQ) confirmed its anti-unionism at a time when Thatcher was hypocritically paying court to the Polish trade union, Solidarnosc. The POA issued a Circular in the GCHQ workers' defence:

> Members will be aware that the Government has taken an unprecedented step to withdraw Trade Union representation from civil servants at Government Communications Headquarters. Whilst the ban does not affect any grades represented by the Prison Officers' Association, it is clear that an injustice done to one section of the Trade Union movement is the reproach heaped on all of us.[5]

1984 was also the year of the government's Trade Union Act on internal union democracy, allegedly aimed at 'giving the unions back to their members' but in fact imposing a series of draconian regulations over strike ballots, and so on. As a letter in the March 1985 issue of the *Prison Officers' Magazine* put it: 'The Government has embarked on a policy to divide and fragment the trade union movement ....' Citing the 1978 Ridley Report,[6] which had advocated the build-up of coal stocks to pre-empt future miners' strikes, the writer argued:

> We are assisting the Government ... by default to achieve their ambition to weaken even further an indolent and divided Trade Union movement. The movement has been bludgeoned by legislation; morale is low. If we wish to take industrial action of the most trivial nature we have to ballot members, giving management 28 days' notice of our intention ... Gone

are the days of the effective short sharp action used responsibly by this Association in the past to achieve its aims.

An example of the government's obsessive anti-trade unionism which directly affected the POA came about when, in early October 1985, a Tory Party political broadcast showed a photograph of Colin Steel, then POA Chairman, as part of a series of photos of union leaders holding up block voting cards. This was accompanied by the commentary: 'the votes of millions of Conservative union members are being given by union bosses to Labour and even more extreme left-wing causes'. The photograph corresponding to the words 'and even more extreme left-wing causes' was of Colin Steel. The broadcast continued: 'It was the [union] bosses' block votes that gave Arthur Scargill his victory at last month's Trades Union Congress ….'

As the POA argued in court:

> By use of the photo of Colin Steel the impression was conveyed that he had voted in favour of a motion from Arthur Scargill at the September 1985 TUC. In fact Mr Steel had never used a block vote, keeps to the POA's non-partisan and neutral party political stance, and had voted against the Scargill resolution.

After the POA's successful court case in December 1985, Colin received an apology from the Defendant, Tory Employment Secretary Norman Tebbit.

'Forced to Look Unreasonable …'

However, in 1980 the trade union legislation had only begun to put a noose around the necks of the movement. The POA national action which began in October of that year took three basic forms: prevention of essential maintenance, leading to a closure of some prison workshops; refusal to carry out certain duties within prisons, and – defined by the government as 'perhaps the most serious' – refusal to receive prisoners sentenced or remanded by the courts. As a result of this last action, the government thundered: 'some 3,500 prisoners are being held in police cells'.[7]

Not all MPs were as hostile. The member for the constituency covering Gartree remarked:

> I urge the Government to think about the possibility of not continually saying 'No' to arbitration, and adopting an attitude that is a little more humane towards Prison Officers. They are not a militant group. They do probably the most unpleasant job in the country ....

Nevertheless, the sanctions were still in force at the end of the year, by which time the Prison Department and Home Office had devised proposals to resolve the dispute. These, which included 'the adoption of a new duty system for prison officers which will eliminate anomalies',[8] were put before a Special Delegate Conference of the POA in mid December 1980. Delegates refused to accept these proposals due to what they regarded as the unacceptable 'strings' represented by the proposed Common Working System (CWS) (see below). Instead, the Conference resolved to maintain the industrial action and to continue to seek the right to arbitration from the Home Office. As the Conference Report put it: 'To say that in the latter part of 1980 the industrial action dominated all other matters would be an understatement ....'

However, there were other matters for the Association to deal with even during this hectic period, primarily that of the suspension of the Civil Service Pay Agreement, yet again, by the Conservative government. This agreement had been suspended by Labour in 1975 as part of its Stage 1 incomes policy (see Chapter 2), and its renewed suspension denied civil servants across all grades a review of their pay. Adding to the unions' resentment, the independent pay research findings on Civil Service pay were denied, despite a legal challenge, to the constituent unions of the Council of Civil Service Unions (CCSU). In response, the CCSU launched a campaign against the government's determination to depress Civil Service pay, 'and as the year drew to a close meetings had been held up and down the country to register the feelings of anger'.[9]

Meanwhile, industrial action by POA members on both a national and local basis over a number of issues continued into the following year. As a leading POA official at the time recalled:

The Prison Service had refused to go to arbitration and the only thing left was to take some form of action ... Even after we'd taken our own form of action nationally on overtime there was further action taken by the membership in selected institutions. We'd never undertaken mindless industrial action – just hoped that governments would honour agreements ... but they didn't ... they created the circumstances to force us to take industrial action. We were forced to look unreasonable ... that's what the Prison Service did to us.[10]

Forms of industrial action varied from one institution to another, but a vivid account from an activist at Pentonville conveys their ingenuity:

I was on the front gate – a vehicle [containing prisoners] pulled up, we said 'We're not letting you in because of industrial action due to finish at twelve o'clock.' The Governor came down [and] he said 'I'm giving you a direct order to let the vehicle in' – we said 'No' ... We were taken to the boardroom which is inside the prison and we sat for our period of suspension in the boardroom while he was taking advice. At five past twelve he comes back in the boardroom ... and said 'I want you to sign these bits of paper [saying] you will not withdraw your labour.' We said 'Don't be silly.' We'd had a ballot to withdraw our labour by saying we weren't going to let prisoners in ....[11]

In another form of action:

it became so traumatic for them – you had 300 staff stood outside the gate [who] should come in at half past seven or before – all at half past seven they start shuffling forward to come through the gate – it's chaos – and then [management] line you up in the passageway and give you a letter which stops you 45 minutes' pay ... Everybody's got the letter, screws it up, throws it in the bin ....[12]

The Killer Instinct?

The Association suspended and then renewed the action a number of times, firstly in early 1981, in the light of the government's CWS proposals. Such suspension provoked dissent from the membership. One particularly disgruntled POA representative from Ford Open Prison wrote in the March 1981 *Prison Officers' Magazine*: 'This whole industrial Action has got to be the biggest farce in history ... To describe it as a shambles would be a mild description.' Others, however, were outspoken in the POA's defence. As the Gloucester branch put it: 'we believe that our action is the right one, because we are fed up with being continually sold down the line year after year. It surely must come to pass that we Prison Officers eventually get a good deal from the Government or do we have to be pushed into the sidelines yet again?'

From a different point of view, the typical difficulties faced by workers on strike were expressed in poetic form:

> ... how long will it all last.
> It's Christmas, I don't want to fast.
> Into the New Year without any cheer.
> My pockets are emptying fast ...

By May 1981, even the Gloucester members were expressing unrest. A further contribution to the May 1981 issue of the *Magazine* noted that:

it would now seem that the 'Industrial Action' which has been in operation since last October has been suspended (More like dead and buried). To say we ... are disappointed must be the understatement of the year ... It's a pity that our NEC did not take a leaf out of the book of miners' leaders[13] to get favourable results for its members ....'

Rather in tune with the later controversy over the 1984 miners' strike, many members felt the problems could have been avoided with a national ballot over action, a view reflected in a number of motions to the 1981 Annual Conference.

A letter to the September 1981 *Magazine* summed up the successes and failures of the action:

The strike is over, the government have won ... In many ways the action proved to be very effective. The technique of the selective strike was developed to a new sophistication ... [But] I am convinced that had we played a bigger part in the industrial action, the outcome would have been different ... To get anywhere with this government you need the killer instinct.

As late as 1983, resolutions to Annual Conference 'deplore[d] the failure to reach agreement under the terms of the suspended industrial action of CDC claims, and instruct[ed] the NEC to negotiate payment immediately ... of all outstanding claims'. Internal dissent characterised the Annual Conferences of the period. As one activist recalls: ''82, '83,'84, Battle of Hastings, we still talk about that. Annual Conference at Hastings became known as the NEC's Battle of Hastings because of the infighting.'[14]

Manipulative Mathematics

Despite the suspension of the POA action over 'duty systems', conflict again arose with the government shortly afterwards on the wider issue of the suspension of the Civil Service Agreement, noted above. The ensuing Civil Service-wide dispute, which ended in August 1981, was described by then POA General Secretary Ken Daniel as:

> one of the longest and most damaging industrial disputes known in the country this century ... With complete disregard for good industrial relations practice, the Government unilaterally discarded our pay agreement for 1981 and future years ... The end result was a lengthy and damaging industrial action.[15]

As indicated, local industrial action had continued throughout the period, whatever the POA strategy at national level. The Wandsworth Report in the December 1981 *Prison Officers' Magazine*'s 'News and Jottings' noted that:

> We are taking industrial action here about manning levels, the staff decided that enough was enough and registered their disapproval by doing controlled unlocking for a while. Some of the things we are asked to do are downright dangerous, such as only two officers on a landing, one taking applications while the other unlocks and locks up etc, no mean feat when you have sixty or seventy prisoners milling about ... There are a lot of things

wrong but nobody in authority seems to care, still if the place does blow up at least the POA will be able to say we told you so ....

By January 1982, the same branch was 'implementing the CNA [Certified Normal Accommodation]'; that is, only receiving the formally required number of prisoners, in order to highlight the acute shortage of staff. In response, 'the department were suddenly able to find us detached duty staff which had previously been impossible!' Interestingly, this confirms the force of a recommendation on strike strategy in the July 1981 issue of the *Prison Officers' Magazine*: 'The strongest action that we can take is to refuse to accept prisoners beyond our CNA figure. This causes the Government to bleed pound notes profusely ....'

POA members at Wandsworth, like those in many other institutions, were increasingly disturbed by the reports of the new attendance scheme, the CWS, which the government had proposed but of which very few details were as yet forthcoming. As a letter to the July 1981 *Prison Officers' Magazine*, headed 'Thoughts On the Proposed Common Working System or Manipulative Mathematics', noted with foreboding: 'Like all my fellow POA members I received the consultative document on "Gross Hours and the Common Working System" and since then have wrestled with its policies and formula ....' The letter continued worriedly: 'Should the proposed CWS be accepted in its present form how many POA members realise that they stand to lose money?' However, the CWS continued to be shrouded in obscurity. In December 1981, the Wandsworth branch could still sum up members' fears with its laconic observation, 'Everybody is wondering when our new scheme of attendance will come in (if it ever does). Feelings are a bit mixed; here some want it, some don't ... we will have to see how a vote goes if we ever get to take one that is.'[16]

Pay and conditions for prison officers were not the only issue facing the POA in 1981. The period was one of immense social unrest, provoked predictably by the draconian Thatcher regime. A senior POA official recalls street riots in Brixton, Toxteth and beyond: 'There were riots in the streets, and they had to open prison camps all over the place ... the mood of the service and our members was reflected in the anger that was felt on the streets of Britain ... Britain was an angry place at that time ....'[17] This anger found its reflection in the mood of the POA rank and file:

> the prison service wasn't shielded from that particular anger – in fact it reflected it in many respects, and because of the nature of that anger our members were saying quite clearly – we have rights too, we want people to fight for our rights, and we are willing to support anybody who's willing to – and that was the kind of attitude that prevailed at the time in the POA.[18]

'Pay Determination by Government Diktat'

By 1982, however, prison officers appeared to be as far as ever from fully obtaining those 'rights'. As newly-elected General Secretary David Evans[19] put it in the April issue of the *Magazine*: 'The Government's pay offer in 1982 has struck at the very heart of unfairness in pay procedures. It has imposed ... limitations of the severest nature ....' The offer consisted of 'no-pay' for some, and increases of only 1 per cent or 2.5 per cent for the 'vast majority', though some senior staff would receive 5.5 per cent. In June 1981, the Megaw inquiry had been set up in order to 'consider ... the system by which the remuneration of the non-industrial Civil Service should be determined',[20] now that the previous Pay Research Unit had been unilaterally disbanded by the government. Commenting on the forthcoming Report of this inquiry, which he acknowledged was to consider 'the widest possible features of pay determination' in the Civil Service rather than the specific position of prison officers, the General Secretary added the warning note: 'The Association's membership were deeply disappointed with the Justice May Inquiry and a repeat performance of that nature could only serve to shatter the faith of Prison Officers.'

By contrast, the Scottish Prison Officers' Association was optimistic: 1982 'could be the one of the most important years ... in the history of the Scottish Prison Officers' Association' with regard to the working parties set up to implement the May Report, as well as the Megaw inquiry. General Secretary John Renton wrote in the January 1981 issue of the SPOA's *Link*:

> There is also the prospect that, in 1982, we may at last see the introduction of gross hours, which will of course reduce the number of working hours for all members of staff. There is, too, the possibility of introducing averaging of pay … Our object should be to strive towards a unified service, and this could be a major factor in that regard.'

In October 1982, however, after having studied the Report, he was less convinced:

> There is no doubt that there are a number of aspects … which are against the interest of Prison Officers. For example, the status of the Wynn Parry formula … has been challenged and it is likely that it will disappear. Whatever its failings may have been the Wynn Parry formula did result in prison officers having their pay claims considered objectively ….

Throughout 1982, discussions had been taking place on the proposals of the Megaw Report. As the General Secretary had commented to the SPOA Conference in October: 'It is clear from that report that the prison officer cannot be expected to be treated any differently from the generality of his civil service colleagues. Our unique position in the labour market is to be ignored ….' As the General Secretary noted in the December issue of the *Magazine*, the emphasis of the Report on the Civil Service as a whole would mean that 'Whatever approach is finally adopted … the 1983 pay round will have to be fought, and won, by the collective actions of Civil Service Unions.' Not only did this go against the wishes of members as expressed in that year's Annual Conference, but, as ever, 'it is clear that future pay bargaining will be both bitter and hard'. Discussions between the POA and the Treasury on the Report covered areas ranging from internal relativities to low pay, industrial relations and arbitration – and, ominously, performance-related pay.

The POA's Annual Report for 1983 saw the Association still highly concerned about Megaw: 'There is no doubt that the Megaw recommendations represent the most serious of challenges to Civil Servants' pay. Prison Officers are no exception to that principle ....'[21] Some of the reasons for that concern are spelt out in a dissenting 'Minority Report' proposed by one member of the Committee of Inquiry, John Chalmers,[22] which points out, amongst other things, that:

> The [Megaw] Report immediately betrays its stance by refusing to identify the real reasons for the breakdown of the pay research system – persisting and worrying breaches by successive governments of the National Pay Agreement culminating in ... total withdrawal from [the Agreement] in 1981. It was this clear breach of the Pay Agreement which caused the bitter and prolonged strike of 1981.

Chalmers also criticises the assumption of the Megaw Report that cash limits set before negotiations were 'inevitable'; the imposition of job evaluation based on job analysis rather than whole job comparisons, and administered by private management consultants; and the Report's ruling against the trade union right to compel the government to go to arbitration. Chalmers also criticised the 'cash limit system' imposed over the previous four years as 'pay determination by government "diktat"'. The proposal to restrict access to arbitration would 'make industrial action all the more likely', and adherence to analytical job evaluation schemes would greatly prolong the period needed to establish fair job comparisons.

Many of the POA's responses echo these criticisms. The General Secretary's Address to the 1983 Conference argues that 'Without doubt the decision of the Conservative Government to abolish for Civil Servants an agreed pay procedure has been most damaging', and notes that as part of the Megaw recommendations the government was now prepared to go over the heads of the NEC and consult with members directly: 'This feature is neither fair or democratic and if it persists into the 1984 pay discussions then quite clearly it signifies the resolve of the Government to continually peg the pay of Civil Servants below that [of] the private sector.' Further:

> The whole question of outside comparisons and the right to arbitration are principles upon which heated and protracted discussion will take place. The case for Prison Officers, we firmly believe, is different to that of other Civil Servants and this has been reflected in our relative pay bargaining positions since the Wynn Parry Report of 1959.

In general, 'The whole question of pay for 1983 and 1984 [was] still outstanding on the Megaw recommendations.'

Meanwhile, continued cash limits were still being imposed on all sections of the Civil Service, and improvements in leave arrangements were 'not as successful as the Association would have liked'. Yet again, a government inquiry had had little or no impact on the daily questions facing prison officers. Towards the end of 1983, the General Secretary was forced to the conclusion that the Megaw recommendations would have greater relevance to pay negotiations in 1985 than either that year or the next.

Discreetly Forgotten?

The Common Working System continued to provoke concern, with the comment from Liverpool that, 'As the Common Working Agreement [CWA] unfolds, different snakes appear to jump out of the basket ... In view of the ridiculous pay offer this year, one would be very surprised if this new working system does have all the financial benefits that we were led to expect.' The Onley branch was 'concerned over the recent pay offer ... when coupled with ... the loss of ASDA [Additional Staff Daytime Allowance] payments in the CWA ... most of our members will suffer a loss of pay as a result (what price progress).' Sharing similar concerns, Portland added: 'It is our unbounded belief that to accept the Common Working Agreement is to accept a pay cut ....' As for the government's pay offer: 'What a bloody insult it is ... It would split this service as never before [with] the temptation for senior members to say "I'm all right, Jack" ... Our NEC must reject with all its power; a pay award must be for all its members, not part.' However, the Shrewsbury branch argued that 'The Common Working System appears to be dying a death at the moment, mainly due to the Department trying to renege on the "agreement" ... It's our belief ... that it could cost them a few bob, and as a result want it ditched as soon as possible ....', and by November 1982 the Northallerton branch could ask: 'What's happened to the CWS? Has anybody heard of it or was it a figment of the imagination, has someone lost his tongue or has it been discreetly forgotten?'

As one prison officer recalled years later regarding the CWS:

> They blinded you with lots of information. Everyone in the service was going to be on this one system. So they did this for about three years – brainwashing staff, sending you on courses, sending people out training – and another pamphlet would come out, this is another form of the Common Working System, and it went on and on, everyone's getting worn out ....'[23]

As late as January 1985, a report from the Maze Prison on 'The Common Working Agreement/37-hour week' pleaded:

> We wait in anticipation for a favourable result in our favour ... All we want Mrs T is to be treated like all other non-industrial civil servants within the Civil Service who are on 37 hours ... come on Mrs T where is this democratic right that you and your Tory Party shout about all the time, or are Prison Officers yet again being classed as second class citizens?

In the same month, the Onley branch commented: 'We are anxiously awaiting the conference decisions on CWA ... It would seem that over the CWA issue the department bought four years of peace for a promise that is not to be fulfilled.'

Nevertheless, during the early 1980s the CWS continued in the background as a possible answer to the problems raised by the FGS, 'Vee' and CDC shift-related issues which had sparked the national dispute of 1980. The ramifications of the strike and its stalled resolution continued. In 1984, a Special Delegate Conference on the 1980 dispute was held at which the NEC reported that negotiations on possible terms for a settlement were now 'at a critical stage'. The leadership argued that negotiations on the CWA and gross hours had taken far longer than expected 'due to the tardiness of the Prison Department after negotiations ended on … the CWA in September 1982' – a reference which explains the apparent 'death' of the CWA in that year. However, the announcement that the Home Secretary had now refused to offer gross hours as part of the terms for settlement of the 1980–81 dispute led to a number of dissenting resolutions at the 1984 Special Delegate Conference.

The 1984 Annual Report records the NEC as declaring itself

> fully appreciative of the anger and frustration being experienced by the membership. However, it is the opinion of the NEC that our responses to the Home Office Prison Department on this issue will need to be positive and properly co-ordinated. In view of this, therefore, Branches are advised to refrain from embarking upon any course of local industrial action at the present time.

Playing with Fire …

Again, however, the problems facing prison officers extended far beyond pay and conditions. The June 1982 issue of the *Magazine* contained another reference to the ever-present issue of prison overcrowding, with none other than the Director-General of the Prison Service, Sir Dennis Trevelyan, describing the problem as 'an affront to civilised society'. Difficulties were compounded by the fact that, at any one time, a number of cells were out of use. As the General Secretary put it: 'When coupled with … the decaying state of many institutions, the Service is facing more than a chronic crisis.' Trevelyan had struck a chord with the POA in his comments that 'the traditional objectives of imprisonment provide no answer to prison staff confronted by problems of overcrowding … [and] increasing numbers of violent and dangerous prisoners'; yet these points, like recommendations in the May Report of 'humane containment' and 'positive custody', were 'empty aims' without a move towards more positive conditions for staff. The argument led back to the POA's ongoing drive to widen the role of the prison officer: 'New buildings will do a lot, but it has to be accompanied by a commitment from the Home Office Prison Department to provide a developing role for Prison Officers.'

The problem of prison overcrowding was compounded, as always, by corresponding staff shortages. As the General Secretary noted, the need 'to ensure that these overcrowded and staff-denuded establishments can function' created the contradictory phenomenon of 'detached duty' in which some prisons were required to send extra officers to the most severely understaffed establishments, thus rendering them in their turn unable to complete their own 'essential task lists'. As a retired full-time official put it: 'In 1982 staff deficiencies were a huge issue. The May Report didn't resolve everything – items outstanding like staffing levels and shift systems continued to bug the service ....'[24] By November 1982, Stoke Heath branch could report that, across the Prison Service, there were 'over forty five thousand in custody now. Allied to a shortfall of thousands of staff ....'[25] In a more hopeful sign, a speech by the Home Secretary to magistrates in April 1983 acknowledged the problems of the rapidly increasing prison population and overcrowding and announced the opening of 14 new prisons employing 5,000 new prison officers. However, as subsequent sections show, this promise was slow in realisation.

In direct contradiction to the overwhelming need for a more stable, full-time staff complement, the 1982 POA Conference reported a new and sinister development presaging much of the Conservative government's future 'contracting-out' agenda with a reference to the possible use of the private firm Securicor to take over prison escorts. As the POA Chair commented:

> If the Prison Department is looking for massive confrontation, then it should continue looking at prisons and courts with a view to taking them from the Prison Service. If there is one area that the Service will go into battle about, it is escorts and courts. To the Home Office I offer this genuine piece of advice: leave it well alone, you are playing with fire.

Unfortunately, as the years to come were to show, this was by no means the end of the issue.

Further concern over staffing issues during the period was provoked by the Prison Department's proposed Review of Management Structure, which the Association warned would 'demand a commitment from the membership of iron determination if they are to protect their positions within the Service'. These proposals appeared to diminish the role of Chief Officers and Principal Officers within the management structure in favour of increased layers of middle management. The POA produced a document on the role of Assistant Governors for the Review in which it argued that the Home Office Prison Department had 'employed far too many Assistant Governors for the tasks available to them'. Local management had therefore tried to establish wider roles for these Assistant Governors, 'often to the detriment of the role of the Chief Officer and the Principal Officer ... One of the current difficulties preventing a clear chain of command based upon functions is the presence of too many middle management grades.'[26]

In 1983, these proposed management changes provoked a serious dispute at HMP Preston, sparked when two Principal Officers (the next grade down from Chief Officer II and one above Senior Officer) had challenged the authority of an Acting Governor by refusing to accompany him on his prison rounds. In response, the Prison Service sent out an angry Notice to Staff (NTS 63/83) giving notice that 'failure to recognise the lawful authority of a Governor ... constitutes a fundamental breach of an officer's conditions of employment'. In response, the POA argued that the Notice had pre-empted discussions on the Management Structure Review; in addition:

> We believe that leaving an institution 'in-charge' of an Assistant Governor is a grave mistake ... [The] sense of timing in issuing the NTS we can only interpret as being calculated to challenge our Membership ... [and] is a direct challenge on the authority and status of Chief Officers and Principal Officers.

The NEC declared itself 'committed to resolving this matter and ... wholly supportive of the Preston Branch'.

Another serious industrial relations issue arose at the Dartmoor branch of the POA, which had been in dispute over unilaterally imposed Manpower Team recommendations which the branch believed would lead to unsafe manning levels. When the branch Chair, Brian Benwell, refused to obey an order relating to these unsafe levels, he was put under notice of dismissal. A call for protest action was unanimously endorsed by the POA, but Benwell was nevertheless dismissed with effect from 31 December 1983. The NEC, 'still of the view that ... dismissal is unnecessarily harsh', instructed solicitors to look into the case. They also decided to send a delegation to the Home Secretary asking him to investigate, and informed the Prison Department that they would instruct POA members to take industrial action in support of Benwell's reinstatement.

Still Attempting to Finalise that Agreement ...

A number of other questions remained unresolved. The Association had been negotiating throughout 1983 over the proposed abolition of the long-hours gratuity, 'and the thorny question of the Common Working System [was] still outstanding'. As the General Secretary put it: 'The whole question of the common working system and gross hours has been ravaging the POA for a considerable time'; a Special Delegate Conference was to be held on the issue before the Annual Conference in 1984. In the meantime, POA Chair Colin Steel noted that, while the POA's national action in 1980 had led to the offer by the Home Secretary of a reduced working week and new attendance system, 'We are ... still attempting to finalise that agreement and that offer.' Ongoing problems with negotiations on the CWS ('which will surprise you all') had, however, led to a meeting with the Home Secretary, and the Chair was 'hopeful that [this] meeting will unblock the stagnated negotiations on the CWS ... hopefully I can look at a Special Conference before the end of the Autumn'.[27]

By later in the year, the CWA had been revised, and 22,000 copies were to be distributed in the first two weeks of September. As part of the new agreement, Agreed Staffing Levels (ASLs) were to be standardised, with all staff calculations to be based on the assumption that every officer worked 40 hours a week; some overtime would still be necessary to cover the 'non-effective hours' for every officer (annual leave, sick leave, training, and so on). This new system of 'contract hours' was a first step towards the ending of compulsory overtime, in which any period of overtime lasting more than ten hours would now be voluntary other than in an emergency. Despite these more optimistic prospects, the General Secretary commented that 'The 1984 pay negotiations will, to my mind, be the hardest discussions the Civil Service unions will ever have with any Government.'[28]

Correspondence between the Council of Civil Service unions (CCSU) and the Treasury in late September appear to justify his foreboding. Although, at a meeting on 5 September, the CCSU had informed the Secretary of State for Employment of 'the deep rooted hostility existing among members in respect of the Government's intransigence on 1984 pay', the government confirmed on the 15th that the cash factor for settlements in the forthcoming pay round would be set at 3 per cent. As the CCCU commented, this announcement pre-empted not only any meaningful negotiations for 1984, but also the earlier discussions on the Megaw Report.

POA documents for 1984 tell much the same story, with the 3 per cent limit on pay 'rigidly applied by the Treasury'. Some hope lay in the decision to give the government's Office of Manpower Economics (OME) the task of collecting data on pay and conditions, including basic pay, merit pay, hours, holidays and 'other remunerative elements', to be used for pay comparisons. A Report was expected in March, after which 'discussions with the Treasury [would] begin in earnest', according to a POA Circular. However, the Circular continues: 'The determination of the Government to maintain low pay settlements continues unabated.'

The OME Report was duly produced and 'reflect[ed], in many instances, the arguments advanced by the Unions on pay factors for a number of years'. However, the government had made it clear that the OME figures would be just one factor taken into consideration among many, 'including especially cost'. At the first meeting between the unions and the Treasury on 17 April, the CCSU presented a claim for 7 per cent based on the OME Report, with a minimum increase of £7 a week, for non-industrial civil servants; while the OME Report recommended an average of 6 per cent, the CCCU cited the fact that since April 1980 the retail price index had risen by 37 per cent and average earnings by 49 per cent, whereas Civil Service pay had only increased by 19.4 per cent. Yet, while Treasury representatives promised to give the claim 'careful consideration', their initial reaction, predictably, was that it was 'far too high'. They also refused to give any advance commitment to arbitration.[29]

On 24 April, the Treasury made a 3 per cent offer in conformity with the government's pay norm, increased to 4 per cent at the top grades and on flat rate pay. This offer was immediately rejected by the Trade Union Side as 'not even ... a basis for negotiation'. On 31 May, the Treasury offered 5 per cent; the NEC recommended rejection, and the membership agreed, with 71.5 per cent voting against on an 87 per cent turnout. The unions recommended that the issue be referred to arbitration but, as it had done previously, the government rejected the recommendation. Despite the POA's stand, however, it appears that the unions eventually accepted revised rates of pay from 1 April 1984 of 4 per cent and 5 per cent.

While no industrial action on the scale of the early 1980s was now taking place, many disputes remained in progress. In response to a question in Parliament, Home Secretary Douglas Hurd reported that:

> In addition to a number of disputes at particular establishments – over overcrowding, staffing levels, the implementation of Manpower Reports, and allowances – there are two national disputes, one relating to procedural issues on Use of Force reports[30] and the other to procedures for internal investigations ... None of the disputes at present involve industrial action.

The apparent lack of overt strike action over pay in 1984 did not, therefore, mean an overall lack of conflict during the year. One typical example was official action at Ranby Prison in March 1984 over the withdrawal of an outside security post known as the 'November IV post' after a contractor had put up a corrugated iron fence which divided the prison, meaning staff at perimeter security posts could no longer see one another. Prisoners had been meeting in the concealed area, which had also been used as a drop-off point for drugs. The NEC argued that the 'arbitrary withdrawal of the November IV post was based on a policy of financial dogma rather than the safety and security of staff and public'. After 'limited' strike action by the Ranby Branch, the Prison Department proposed a 24-hour patrol of the perimeter as an interim measure, leading to a return to work.

However, conflict at the prison resurfaced in November, this time over manning levels; the action led to discussions in the House of Commons, with the Home Secretary reporting the possibility that the staff at Ranby would walk out on total strike in December. Yet when MP Joe Ashton asked the Home Secretary whether he was satisfied that a breakout by two prisoners from Ranby had not been due to the reduced surveillance of the perimeter fence, along with reductions in staffing, the answer came: 'We are satisfied that this escape was not due to any of the factors described by the Hon. Member.'

The POA's relationship with the authorities remained wary. After a letter was received from the Prison Department regarding a proposed Working Party on Communications between Management and Staff, the NEC decided to treat the matter 'with the utmost gravity. Should any member of the Association co-operate with working committees of this nature, it is the NEC's view that [this] would allow our employers to undermine [established and recognised] negotiating structures.' In fact, the NEC 'expressed amazement that the Home Office Prison Department could authorise the setting up of such a Working Party without prior consultation with the POA'.[31] Later in the year, the Prison Department published a report on its Review of Management Structure, which had already been implicated in the serious dispute at Preston described above; the NEC urged branches to refrain from taking part in local discussions until they had concluded their consideration of the document.

More disappointment at Prison Department policy came with a revised Disciplinary Code which failed to overcome the many weaknesses in previous versions. As General Secretary David Evans pointed out, a major example of such weaknesses was that those bringing charges against a prison officer were not required to prove the officer's guilt beyond reasonable doubt; the new Code made no improvement on this. As the General Secretary put it: 'There has to be a procedure to discover if a case against an Officer can be proved beyond reasonable doubt. There must be no point at which "a friend" must prove an Officer's innocence ....'[32]

In addition to the weaknesses of the Code, in many establishments, governors were adopting practices which undermined even the basic rights specified. For example, officers accused of a misdemeanour were being called for interview with the governor and middle management; following this, the prison officer would receive a brief note recording that the interview had taken place and its details. Such letters were then placed on the officer's personal file. As the General Secretary pointed out, these practices were 'oppressive and intimidatory', particularly as there was often no provision for removing the letter from the record. In the light of this and the continued weaknesses of the Disciplinary Code, the Association advised its branches to instruct their members not to cooperate with these processes, to inform their governors of this advice and to inform POA HQ of any disciplining of members which breached these guidelines. In June 1985, Lowdham Grange duly reported:

> We are disgusted over inmates being used to give evidence against ... staff ... charged under the Code of Discipline when it is the Governor's policy not to use inmates to give evidence against other inmates. We hope the NEC will pursue this with the utmost vigour ....[33]

Despite such injustices, there were grounds for optimism during the period. Significant increases in staffing announced in late 1983 and early 1984 provided, in the POA Chairman's view, 'a background of confidence against which everyone can together tackle the immediate issues which lie before the Service – the need to bring discussions to an end on the Common Working System and the impending report of the Review of Management Structures'. A 1984 speech by the Home Secretary to Annual Conference seemed to endorse this view:

> I will not deny that there have been times in the past when industrial relations have broken down. Many of you will recall the industrial action

taken by Prison Officers in the winter of 1980 to 81 when, at its peak, 5000 inmates had to be held in police cells ... However, the picture has now altered radically ... The Service can look forward to real improvement, not only in its working conditions, but also ... in the quality of its work and in job satisfaction.

Men in Charge of Animals?

An early indication of these promised improvements came in October 1983, when a speech by the Home Secretary referred to significant increases in staff: 'In May 1979 there were about 15,700 prison officers ... now there are 17,750. By March 1984 there will be 18,065.' Soon afterwards, in February 1984, he announced 'a very substantial increase in resources for the Prison Service', stating that 5,000 extra prison officers would be recruited between 1 April 1984 and 31 March 1988, of whom 1,230 would be needed 'to man new or refurbished accommodation'. The increase in staff was promoted as potentially dealing with the 'excessive amounts of overtime' carried out by prison officers.

The Home Department also announced that the prison building programme had been accelerated to provide 6,600 places in new prisons and 4,000 through redevelopment in existing prisons. Broadmoor was being completely redeveloped on its existing site, beginning in February 1984 with completion in autumn 1986. While welcome, these decisions of course reflected the inexorable increase in prison population, now at well over 40,000 and expected to reach 47,000 by 1990.

Prison officers could also find some satisfaction in their endorsement by the eminent and longstanding prison reformer Lord Longford, who spoke at length in a House of Lords debate in March 1984 on the need to expand the welfare role of prison officers. As Longford put it, referring to the 'uniformed branch' of prison staff: 'They are doing a difficult job ... and they are doing it with honest zeal ... yet they are curiously isolated and neglected in public discussion.' Longford remarked that 'The idea of giving [prison officers] a more constructive role has been around for a considerable time ....' Referring back to 1955, when he had opened the first House of Lords debate on prisons, he recalled:

> The argument was that in future Prison Officers should become more like social workers – not just turnkeys ... I said that 30 years ago and better men than I have said it since. However, I cannot see that any progress in this direction has been made in the last 30 years.[34]

Criticising what he termed a 'mania for security' in the wake of the 'disaster' of the Mountbatten Report, Longford went on to describe the May Report also as 'profoundly disappointing' in its approach to the prison officer's role.

However, despite his pessimistic characterisation of the current Home Secretary, who, according to Longford, 'sees Prison Officers as little more than gaolers', he suggested that prison officers themselves

> seem anxious to break out of their isolation and make closer contact with the public outside – including politicians ... Their General Secretary ... is certainly a live wire – and ... he is by no means alone. Officials of the Prison Officers' Association to whom I have spoken recently have expressed themselves as fed up with their public image ... Two local officials recently said ...'At the best we are presented as men in charge of animals, but quite often as animals in charge of animals.' ... There is much force in that comment.

In fact, the reality of relations between prison officers and their charges was often significantly different. As one officer wrote in the *Magazine* a year or two later, 'Prisoners, generally, are genial people and the prison system has cause to be grateful for their good humour.'[35]

While he had long been supportive of prison officers, Longford's close recent contact with the General Secretary and other Association officials reflected the POA's increasingly high public and political profile. In early 1984 the NEC had held a Parliamentary reception attended by over 100 members of both houses. Parliamentary contacts increased to an extent that 'resulted in a dramatic increase in Prison Service coverage in both Houses', according to the 1984 Report. In 1985, former POA official Ted Graham, now Lord Graham of Edmonton, related in an article headed 'Lifting our Parliamentary Profile' that the POA was 'embark[ing] on a programme of lifting its profile at Westminster' through an annual reception, series of lunches and other events such as talks on different types of penal establishments. He urged the need for more MPs to visit prisons, at least in part because 'The current dreadful over-crowding can explode into a civil crisis very quickly and all MPs should be made aware of the conditions under which prisoners and prison officers are forced to exist ....'[36]

This Degrading Practice ...

This higher public profile, prefaced by the much greater media interest in prisons and prison officers from the late 1960s onwards (see Chapter 2), prison officers and the POA highlighted in the previous chapter, generated an increasing 'campaigning' role for the Association on prison-related issues. One such major campaign in the early 1980s was the fight to end slopping out; the POA

> believed that this practice was abhorrent and that we should try and ensure that our case was presented to others of like mind in trying to stop this degrading practice ... We took the argument to the TUC and to political parties at their conferences - we did all we possibly could to make sure this practice ended.[37]

In the account of one POA activist:

> The POA ensured civilised facilities for prisoners - I don't think that's been recognised. It was us that forced out slopping out – it was the POA that forced in integral sanitation ... Our attitude was 'Why should prisoners have to put up with this and why should we have to slop them out – it's unhygienic ... [and] a dreadful way to treat prisoners.' You should treat prisoners the way you should treat yourself. So that was forced through and we were all agreed on that because it improved our working practices.[38]

In 1985, a pilot scheme for 'integral sanitation' in Stafford Prison was launched.

As the same activist pointed out, prisoners and prison officers often had joint interests in the reform of such issues, as well as with the improvement of facilities such as canteens:

So that [ending of slopping-out] was forced through and we were all agreed on that because it improved our working practices. We did that as a force ... [as with] the canteen, which improved our working facilities and improved their living conditions. When the POA amalgamated with prisoners over working conditions and prisoners' conditions we were almost always successful. What would happen is you would put the resolution forward at POA Conference – you would then get the publicity through the press and then other societies would pick that up along with the Executive.

Another achievement in the health and safety field was signalled with the POA's successful campaign against the use of polyurethane mattresses in prison cells, which emitted toxic fumes in the event of cell fires. In 1982 the Association could report that it had 'finally convinced the Home Office Prison Department that more speedy and effective action is necessary if we are to avoid a major catastrophe'. The Home Office Prison Department had now issued two types of smoke protection hoods on an experimental basis: 'This, hopefully, will be just the beginning as we believe that a safer mattress with no emission of toxic fumes is the only answer.'[39]

By 1983, the NEC could report to Annual Conference that 'a scientifically treated polyurethane mattress [had] proved acceptable as a replacement ... the treatment process had reduced the risk of toxicity to an acceptable level'. At that year's Congress, the TUC gave its support to the campaign. Deliveries of the new type of mattress began in June 1984 and were expected to be completed by November. Unfortunately, the issue resurfaced in early 1985 with the use of an equally toxic substance, polypropylene, for mailbags; at Parkhurst, prison officers suffered long-term effects from toxic smoke after a cell fire was started deliberately by a prisoner using polypropylene mailbag material. One officer 'came close to losing his life'. The POA branch at Parkhurst sent out a message through the Association: 'Following a serious cell fire here on 11 January 1985, we would wish to warn other branches of the dangers of having inmates sewing the POLYPROPYLENE type mailbags in their cells.'

It was early in 1984 that the first warning of a still more serious hazard, Acquired Immune Deficiency Syndrome (AIDS), was circulated by the Association with the words: 'Many of our members will be aware of the growing concern about "AIDS" and the possibility of the condition being introduced into penal establishments.' As one senior officer recalls:

> That was the beginning of the problem with AIDS, and at the very beginning, like the word cancer, it frightened everybody ... Dealing with those fears was very difficult and we tried to have a campaign to ensure that there was information to everybody ... and to devise [safe] practices ... we were dealing with all those issues at that time, and there's no doubt that from the early 80s on we were dealing with tremendous fears about this.[40]

In early 1985, the POA issued a press statement on AIDS: 'Prison Officers are at greater risk of infection ... resources must be made available which will better enable the Prison Service to cope with this frightening issue.'

An additional health and safety issue of great concern to the Association was increasing drug use in prisons. At a 1984 Whitley Council meeting, the Trade Union Side reported that they had sent a questionnaire to their branches, 81 per cent of which had identified the problems as very serious. There was a mismatch between Department and Trade Union Side figures; for example: 'While the Department showed two incidents with five finds of cannabis at Wandsworth, the Trade Union side's research showed 85 finds of which six were class A controlled drugs.' Not surprisingly, this issue was to resurface during the years to come.

Finally, a development which contributed to the safety of both prison officers and inmates in helping staff deal with prison violence in a more sophisticated way than before was the introduction of MUFTI (Minimum Use of Force Tactical Intervention) squads in the early 1980s. As an NEC member recounted:

In the 60s and 70s there was no riot training for prison officers. There was no specialist equipment ... All you had available ... was a small wooden stave for yourself or a long wooden stave which we called a riot stick. If you look at where we are today with our intervention squads, the training they have ... we've come so far ... And I think the POA did a lot to move all that forward, trying to get training for our staff, trying to get protective equipment so we are as professional as we are today.

After the major incidents of the 70s the POA and Prison Service talked and realised there had to be a sea change, there had to be proper training, proper equipment, and the first stab at it was when we got what we called MUFTI. You had teams of six ... We were provided with shields [and] you went forward with your shields a bit like the police do. You didn't have machine guns or anything like that ... A lot of it was more about the visual effect – when you get an intervention team going that have got helmets on and all the protective gear, the very visual presence makes people think twice.[41]

The first use of MUFTI squads was mentioned in Parliament in 1983, when David Mellor reported for the Home Office that:

MUFTI teams have been deployed since 1 January 1982. This was during an incident at HMP Aylesbury when a number of prisoners refused to return to their cells in protest at certain aspects of conditions at the prison ... Two MUFTI teams ... were deployed in sight of the demonstrating prisoners, who agreed to return to their cells ... One officer was slightly injured.[42]

'A Killing They are Going to Make'?

A major issue of the mid 1980s was the proposed 'discount sale of quarters', mentioned in the *Prison Officers' Magazine* of June 1982 when one contribution from Featherstone, under the heading 'Purchase of Quarters' reported plaintively:

Officers at this establishment expressed an interest in this scheme and duly asked for the District Valuer to come along and value their quarters. They waited and waited and waited ... It is amazing that everything moves so slowly especially when we are led to believe the Home Office wishes to dispose of quarters as quickly as possible.

By 1985, however, the issue was considerably more to the forefront, with some branches expressing strong disapproval. The POA representative at Ford, for example, argued: 'I cannot see the scheme being a success and feel it will be kicked into touch – which is where it deserves to be.' Maidstone were even more critical: 'For the first time in memory the Maidstone branch have found it necessary to censure the NEC. This has been brought about by their totally defeatist recommendation ... on the sale of quarters ....' Aldington branch also expressed dissatisfaction over the issue, and from Ashford came a 'Poem on Discount Sales':

> ... Why are they so keen to sell
> Because they're going to do quite well,
> A killing they are going to make
> If this offer we should take.
>
> They will sit up there and smirk,
> They know you have to come to work,
> That monthly mortgage that you pay,
> Will let them make the rules of play.[43]

A letter in the same issue, headed 'Discount Sale of Quarters – End Result?', argued shrewdly that the Prison Department 'offer' has 'had staff at each other's throats as to what was in it for them ... to gain anything, many would probably have to give a lot'.[44] One writer in the March issue referred to the 'tardy response ... to the National Ballot on the Discount Sale of Quarters'. The letter argued that, since 1981, 'two issues above all others have concentrated the hearts and minds of the Executive and members alike: the Discount Sale of Quarters and CWA/CDC'.[45] Yet there had been a low turnout on the ballot. Another letter noted that 'lo and behold the "package" contained a change of terms in the Rent Allowance ... Any officer should have the right ... to buy his house, but Rent Allowances should [not] be discussed ... in the same breath ....'[46]

The 1985 POA Annual Conference saw a number of resolutions on the issue, none of them favourable. Stoke Heath, for example, 'severely censur[ed] the NEC for the negative handling of the

Discount Quarters Policy … knowing that it was detrimental to the long-term interests of the membership'; Holloway asked 'That industrial action be taken by this Association if discount sales are forced upon us by the HOPD [Home Office Prison Department] with any loss to pay or adverse effect on our conditions of service.' In fact, as suggested in the POA's Parliamentary Report, the national ballot over discount sale of quarters had rejected the policy; a Home Office official had replied to a parliamentary question that 'A proposed change in conditions of service including provision of discount sales of quarters to occupants was *not* accepted on a recent ballot of members of the Prison Officers' Association, but surplus quarters may be purchased by occupants at current market value' (emphasis added).

Criticism of the policy continued. In September 1985, 'disposal of quarters' appeared as one of a list of complaints against the NEC. Many of the concerns were over lack of information from the Association. 'News and Jottings' from Risley in the *Prison Officers' Magazine* commented that 'It is hoped that by the time these Jottings appear in print that all Branches will have received information about the sale of quarters and other subjects which have been the causation of much rumour and speculation throughout the Association.'

The reason for the opposition? As the Home Office official had stated, 'Prison Officers occupy quarters rent-free as a condition of service or, subject to permission, may live in private accommodation with the benefit of a housing allowance.' This was a valuable advantage which many members, despite Thatcherite ideology on the wonders of home ownership, were canny enough to appreciate. Looking back, POA activists listed the advantages. As one recalled: 'I went for the Prison Service because it was equal opportunities … and there was free housing then.' Her fellow-officer added: 'Three-bedroom flat five minutes' walk from work for which I paid a very small rent ….'[47]

Both spoke of the 'comradeship' generated by living in prison quarters: 'if anything with the comradeship and getting to know each other [it] was easier – it helped you cope with the pressures of all the hours'. As this suggests, important non-financial advantages of free or low-rent quarters close to the prison included a 'community' atmosphere, with much use of an on-site social club: 'You'd get in the club, you'd be talking about the day ... Because the quarters were next door ... we did tend to socialise together.' His colleague added:

> You supervised each other. So if you saw someone wasn't doing very well, or becoming emotional or suffering domestic problems or something traumatic at work, a death ... or whatever, you'd be able to support that person ... Some of the things that you'd like to see today such as the community support can't be reproduced because we don't have the same facilities. They don't have housing now, they don't have clubs ... So it's going to be harder now for staff coming into the service, and also as a POA rep, because at least you could go into the club and get the feel of how staff felt ... in the club you had more freedom.

As one summed up the issues: 'Quarters have all been sold off. So now [prison officers] don't get anywhere to live, have to buy it themselves ... I would not have been able to join the Service if they hadn't given me somewhere to live ... They've lost a major thing there.'

Another official raised a different point:

> People were against the discount sale of quarters - why? One thing with quarters is ... all the quarters had alarm bells. If you take the Parkhurst riot, if you hadn't had quarters that night people might have lost their lives because when the riots started the alarm bells went off so that meant all the staff went out. I don't think the prison service has come to terms with the discipline code of people living out of quarters – when you lived in quarters you were in a very insular society, you didn't come into contact with people living outside ... [But] now they recruit locally, people live in the local community ... and very often your next door neighbour could end up in prison [but] you're not supposed to talk to them when you're outside – the discipline code says you can't mix with inmates.[48]

A Collision Course ...

Meanwhile, the problems with excessive overtime which within a year would lead to the 'Fresh Start' proposals, with their central inducement of discount house purchasing, were finding increasing expression. As a letter from a Ford POA member put it: '"Now is the Winter of our Discontent' Shakespeare once penned and I have a feeling he might have penned it specially for us in the Association judging by ... the Overtime Agreements Task Cuttings ....'[49] This referred to Home Office instructions set out in a January 1985 POA Circular on local overtime agreements: 'Governors ... who are experiencing difficulty [re] staff exercising their right not to extend their shift [should] renegotiate their local overtime agreement and ... dispense with the need to employ other staff on an overtime basis to cover the shortfall ....'

The POA issued a warning that this letter should be read in conjunction with its own 1984 Circulars on the question, while the representative from Ford added a warning on a broader note: 'We are set on a collision course ... Money must no longer be the be all and end all, we must be prepared to sacrifice the pound notes.'[50] However, it was perhaps understandable that prison officers sought extra overtime. The March 1985 issue of the *Prison Officers' Magazine* recorded that the POA claim for a 12 per cent increase had met Treasury insistence on 'still maintaining [its] 3% position'. In vain, the Association had 'stressed the importance the Association placed upon a separate pay bargaining procedure for prison officer grades, and the weight given to this position by both Justice Wynn Parry and Justice May'. In April the General Secretary reported that the Treasury pay offer had been rejected as 'bearing no comparison' to the POA claim.

While overtime pay could temporarily remedy this forlorn situation, some of the problems to come were heralded by a letter in the *Magazine* from Rampton branch which referred to the 'days [of overtime] we have been owed since 1980 ... Our whole holiday system is a farce with people having summer leave in November.'[51] Yet a Report of the Whitley Council meeting of July 1985 included a POA statement that its membership was 'motivated largely by their level of take home pay and any attempts by the Official Side to reduce this, such as removing opportunities to work overtime, would have the obvious result of industrial action on a massive scale'.

'Anger' ...

At the same time, however, POA instructions on overtime were described as a 'mockery. As a letter to the *Magazine* put it:

> On 31/1/85 I was ordered in to do a shift extension until 21.30 ... There were ... staff already on duty willing to extend but they were not allowed to do this ... The advice given to me by our NEC was like a kick in the gut ... [It] came back with the answer to work if ordered to do so ... This, colleagues, takes my right and yours to refuse overtime away, and makes a mockery of POA [policy].[52]

Indeed, motions to the 1985 Annual Conference were critical on both pay and overtime questions. Bedford branch, for example, moved that 'This conference registers its severe criticism of the NEC for their handling of the 1984 pay negotiations and now mandates the NEC to seek a substantial basic pay rise for its members and in so doing use all the power at their disposal including industrial action.' Another motion, from Durham, linked the ongoing issue of 'duty systems' and the CWA to the overtime question: 'Because of the breakdown of the CWA negotiations there is still overtime built into the Vee Scheme which is contrary to the principles of the voluntary overtime agreement. I therefore propose that the built-in overtime within the Vee Scheme becomes completely voluntary.'

In the July 1985 *Prison Officers' Magazine*, the Manchester branch noted: 'The conference is upon us again and we still are no nearer to our pay settlement. Our NEC seem to allow the department to back them into a corner then "MUG THEM".' The CWA also came under fire, with a letter from the Aldington branch secretary commenting drily: 'My members here are particularly pleased with the NEC's ability to negotiate them a forty to fifty pound loss when they work a set of night duties.' The Ford branch secretary was equally satirical: 'The one question I have is how the NEC accept a system which when first produced as part of the ... Common Working System included paid meal breaks and when finally agreed [includes] no sign of a paid meal break?'

By July 1985, a speech by POA Chairman Colin Steel referred to 'the decision of the Home Secretary not to offer the CWA package on the grounds of expense', and a letter from a prison officer at the Leyhill Training School, now slated for closure, appeared to confirm this: 'With the department's withdrawal of the C.W.S. and gross hours this reduced the number of staff required but we were still given to understand there would be a need to train the staff remaining ....'[53]

These complex and interrelated issues were summed up in an explosive letter in the *Magazine* headed 'Anger'. Addressed to the 'Gentlemen of the NEC', it declared:

> You are now identified as the most ineffective negotiating team in the whole of the trade union movement ... Why don't the NEC get off their knees and assist branches to their feet, regain all of our dignities ... as they did in the heady days of 80/81 when they showed the attributes of leadership?[54]

The writer referred to the 'abhorrence ... I felt when I read POA circ.134/84' (which had called off industrial action over pay), and added:

> Surely now that the Home Secretary has decided not to offer the new hours of attendance and in consequence withdraws [the government's] package deal...now that we will not be offered gross hours ... the afore-mentioned Circular should have concluded with 'Therefore the suspension of the industrial action is lifted and all branches directed to return to the industrial action they were performing prior to suspending the action [in 1981].'

The writer questioned the plausibility of the NEC's statement in a 1984 Circular that there was a likelihood of duty credits being honoured: 'There is no likelihood of this government in a gesture of goodwill paying a CDC claim that Justice May stated was invalid and sparked off the industrial action ....'

... And 'a Few Flowers'

Such fury is not unusual amongst lay members in a democratic union where, as one POA activist noted:

There's a national policy, but if for any reason that national policy's not being adhered to you can still operate independently ... You're not totally dependent on the NEC or the rest of the branches to support you – you can operate individually provided you're sticking to the rules. I think [that] makes the union stronger, because the NEC can't impose something on an individual branch unless it's a national direction and they can only do that by permission of the whole entity ... and in reverse, if a committee locally wants to have a go at the NEC ... you can do that.[55]

Meanwhile, there were many glimpses of appreciation from the membership. The Chelmsford branch noted that:

Our CDC payments will be disbursed to us in a very few days' time ... [thanks to] our POA committee. Not forgetting our NEC for their dogged persistence in hammering away at this matter ... quite a few people are handy enough with their brickbats for the NEC, time a few flowers were strewn in their path.[56]

Wormwood Scrubs reported 'payment in full of CDCs';[57] Wandsworth announced 'the payment at last of the longstanding CDC claim',[58] and the Aylesbury branch also noted that their CDC payments had been settled.[59] In November, the Risley branch noted:

It is sad to read some of the comments in the Jottings ... which are critical of the National Executive Committee, while I agree it is frustrating, at times, [that] we do not have up-to-date information, from recent personal experience I can vouchsafe that my enquiries at Cronin House have been met with one hundred per cent cooperation and information.[60]

And Preston weighed in with:

a word of praise for the ... POA Magazine ... January's 75th Anniversary Issue was first-class and reading the notes of yesteryear made one realise the great steps forward by our association over the years. No longer are we a secret society, but a vigorous force who do not let management ride roughshod over us. Long may it stay that way.[61]

'Akin to a Vulture ...'

Nevertheless, serious problems continued. In 1983, a Prison Department Circular had announced the introduction of a Prison Costing System and had outlined four stages for moving towards local budgetary proposals. In May 1984, the General Secretary reported that the first three stages of this system had now been implemented, requiring a move towards local budgets and local responsibilities which was 'clearly believed by the Home Office to provide a ... framework for allowing the Prison Department to stay within budget limits'. In 1985, Home Office minister David Mellor spelt out the main aspects of the policy in an answer to a Parliamentary question on improving the efficiency of the Prison Service: 'In particular priority will be given to ensuring that prison service staff are deployed to the best possible effect and with less reliance than at present on very high levels of overtime.' Other measures included: a system of annual performance reviews, a computerised costing system installed in April 1983 'and still being developed', and 'a system of local budgets, targeted for implementation from 1st April 1986, to give greater responsibility to local management for the effective control of expenditure'.

As the General Secretary summed up the proposals: 'It is now clear that far too great an emphasis is being placed on management systems within the financial proposals and far too little given to planning the service.' A 1984 Prison Department Circular, for example, had included machinery for governors to be made accountable directly to the Prisons Board 'for the operations of [their] own establishment'; meanwhile, further Circulars indicated that 'task dropping will become a permanent feature of the Prison Service', and a letter from the HOPD re 'task lists' had questioned whether 'manning levels [are] too high ... in particular parts of the establishment?' In response, the General Secretary confirmed: 'The POA has a clear policy – to protect the essential task list. This policy protects inmates and allows for some measure of acceptable standard on essential services.'[62]

But implementing the policy was a different matter. As the Wymott branch noted in August, referring to broken promises on CDC payments: 'Our NEC should always be mindful of the type of management we are now dealing with … Is there any point in negotiating with these people?' Leyhill reported that 'A few years ago we experienced budgetary control … now under a new heading we have financial limits … We at this establishment have to slave 64 hours per week to keep within the bread-line.' From Bristol, POA activists related:

> At the time of writing we at Bristol are now working to the 'Budgetary Control' and boy is it a control. No weekend working at all, and because of the miserly wage we get, it can make a big difference to a family man or an officer on a big mortgage … [I]t is a case of we have given them their 'C.D.C' payments, now let's take it back off them in other ways ….

Coldingley wrote:

> April saw the start of 'Coldingley's Costing Experiment', whereby Head Office gives us a budget in order to 'assess the possibility of costing at local level'. Not very well received would be an understatement. Morale was low but this is 'the pits'.[63]

In June, the Stafford branch reported on the return of the Manpower Review Team: 'Be under no illusions, however tight a ship you carry they still want cuts but they call them savings.'
At Bedford Prison, management had:

> imposed budgetary controls on us…without consultation or negotiations … Needless to say that after a ballot we embarked on industrial action … What are they trying to do to us, these people who sit in high places? Here we are at Bedford, like so many other establishments, understaffed and struggling to man the prison, when all they want to do is cut our hours even more.[64]

And the Glen Parva branch summed up the problems in November:

> To all colleagues the length and breadth of the country we stand firm against the current climate too lightly depicted as 'Budgetary Control'. More aptly as akin to a vulture picking at the bare bones of our once professional and respected service.[65]

More Fertiliser from Above

There were a number of further troubling aspects of budgetary control, some still in their infancy but to come to fruition only too soon. One of these was incipient privatisation. In 1985, Park Lane hospital branch warned:

> Privatisation is still with us somewhere, and members are reminded that they must protect their jobs at all costs, and not to become complacent because the Health Service[66] is finding out it's a lame duck. We are not out of the thick of it yet and more fertiliser is bound to come down from above.[67]

A further letter in the November issue of the *Prison Officers' Magazine*, headed 'Queen Bees or Worker Bees?', noted the encroachment of private contractors in the NHS and Prison Service (as with the use of Securicor referred to above).

A further impact of budgetary control was a cut in the number of prison workshops. In July 1985, POA General Secretary David Evans referred to a Prisons Board document announcing the closure of 70 prison workshops on the basis that they worked less than 15 hours per week. This was 'a document where the ultimate demise of Prison industries is camouflaged by seductive phrases'. The closure of a range of other workshops on grounds of 'over-manning' was also to be considered. In August, the General Secretary raised the issue of new technology, which would 'allow a much more refined system of cost comparison ... The HOPD estimates that ... computers will reduce the present 340 tasks by 50% ....' The policy of the POA, as agreed at Annual Conference, was to obtain 'complete ... involvement by Prison Officers' in the new technology and to 'resist most strongly any reduction in manning levels'.

A 1984 Report on managing the long-term prison system had illustrated 'the very subtle way in which financial restraint has become the prime consideration'. While the dispersal system set up in the wake of the Mountbatten and Radzinowicz Reports to deal with high-risk prisoners had been 'tremendously successful', the government's Control Review Committee had now stated that the system was too big and that a significant proportion of 'dispersal' prisoners could be contained in less secure accommodation. This, argued Evans, would 'expose the staff and public to unnecessary risk'. He concluded that 'The essential weakness of applying cash limits to the Prison Service is to believe that the full range of its work and activities are predictable ... [and] to ignore a fundamental fact – *48,000 prisoners are not volunteers in the System*.[68]

Modern Maths

In an ominous endorsement of this point, MP for Stretford Tony Lloyd asked in Parliament in the summer of 1985: 'Is the Leader of the House aware of the tremendous pressure which is building up in Strangeways Prison[69] in Manchester which now holds nearly twice as many people as it was originally designed for ...?' Prison officers at Strangeways had recently passed a motion of no confidence in the governor; Lloyd demanded an independent inquiry or for 'something to be done' regarding the 'realistic grievances' of prison officers and inmates.

Yet staff shortages continued. Huntercombe Prison reported a

shortage of required officer grades of 28% and rising ... We are now at a state where we feel that we can no longer give undertakings to work unreasonable amounts of overtime to keep the ship afloat ... It seems that money has become far more important to the Government than safety and health of prison officers.[70]

A Manchester POA representative commented: 'The department keep saying that recruitment is increasing, well in 1982 we were just 12 staff short now we find ourselves in 1985 with 83 officers short, if this is the department's idea of improving staffing levels I was definitely taught the wrong formula at school (albeit a long time ago).' In August, the Aylesbury branch noted:

We keep hearing about 5,000 new staff to be employed ... [but] with no new staff ... in the foreseeable future ... one wonders if the department really intends to take on more staff, especially after hearing about Budgetary Controls [which] will have dire consequences ... It was suggested that nationally this may be a rough year for our membership and so it is turning out to be.[71]

A similar situation was reported at Cookhamwood:

> The staffing level here is reaching…dangerously low…By the summer we shall be almost 40% below strength! The department don't seem to want to know, as long as we are ticking over the proverbial blind eye is turned. Even with so few staff there is still talk of overtime cut backs…All this and still no decent increase in basic pay in sight.[72]

A comment from Leicester shrewdly noted the connection between staffing shortages, overcrowding and budgetary control:

> Budgetary Control is with us once again. The people who impose these financial restraints should really have a day out and come to visit Leicester, ideally at slop-out and mealtimes … Governors are being told … if you can't run your prison within the budget imposed you will be replaced by someone who can. So much for the Home Secretary's statement [that] the Prison Service is a growth industry. Well, at least he is half right. The inmates are on the increase in their thousands …[73]

In August, the *Prison Officers' Magazine* Parliamentary Report recorded ex-POA official Lord Ted Graham asking about the progress of the prison building programme 'at a time when the prison population, at 48,100 is the highest on record',[74] and in September the Chelmsford branch noted: 'As yet we have not seen any of the 240 extra staff that the Home Secretary promised us.' In the same month Preston officers reported a 'steady depletion' of staff.[75] In October, Lewes listed the problems:

> Due to the serious shortage of staff at this establishment we still have the problem of limited alerts being called and staff having to work overtime… against their wishes … Our problems … are the same as experienced at most establishments, namely overcrowding, understaffing, overtime budgets and lack of work for prisoners.[76]

The Northeye branch summed it all up:

> The Prison Service is now run by Accountants, who believe they can 'quantify' the unquantifiable, and have introduced us to their 'Modern

Maths'. Step One: Overcrowd the Prisons and pressurise the Staff ... Step Two: Close down Prison workshops and deprive inmates of work ....[77]

Other problems related to the 'Modern Maths' were recounted by the Onley branch:

Major works at this and other establishments are being held up for the time being to contain a large overspend ... At Onley we have had improvement work put back year after year ... potential health and safety hazards have been identified by reps and agreed by management as a danger to health but still exist because of lack of cash ... We have reached crisis point in this service and this situation has been brought about by a combination of penal policy and years of neglect and financial famine.[78]

The Brixton branch summed it all up in a poetic appeal 'To the Boss':

> ... Conditions of service are worsening,
> What more from us, can you take,
> For most of us have discovered,
> The icing, has disappeared, from
> The cake.[79]

'A More Positive and Militant Prison Officer Grade ...'

It was hardly surprising that these conditions fomented conflict. In the August 1985 issue of the *Prison Officers' Magazine*, Highpoint staff noted: 'Morale is off the scale ... the way routines have been imposed without any true consultations (whatever may be claimed) have totally shattered any small remaining spark of ... confidence that may have survived the rigours of recent times ....' Nottingham referred to 'major problem areas of unsafe manning levels', and a recent assault on a prison officer was related to 'wilful reduction of the Essential Task List and manning levels beyond and below minimum standards of safety'. Before long, the anger broke out into threats of action: Wakefield reported: 'Re budgetary control, high attendance at branch meeting and resolutions threatening industrial action and an overtime ban on weekend shifts served on the Governor.' The overtime ban took place on the weekend of 8–9 June, and 'had the desired effect ... These events highlight that this branch does not enter into Industrial Action lightly and it is only used as a very last resort.'

In the September *Magazine*, Park Lane noted that the prison hospital 'may be entering a period of industrial unrest', while in October POA members at Albany reported that they were 'taking industrial action in response to the budgetary control, grandly known as Management Financial Initiative'. Liverpool reported a 'very close' vote, with a majority of only six against taking 'a pre-determined course of industrial action in response to ... the task list and descending order of priorities list'. Onley called for national industrial action over cuts in the task list:

> The branch are not prepared to accept those cuts that are proposed...In a recent ballot over cuts in the ETL [Essential Task List] this Branch decided not to take local industrial action as a large number of members felt that any local action would only make us vulnerable ... Many of our members felt that any action should be controlled and directed nationally over such an important issue as the ETL, although it is possible to understand the reluctance of the NEC to hold a ballot for national action at this moment ...

In the December *Magazine*, noting the recent replacement of Borstal and the detention centre systems with a Youth Custody programme, the Portland branch secretary wrote:

> Staff morale ... seems to be at an all time low. Since the demise of the Borstal system we seem to be engaged in a constant struggle to maintain control. Staff shortages effectively ensure that we are unable to man working parties, and manning levels are less than safe. Assaults on staff have risen ... Who knows where it will all end? Soon, we are expecting a visit from the Director General, and on the same day we are holding a ballot on industrial action ...

The anger over deteriorating conditions for prisoners and staff increasingly fomented a wider political awareness. As the Wymott branch argued:

The cuts in the Prison Service are nothing to do with eliminating waste, but purely and simply another avenue by which this government can raise money so they can reduce income tax, with the hope that they will get re-elected. We in the prison service are already bearing the brunt of the Government's failure to reduce unemployment, which is one of the major reasons for our huge and growing [prison] population ....

In May 1985 in the *Magazine*, the Canterbury branch secretary had sardonically noted: 'Business ... is brisker than usual of late. It would appear that now the miners' strike is over, the police have more time to execute non-payment warrants and they are doing so with a vengeance. We are constantly full to bursting ....'

The same branch more soberly, and with majestic rhetoric, reported:

deep frustration and anger at the off handed manner that we prison officers are dealt with ... the Home Office Prison Department have used and abused us, attempting to carry out government Policy that at times is so ludicrous our heads spin with a dizziness borne from the inability to foresee just what they are attempting to achieve. What HOPD will achieve will be the emergence of a more positive and militant prison officer grade ... The full might of the prison officer grade has yet to be felt by the HOPD and woe betide them when they force us into that final corner ... The political animals that were once our leaders in HOPD will have to dig their burrows very deep because when the Government has finished with us it will turn like an angry tiger to devour the HOPD, it will slash and cut deeply into the once hallowed ground of what is now the bastion of safety and serene power of the HOPD, the present cutting tool of a cost cutting government.

In the meantime, like most examples of withdrawal of labour, local industrial action was beginning to bite. In the November 1985 *Magazine*, Albany reported on the impact of their industrial action against financial restraints, which had taken the form of 'delaying the unlock, not manning workshops, and not working overtime'. As the branch secretary recounted: 'Once the action started and the powers that be realised that Albany meant business, new talks ... took place ... The outcome ... was that management re-checked their figures and decided that they had made a calculation error, and that the restraints would not after all affect Albany.' Highpoint could record the same process. The prison

> has gone from a quiet backwater to a place of major importance and is something of a political hot potato ... Basically our manning levels are inadequate for a prison of uncontrolled growth ... However there are none so blind as those who do not want to hear, and it was the intention to increase the population quite substantially ... In the best traditions, this was scheduled for a period when savage cuts were imposed without any prior consultation. After a short burst of industrial action, people in high places decided to talk and those talks are slowly proving fruitful.

Before long, as urged by the membership, a number of disputes were taken up by the POA at the national level. In August, answering a parliamentary question on industrial action in the Prison Service, Home Office official David Mellor replied:

> In addition to a number of disputes at particular establishments over local matters such as manning levels and efficiency improvements, there are four national disputes relating to procedural issues on the use of force reports, procedures for internal investigations, non-cooperation in the use of radio-pagers and non-cooperation in supply of statistical information regarding movements to courts.

The 'Fish and Chip' Dispute

In 1986, 'the mood of prison officers was still affected by their experiences in the previous year', according to a retired senior official; yet 'departmental instructions were geared towards further financial restrictions on the Service and a direct attack on prison industries. Overcrowding continued, and the Prison Service continued to attack individual members who were refusing to work excessive hours.'

Major industrial action was a predictable result, and in 1986 the POA organised a national ban on compulsory overtime sparked by the government's new Financial Management Initiatives policy, which set yet more cash limits and decreed that overtime could only be worked if it was compulsory. In response, the POA, arguing that the Prison Department had ignored ACAS advice in unilaterally changing pay-related terms for prison officers, banned compulsory overtime at selected institutions.

Once compulsory overtime was withdrawn on a national basis, the situation became serious in these significantly understaffed prisons. The dispute 'led to serious disturbances and rioting; in particular, severe damage was caused at HM Prisons Bristol, Northeye in Sussex and Erlestoke in Wiltshire, where there was also a mass escape, and at Lewes and Wymott in Lancashire'.[80] As NEC member John Boddington summed up the issues:

What brought it all to a head was the Prison Service [was] clearly understaffed and it was driven by overtime. A Prison Officer had no option but to work overtime. You had a 40-hour week at the time but if you were needed to work 80 hours you had to work 80 hours and you had no option … Clearly the Prison Service wanted to cut back on the overtime because it was costing an awful lot of money, but it was also a big weapon for the POA because prisons couldn't run without overtime. You didn't have the staff. It affected the regime and would have led to great unrest, and that's what actually happened in 1986 when we banned overtime.

It lasted 24 hours and you had prisons burning up and down the country. There was unrest in about 40 plus prisons, and Earlstoke … had about 21 prisoners escape when the overtime ban was on. It only lasted 24 hours, but it led to the first Industrial Relations procedure between the POA and the Prison Service ….[81]

During this period of the ban, a bizarre episode, subsequently known as the 'fish and chip' dispute, took place at Gloucester Prison, where over-enthusiastic governors and their deputies locked out a startled night shift of prison officers from their posts. As the POA document *It Need Never Have Happened* recounts:

The prison was handed over to night staff in a normal way whilst the governor remained in his office. At approximately 10.10pm on the 28th [April] the deputy governor arrived at the outside gate stating that he had a fish-and-chip supper to deliver to the governor. Hiding behind the deputy governor were four assistant governors … When the gate was opened they

rushed into the prison taking the keys off the Gate officer and handing to
him a piece of paper with the following words on it:

> You are now occupying the gate against the instructions of the governor
> ... Any attempt physically to stop the operation of the gate now could result
> in your instant dismissal.[82]

As the POA document comments: 'Such dramatic and childish
over-reaction clearly demonstrates the degree to which a "bully
boy" mentality had taken over the thinking of some Prison
Department officials ....' In response, however, the NEC was
forced to suspend the national action on 1 May; the Home
Office responded by instructing the governor to restore the ETL
which had formed part of the Gloucester dispute. Although the
Gloucester governor himself 'flagrantly disregarded' this decision,
another motive for the suspension of the overtime ban was to
restore order after the series of riots and disturbances caused
by its disruption of prison officers' normal duties. The Home
Office 'responded positively' to this by organising a series of
meetings chaired by Sir Brian Cubbon, a Secretary of State at
the Home Office.

These meetings led to a procedure known as the 'Cubbon
formula', which went well beyond the existing Whitley Council
machinery to establish a specific local disputes procedure between
the POA and the Prison Service:

> Up until then there wasn't any mechanism really for dealing with local
> disputes as such. Every branch had a Prison Service 'note' which set
> out arrangements re facility time for officials – so that was in place, but
> this Cubbon formula was actually to deal with disputes and that was
> the forerunner for everything else that we had, the industrial relations
> procedural agreements ...[83]

The three factors of the national overtime ban, the ensuing
prison riots, and the establishment of the Cubbon Formula are
between them defined as generating the 'Fresh Start' proposals of
1987: 'The Cubbon Formula brought in the negotiations about
Fresh Start which did away with overtime and established the

new working practices at the time.'[84] And yet another government inquiry was involved:

> The aftermath of the 1986 national dispute led to the Hennessy Inquiry, whose report emphasised that the whole prison system survived only because it was driven by overtime. The government response was Fresh Start, the main thrust of which was to 'buy out' the overtime culture.[85]

'The Sins of "Fresh Start" ...'

As a senior retired official recalls the process:

> We had a letter from the Prison Service announcing they were intending to have negotiations on a concept called Fresh Start ...
>
> Both sides had agendas – we wanted to make sure that we had proper pay and conditions – their side wanted to do away with overtime. But [they proposed]to include an average of over 16 hours per prison officer into the pay and to have a period of five years where two hours were knocked off the working week in order to reach a stage come 1992 when everybody was working a 39-hr week ... They also agreed to a policy of discount sales of quarters, which came on the back of Margaret Thatcher's idea of selling off council houses to their residents ... and our members wanted [that]. There wasn't as there is today a clamour for quarters. They decided there and then that they wanted to be a part of this agenda for change towards house purchasing ... because house purchasing before was a very very difficult thing for a prison officer to achieve ... Lenders [then] wouldn't give you more than two and half times your salary, and two and a half times your pay in those days wasn't a lot of money ... People wanted to be part and parcel of that house purchasing scheme and they flocked in droves in order to obtain them. It was a massive inducement.[86]

The 'Fresh Start' package represented a radical overhaul of working practices in the Prison Service, introducing, amongst other things, 'a joint commitment to team working'[87] – relatively novel even in industry at the time – and widespread restructuring of grades, including the removal of the most senior rank of uniformed prison officer, Chief Officers I and II. However, by far the most significant measure was the introduction of a basic working week of 39 hours and the removal of compulsory overtime, to be bought out over a five-year period during which any time worked above 48 hours a week would be compensated through Time Off In Lieu (TOIL). As one analysis sums up the changes: 'In essence Fresh Start was an attempt to achieve a 15 per cent cost saving by a radical restructuring of working rotas. It also attempted to reduce the working week for prison officers from an average of 56 hours to a maximum of 39 hours ....'[88]

There was opposition from both the POA and the Prison Governors' Association on the removal of the Chief Officer grade, but initially the Fresh Start proposals overall were greeted with enthusiasm by both POA leadership and members, who voted in favour by 80 per cent; the only POA branch to vote against was Wandsworth, which continued to have disagreements with the NEC for some years. The Northern Ireland region of the POA also fought a long battle against Fresh Start, rejected as 'giving management too much control'; eventually a separate agreement known as 'The Way Forward' was signed.

This oppositional stance may have been vindicated. As so often, the promise held out by Fresh Start did not match reality, with implementation

> often problematic...in practice, the Fresh Start provisions in respect of hours were often not realised. Many prison officers did not obtain a basic working week of 39 hours (net) by 1992; nor were they given time off in lieu for hours above 48 per week ... largely because the prison population continued to rise.[89]

As John Boddington of the POA NEC put it: 'Where I think Fresh Start floundered was that although the hours were reduced the amount of staff required to take account of that wasn't actually put in because the money wasn't forthcoming, which brought Fresh Start into disrepute.'[90] Similar disadvantages were noted by the Scottish Area Assistant Secretary, who was

> on the committee at Barlinnie when Fresh Start was first mooted ... England went for rolling implementation, whereas in Scotland we went for the 'big bang' ... The vote for Fresh Start was overwhelming, because before Fresh

Start we were working something like five double shifts a week – Fresh Start was going to be our method of reducing that with a reasonable level of pay ... but members became disillusioned, because of the application of Time Off In Lieu ... and banked hours. You could work additional hours and get TOIL, but most of the hours were in the summer months when you wanted time off. So that was an imbalance.[91]

As another POA activist put it more robustly: 'Fresh Start was bribery ... because a) it had all this in it it about TOIL ... and b) right to buy ... I ended up buying a house in North London for about £98,000 – very cheap for this area. Suddenly I'm a house owner. Of course I put my cross in that box.'[92]

However, as shown earlier with the first moves towards discount sale of quarters, the 'bribe' was not without its disadvantages for prison officers:

One of the things Fresh Start did was it gave an officer permission to live wherever they liked as long as they could get to work on time. You have [London] officers living at Clacton, Bedford, Surrey, so when they've finished work they don't want to socialise. So we've kind of splintered ourselves. I think the last time the staff attempted to organise an annual reunion it was a disaster because they had no club to use ... There was a very strong club at Holloway and it's now a locker room.[93]

This was confirmed by the Scottish POA official:

It was easier when we had quarters because most of the staff congregated in quarters, so there was less travelling time – after Fresh Start they were further afield so it was like a double shift travelling from home. There was no opposition to the sell-off ... but it affected camaraderie among staff, in the officers' club. Previously, you didn't have to drive home at night. Afterwards, the comradeship went.[94]

The London interviewees also noted internal changes to the organisation of work with the new package:

Since Fresh Start [prison officers] have been more scattered ... Until 1987 officers ... were spread all over the prison ... And everybody met on the centre, at break-off time ... to have a chat about the day – now one of the sins of Fresh Start is everyone's become group-oriented to their area of work, so they only worry about that area, and they'll stand and watch another area suffering to get finished but won't see it in their role to go over and help them so we can all go home together. Prior to Fresh Start, if you could see that another wing was delaying going home you could go and help.

The sale of quarters had other serious implications for prison officers:

What the Prison Service did was they stopped paying for people's first move ... And we actually had people putting tents up in people's garages and things like that. It was terrible ... Before Fresh Start you got subsistence, you were paid so much a night until you were able to move and then when you moved they paid your removal bills ... That all ended – they just stopped that ... it was government diktat.[95]

Nor did Fresh Start appear to address the problems of severe overcrowding which continued to provoke violent prisoner unrest, particularly in Scotland, where a number of serious riots took place in which prison officers were taken hostage. According to the Scottish Area Secretary:

Four officers in Barlinnie were held hostage – we had hostages in Perth, Edinburgh. It almost felt like a concerted effort, like someone was coordinating it. So much so that the Secretary of State ordered a complete lockdown of the service. There were conspiracy theories that it was being organised from outside, it seemed as if when one place was resolved another would start up. There was a lot of overcrowding at the time – it might have just been the combination of prisoners we had at the time ... There were some pretty bad riots down south, but this seemed to be a concerted effort, just one after the other.[96]

In 1987–88, prison officers at Barlinnie stopped prisoners coming into the jail:

We refused to take any more, we'd got too many, so we turned the police vans away – we said take them away, put them in police cells – we filled the police cells in Scotland, they threatened to arrest us! It happened at the same time as the riots. That was one of the things that was bothering us – the overcrowding. We'd already written to the Director of Prisons saying what are you going to do about it ... He said overcrowding doesn't make any difference, you've still got to take prisoners.[97]

'They Ran Their Own Wings ...'

Meanwhile, events in Northern Ireland, where prison population had more than trebled in recent years, continued to 'out-do' even the horrors of prison riots and prison officer hostage-taking. At a POA Conference in early 1980, POA General Secretary Ken Daniel referred to a recent 'brutal attack on four prison officers in Belfast' as well as injuries sustained by prison officers Agnew, Beattie and Rogan.

As the 1980 POA Report noted:

The year under review saw once again the murder of our colleagues in Northern Ireland. There had been a hope of de-escalation in the province but unfortunately, once again, these hopes were dashed ... the problems being faced, on a daily basis by the wives and families of our members in Northern Ireland cannot be equalled. We ... assure them that they are not forgotten.

In March 1981, the *Prison Officers' Magazine* reported the murder of Cecil Burns on 30 December 1980. In the ensuing seven years, five more prison officers were to lose their lives, culminating in the murder of Civilian Instructor L. Jarvis, blown up by the IRA in a boobytrapped car in March 1987. In October 1982, Miss E. Chambers from Armagh Prison was killed by UDR crossfire, while the 1983 POA Annual Report noted 'the murder of James Andrew Ferris in the execution of his duty at HMP Maze Cellular on 25 September 1983'. On 17 February 1985, Principal Officer Patrick Kerr was killed outside St Patrick's Cathedral, 'brutally gunned down after leaving Mass with his children by the IRA', as the Maze Cellular branch reported.

Not only prison officers but also their families were targeted. In July 1985 a report in the *Prison Officers' Magazine* from the Maze Compound noted:

Terrorism in Northern Ireland is something that has been going on for a long time ... but when it come to your own doorstep it is particularly hard to accept. Sid Smith, a long serving Prison officer in the Maze who was recently medically retired had a young son called Garry who wished to make a career with the RUC and because of this he was brutally murdered by terrorists.

Finlay Spratt, Northern Ireland POA Area Chairman, recalled that prison officers

had very little input into the paramilitaries' treatment – they ran their own wings. We were their messenger boys. The POA looked after Prison Officers' safety in their homes – bullet-proof vests, firearms, spyholes, bullet-proof windows, cameras. But there were very few murders at home – they happened going to or coming from prison. All we could do was respond when an incident happened – we would shut down visits for three days after an incident.

Prisoners realised that killing an officer would get them what they wanted. If a Prison Officer was shot, NI Office would concede the prisoners' demands ... If you were an officer in the Maze and you did your job you were a target. If they couldn't get you, they would pick a softer target ... Prison Officers were used as cannon fodder, and there was very little support from the Northern Ireland Office.

The Area Secretary himself had had a banner reading 'Rest In Peace' held up behind him by Loyalist prisoners who jeered at him to get his boots polished because he would be walking behind a coffin. Loyalists took photos of his house.

The POA was always about staying alive, representing our members and protecting them the best we could ... We were forgotten about while political decisions took lives. We as an Association were left to bury our dead and look after their widows ....

In 1985, the POA set up the Prison Service Trust to take care of the families of murdered officers.

'Aware of the Difficulties ...'

On 25 September 1983, a disastrous event which took the life of one prison officer, J.A. Ferris, and traumatised many others, was the escape of 38 paramilitary prisoners from the Maze Compound. Although the inquiry into the incident, headed by Sir James Hennessy, reported that 'staff at the Maze were complacent about security and ... there was widespread laxness and carelessness in the performance of duties', Hennessy nevertheless 'specifically commended a number of officers, including officer Ferris who lost his life'. During the Parliamentary session which heard the Hennessy Report, there were references to 'a collapse of morale' among staff and 'difficulties over various issues with the Northern Ireland Prison Officers' Association' by the then Secretary of State for Northern Ireland, James Prior. In sharp contrast, one MP, Peter Archer, described representations by prison officers on problems in the Maze as 'falling on deaf ears'.

Out of the accusations and counter-accusations, perhaps the best sense can be made from a statement in October 1983 by John Hall, then Assistant Secretary of the POA, on events leading up to the escape.[98] After describing the historical background from 1972 to October 1981, when the government made concessions to paramilitary prisoners including freedom of association and the right to wear their own clothing, the Report described a meeting with James Prior and Lord Gowrie, a minister in the Northern Ireland office at Stormont, at which the POA pointed out that 'without staff to implement the proposed changes difficulties would arise in control and movement and overburden prison staff'. The announcement of the concessions had come just after an escape at Belfast Prison which had 'clearly indicated that the control and security elements left much to be desired'.

The POA reported that after 'control by prison authorities was relaxed in order to resolve the difficult situation of getting inmates to resume work and respond to prison rules', the situation was 'exploited to the full' by the inmates; cases occurred where 'officers ... not acceptable to the inmate body were requested to be removed [and such] officers ... were in fact removed by prison authorities'. According to the statement, prison staff were in 'no doubt ... that command structures [among] paramilitary inmates exist and [are] tolerated by prison authorities'. In response, prison staff at the Maze had continually raised security concerns and were as consistently frustrated.

Notes from POA meetings for the period October 1981 to September 1983 show that in early 1982, POA requests for extra officers to cover the 'blind spots' in the metal workshop, clearly a major hazard, were refused, as were 'search facilities for random searching'. In August 1982, when the POA 'expressed consternation and fear among staff and indicated proposed internal disruption by inmates', the governor simply stated that the Northern Ireland Office 'were aware' of the issue. Requests for extra staff were again refused on the grounds that such fears were simply 'hazards of the job'. By September 1982, the POA was taking industrial action because requests to lessen numbers in H blocks had been ignored. Yet the situation continued to worsen. In November, the POA 'expressed concern over the standing down of hall guard posts, essential when inmates were returning from workshops', and requested a return to previous staffing levels. This was 'not forthcoming'. In December, the POA again expressed concern over the high number of inmates in the H blocks, in reply to which the governor simply stated that the 'situation was under constant review'.

And so it went on. Throughout the early months of 1983, the POA continued to question the reduction of manning levels and to warn of overcrowding, to no avail. After three officers were assaulted by eight inmates in February, officers asked for 'controlled movement' of prisoners, only to receive the bland reply that the governor was 'aware of the difficulties and noted [their] concern'. As the Report summed it up: 'Over the period 28th July 1983 – 29th June 1983 some 13 meetings took place … at which no less than 30 approaches were made by the POA with reference to security, manning levels and controlled movement. Staff were fully aware of the inherent dangers and … made management aware of these dangers' – clearly, to no avail.[99]

Matters came to a head when the authorities responded to a 'segregation movement' by Protestant prisoners by transferring many Protestant inmates to Magilligan prison. In the process, 'The Maze Cellular became top heavy with Republican prisoners

... even though [this was not] Government policy ... It is at this point that effective control was lost, and plans by inmates could be made ready for implementation.'

Hall concluded his statement with a summary of the 'Factors making the Maze escape possible'. These included the

> failure of the prison regimes to effect clear policy re segregation, thus allowing for organised paramilitary activity; ineffective manning levels that stretched the capacity of staff to control inmates; failure by the Maze governor to implement necessary security measures despite repeated POA representations; overcrowding of H blocks, and lack of precise guidance to staff on security issues.[100]

Much of this was confirmed in questions in Parliament in the wake of the Hennessy Report. For example, Peter Archer MP noted a Circular from the Head of Personnel for prisons in the province which urged governors 'to approach all proposals for extra tasks to be performed in your establishment with the firm intention of avoiding any step which entails a demand for extra staff'. Additionally, the 'saga' of the main gate, which prison officers at the Maze had noted as unsafe following the escape from Belfast prison, had begun as long ago as 1978. As Irish MP Ken Maginnis commented: 'Can we view with less than utter scepticism ... [the] wait from 1978 to 1984 for alterations to the main gate?'

As the POA Report concluded: 'The escape of 38 inmates on 25th September 1983 left many questions to be answered.'[101] Yet those questions continued to be neglected, with ongoing consequences for the lives of prison officers working in Northern Ireland. Perhaps the only truly consoling factor could be found in the ongoing solidarity shown across the POA for those enduring the dangers and the tragedies of prison work in the province. As a joint message from all the POA branches in Northern Ireland put it:

> We would like to express our sincere and humble gratitude to the many branches and individuals throughout the Service for their countless messages of condolence, donations and the steadfast support given to

Mrs Ferris, widow of the late Officer James Andrew Ferris and their children following the brutal murder of her husband in the execution of his duty at HMP Maze Cellular on the 25th of September, 1983. Also for the many messages received wishing those injured in the incident a speedy recovery. It is at times like these when words like 'unity is strength' really portray their full meaning and show the magnitude of the comradeship that exists within the Prison Service as a whole, and makes one proud to be a member.[102]

Equal Opportunities

On a more cheerful note, the mid to late 1980s saw major moves in the direction of increased equal opportunities in the service for women, ethnic minorities and other underprivileged groups. As NEC member John Boddington, one of the major proponents of these moves, recalled:

Up until the 80s, '87, '88, if you were a male prison officer you were sent to a male prison, if you were a female you were sent to a female prison. In 1988, after a motion at conference, the POA opened up negotiations with the prison service and we had what was called the 'cross-sex postings agreement', which allowed female officers to work in male prisons and male prison officers to work in female prisons ... Which was a major change for the prison service and certainly a major leap for the [POA] which was always seen as a male bastion.[103]

An early sign of the changes occurred in 1985, when Wandsworth Prison 'saw something of a historic "happening" ... We had our very first female Officer working inside the Prison for the first time in over one hundred years'.[104] In June 1985, Park Lane reported that, as part of an increase in POA representation for the four special hospitals, Broadmoor, Rampton, Moss Side and Park Lane, all of which employed large numbers of female staff, a new consultative committee was charged with 'looking after the interests of the women Trade Unionists in the POA'.

More explicit changes

came about as a motion to conference. In 1986 we had for the very first time a female elected to serve on the National Executive ... there were none before that – [and] there was a recognition that we needed to move into the twentieth century ... You had female officers with great potential who could never achieve because they could only work in female prisons, and there's only a handful of female prisons ... It met with resistance in some quarters of the membership even though it went through Conference that indeed it would happen, that females would work in male establishments. To me it was one of the major significant steps for the union ... It wasn't till the 80s that we had an Equal Opportunities policy for the POA, which we'd never had before, and also a Race Relations policy.[105]

Other POA activists saw equal opportunities as one of the POA's main achievements:

Equal Opportunities for men and women ... It wasn't the [Prison] Department that said 'We'll do this', it was the POA did it. It was the POA that passed the resolutions that women should work in men's establishments and resolutions about the treatment of minorities ... Women in male establishments started in '87–'88 – Holloway was the pilot, we did it first. We had the first female officers working in a male establishment, Pentonville – one of them is still in the job.[106]

4

1988–2000: FROM THATCHERISM TO NEW LABOUR: PRIVATISATION AND UNION REPRESSION

As the previous chapter has indicated, problems with 'Fresh Start' began almost with its implementation in May 1987. By the end of the year, the Association was already 'in dispute with the H.O.P.D. on issues relating to Fresh Start', according to the POA Annual Report. As the entry added: 'We believe that these problems are not insoluble … However, we look to the H.O.P.D. to honour agreements and understandings reached between us, otherwise the problems will remain unresolved.'

This, of course, suggests that the Department had already failed to honour such 'agreements and understandings'. One of these, central to Fresh Start, was that prison officers would receive appropriate Time Off In Lieu (TOIL) for any extra hours they were asked to work. As shown in the recollections of an NEC member, this very quickly became unworkable, if not farcical:

> TOIL became more of an issue with Fresh Start. Because you're conditioned under Fresh Start to 39 hours, if you require to work more than 39 hours there's no way that can be paid. So if instead of 39 hours I needed to work 47 they can't pay me money because there's no facility under Fresh Start so they have to give me eight hours off, which created its own problems because there's no way to give me eight hours off. So there was one stage in the 1990s when the Prison Service was in debt to its employees probably to the tune of 20,000 hours or even more … At one stage they were in debt to their staff, if you worked it out in monetary terms, something like £30–40m in unpaid overtime.[1]

One of the issues indicated here was that prison officers were routinely 'required' (rather than chose) to work extra hours – a clear pointer to the problem that the Home Office was not prepared to back the new system with appropriate levels of new staff. Not surprisingly, therefore, industrial relations in the Prison Service saw little improvement in the later 1980s. As a report into the 1990 Strangeways riot (see below) commented regarding Fresh Start, its implementation in practice had resulted in prison officers 'believing that the Prison department had "moved the goal posts" and reneged on parts of the deal. This led to many Prison Service Staff becoming resentful, feeling that they had been cheated and that they had become the victims of the use of "weasel words".'[2] A comment in the Scottish POA magazine *Link* referred to the aftermath of Fresh Start as 'A year in which the whole Service appears to have been tossed up in the air like a pack of cards, hoping they come down in the right and proper place.'[3]

The Northern Ireland area of the POA continued with its uncompromising rejection of Fresh Start as a whole until well into 1988. The area's tough stance brought a number of concessions from the Northern Ireland Office, incorporated in a revised offer, but this was rejected on the grounds that 'the response does not concede crucial areas such as the *retention* of the rent allowance and compensatory grant in their present form'.[4]

Despite a very different response in England, Wales and Scotland, with the enthusiastic vote which a *Financial Times* article had predicted would 'put an end to Home Office fears that hardliners ... would mount a successful rearguard action against acceptance',[5] a letter from the Prison Service dated May 1988[6] refers to national action over what were clearly violations of 'Bulletin 8', the document setting out work rules under the Fresh Start proposals. The results of a national POA ballot, announced in January 1988, had pushed the Prison Service into negotiations over three central issues: manpower, 'civilisation', and the interpretation of Bulletin 8. On the first, the letter referred to a decision earlier in the year 'to recruit 1360 additional officers in 1988–9', but added: 'As a result of the Home Secretary's statement to the House of Commons just before Easter we are now uncertain about just how many of the additional officers will be recruited in 1988–89.' It was hardly surprising that the POA saw the need for continued action to pressurise this continually vacillating government.

The Prison Service letter went on to say that 'civilianisation' (the process of transferring more aspects of work to posts outside the Prison Officer grade), had 'gone ahead by local agreement in areas such as prisoner canteens, officers' messes, staff car park attendants. We are committed to continuing that process ....' While concerns about 'civilianisation' had at one time related to the growing incursion of professionals like social workers and psychiatrists into the prison officer's area of work, the process was clearly now coming dangerously close to privatisation in many areas. This had also led to some conflict between the POA and other unions involved in the Prison Service, such as the General, Municipal and Boilermakers union (GMB). In July 1989, the POA National Chair, John Bartell, wrote to the Secretary of the Trade Union Side on the Home Office Joint Industrial Council: 'I have to say that there is growing anger and resentment amongst our members that you should be seen to be apparently involved in a process of poaching jobs from the members of a TUC affiliate. It is POA policy to oppose any further erosion of Uniformed Officers' Jobs ....'[7]

The Prison Service letter concluded:

On the interpretation of Bulletin No 8 we have had many hours of talks ... The experience of these negotiations has convinced us that it was a mistake to seek to elaborate on Bulletin No 8 so soon after it has come into use ... For the time being we are convinced that it is best to stick to Bulletin No 8 as it was agreed between us ...

In light of this, the Home Secretary and the Prisons Board invite the NEC to recommend to the POA's members that steps should be taken to lift the current industrial action.[8]

The latter was clearly the Prison Service's main objective. However, the polished Home Office language could not hide the fact that prison officers had genuine grievances only marginally addressed by the points listed above. As a result, justifiably, national industrial action continued (short of outright strikes).

During the same period there was also a series of local disputes over inadequate staffing and other issues. In 1988, an eight-week-long strike at Holloway Prison over manning levels continued unofficially after 'the NEC bailed out', allegedly for fear of 'Maggie Thatcher ... [The branch Secretary] was less frightened of Thatcher than the NEC were ... we went back under our own steam.'[9]

In this case, Holloway Prison management's unilateral action resulted ultimately in a significant reform for prison officers when, even after the return to work, some Holloway prison officers were suspended without pay: 'When we went back to work they tried to introduce things and staff refused to obey that order ... and as each one did they were suspended without pay ... 17 of them.' In response, the Holloway branch secured a judicial review of the action in the name of

> a young female prison officer [who] put her name on the court paper ... They went to the High Court and they won that Judicial Review, *Attard* v. *Home Office* 1989. Since that day of the review, when an officer is suspended they're on full pay, because the judgment was that they're not guilty till they're found guilty – how dare you stop their pay? That judgment is used now, it's written in the Code of Discipline ... That Judicial Review nearly 20 years ago has now meant that officers suspended will be paid ... There's people been suspended for up to four years on full pay. If Holloway hadn't gone out on a limb in '88, '89, if they hadn't taken that action, we'd not have got that.[10]

In a more sober assessment, an industrial relations expert wrote:

> The formal equality of a contract of employment ... [for] prison officers as Crown employees is undermined by a sea of rules, regulations, instructions and disciplinary procedures ... these rules [can] become a source of conflict [as in] *Attard* v. *The Home Office* 1989, where the governor of HM Prison Holloway incorrectly used the *Staff Handbook* as a source of law for invoking a disciplinary procedure.[11]

In 1989, a still more serious local dispute, made worse by a management lockout, took place at Wandsworth Prison. As shown in the last chapter, Wandsworth had gone 'out on a limb' in opposing Fresh Start, mainly over the key issue of staffing levels. As a letter in October 1987 to the Association from the Wandsworth Branch put it: 'Our problem is MANNING LEVELS and I can understand that many of you will be saying that your problems are the same. That is why we have to ensure that the problem is taken seriously by the Department before one of our colleagues is seriously injured or worse ....'

This was followed by an undated letter which recounted the branch's attempts to have a section of the prison closed down 'to offset the short-falls in the main Prison'. This strategy was by no means unheard of: 'We understand that there are Branches who have closed down sections of their establishment in order to create sufficient staff to run safely.' However, despite support from the Wandsworth governor and the Prison Department's own proposals for 'similar strategies in other establishments', the Department had rejected Wandsworth's application – a move which left the POA branch with the 'belief that the Department are manipulating this Branch into a corner with a determination to "Take our members on"'.

Take them on they did. The POA members' stance was met by a ten-day management lockout during which 300 police officers were drafted into the prison. As a POA activist from Wandsworth during the period, Bryan Goodman,[12] recalls:

The dispute started on 29 January 1989 and lasted until 8 February 1989. There were over three hundred members of staff – all the uniformed grades – suspended for those ten days. They were ten very difficult days dealing with a dispute between the Wandsworth branch of the POA and the Home Office Prison Department, which was at that time front-page news in the daily papers. The branch was also dealing with a rift between ourselves and the elected POA leaders, who as far as we were concerned were not forthcoming with the support that we needed at that time. This did cause a serious rift in our relationship with the NEC and one that would cause a lot of heartache. However, a lot of water has passed under the bridge since then and we have all moved on, as we had to do in order to survive as a united organisation.

There had been a long lead up to the dispute, involving safe manning levels and the introduction of more prisoners. At the time there were over a thousand prisoners housed in police cells, due to the overcrowding prevalent in the prison system as a whole. We felt we could not take any more prisoners without an increase in staffing levels. Fresh Start had also been introduced and Wandsworth had voted against it; we had objections that it was a five-year deal and that it was linked to the discount sale of quarters. In any event we finally got onto Fresh Start after we had agreed the shift systems and local agreements with the governor on 3 June 1988.

Some of our fears were realised when the prison regime was constantly being cut due to lack of staff. There was by now difficulty recruiting staff, partly because they could no longer look forward to living in a prison quarter as these were being bought by staff under the discount sale scheme, which meant that staff being transferred in had no accommodation and property prices were high, making it difficult or, to some, impossible to buy.

We continued to experience staffing problems and took various forms of action in order to ensure that our members were able to operate in a safe environment. We had heard many whispers that the Prison Department were looking for a dispute at Wandsworth, and that in fact they were going to put the police in to run the prison. The Committee and myself approached the governor and asked him if there was any truth to this rumour. He told us that there was not and that he had made it perfectly clear to the minister that he would only run Wandsworth Prison with prison officers, he would not consider running it with anyone else.

[However, he was sacked for his pains]; the HOPD of course found a governor who was prepared to lock us out and use the police to run the prison. This man arrived on 5 December 1988 and left us in no doubt what was in store for us. He initiated new shift systems and manning levels, which would be subject to a short period of consultation, and if no agreement were found they would be imposed on 29 February 1989. We were not going to be allowed to have this dispute resolved via the recognised disputes procedure, the Cubbon formula. They simply chose to ignore it. As far as we were concerned this was in breach of a national agreement.

We were unable to agree to the new shift systems and argued that we already had agreed systems and manning levels that had been signed on 3 June 1988. But they were simply not interested in any of that; they were prepared to drive a coach and horses through all of our recognised agreements that were enshrined in the Fresh Start document Bulletin 8.

Wandsworth Staff were adamant that they would not work the new systems; we considered them to be flawed and unsafe. On Sunday 29 January, all staff scheduled for duty went into the prison and were met by a number of governors who ordered staff to work the new shift systems or be suspended from duty. All but a few told the governor that they were not prepared to work his new shift systems. All staff who took that stance were then promptly suspended from duty and issued with a suspension notice as they left the prison. As it was officially my weekend off and I was therefore not scheduled for duty, I was not issued with a suspension notice that day, but I was the last member of staff to leave the prison; as I left I was greeted by a governor who took great delight in telling me that I was not going to be suspended – I was going to be sacked. I firmly believed that this was their intention.

We immediately went to the Officers' Club and 'set up camp'. We were concerned that even though the union leadership were fully aware of the likely outcome, there was no NEC presence. Eventually an NEC representative arrived in the afternoon having been sent from way up country, which was strange because he was not our delegated representative, who lived only a short distance away. There was another NEC representative who lived nearby and was actually a Wandsworth member of staff; however, neither of them attended and we were not impressed by this.

Following our departure, hundreds of Metropolitan Police were bussed into the prison to work alongside the governor grades that had also been sent from all over the country to staff the prison. On a daily basis there were about 600 police officers staffing the prison and even then they were unable to unlock the whole prison at the same time. We would normally operate the prison with an average of 120 staff and unlock the whole prison at once. The governor and HOPD gave many press conferences throughout the dispute and advised the country that everything was under control and the prison was running smoothly. We knew that this was far from the truth of the matter.

We now know that part of their plans to deal with the situation included the police being informed that the POA at Wandsworth 'were extremely militant'; they were told not to expect any cooperation from POA members and to be 'prepared for open opposition and hostility'.

Perhaps because of our stand on overcrowding and opposition to Fresh Start, along with other issues, Wandsworth POA was seen by many as being militant and unreasonable. I have to say that that is not a view I share or one that can be justified. Like many other branches at that time, we were a very strong and committed branch. We were good policemen of POA policy and were unwilling to implement any systems or procedures that were against POA policies. For that we were castigated many times, but we make no apology for standing by those policies. They were all properly constituted motions that had been passed by various Annual Conferences over the years and had therefore become POA policy. We did not consider that because some branches were in breach of some of these policies that we also had to fall in line, and therefore we stood firm.

Of course nothing that the police had been 'warned' of took place and there was no hostility shown towards the police, or any staff that had agreed to work the new systems. With regard to the police, we did not like the fact that they were carrying out our duties but we fully understood the position they were placed in. We were aware from sources that we had that there was even talk that a number of police were going to refuse to enter the prison. As far as we are aware this did not transpire. We actually had a very good relationship with the Police Federation who were obviously not happy that they had to be there.

Wandsworth staff maintained a presence outside the prison throughout the dispute. We were told initially that it would be dealt with under the Codes of Practice concerning pickets under the Employment Act 1980, but this was never used and in fact the police very quickly withdrew their presence outside the prison. They could see that people who were going into the prison were not being harassed or abused by suspended staff. The Police Federation were also making their objections to being used in an industrial dispute and wanted their members out as soon as possible. They had acted similarly in previous disputes which they were used to cover, such as the ambulance strikes.

We were encouraged by the numerous messages of support we received from other branches that were ready to come out in support of us. Looking back, I think one of my biggest regrets is that when branches were phoning to ask, 'Do you want us to come out with you?' my response was, the NEC will give you the call when the time is right. Wait for their call. Of course, that call did not come. Hindsight is a wonderful thing, but I wish now I had taken them up on their offers of support. Things would have turned out very differently I am sure.

I am still firmly of the view that if immediate national industrial action had taken place, it would have been impossible for the HOPD to cope. They were struggling to cope with staffing one Prison as it was. They did not have the resources available to deal with a national action.

There were Conference motions that had been passed that said that immediate national industrial action would take place in the event of any branches being isolated. Others will have to answer why these were never implemented in our support.

We were aware that a coachload of prisoners was to be transferred from Wandsworth to the Isle of Wight Prisons. We had received intelligence that one of the ploys to be used was to completely empty Wandsworth Prison and leave us outside of an empty prison. I phoned all three IOW prisons and spoke to their branch officials. I pointed out that it was our view that if they accepted these prisoners that would leave the way clear to begin to empty the prison and we would be lost. All three branches made it perfectly clear that they would not under any circumstances be accepting these prisoners. They were true to their word and Wandsworth owe them a debt of gratitude for the stance they took that day. The busload of prisoners and exhausted and angry governors finally had to take the prisoners to Lambeth police cells overnight as they could find nowhere else to house them.

Staff were not being paid and many were extremely concerned because we didn't know how long this dispute would last. We were extremely pleased that the NEC provided the members with about £53,000 from the 'strike fund', to enable members to pay their bills and look after their families.

We finally arrived at an agreement that put us back to work with a transitional agreement. We returned to duty at the prison on 8 February. It is a testament to the professionalism of the staff that within the hour the whole of the prison was returned to normal with most prisoners pleased to see us back. Of course, we gained a good deal of information from prisoners about the chaos that had reigned for those ten days.

We were firmly of the view that this was a contrived dispute intended to smash the POA. If indeed that was their aim, then they had failed miserably.

In fact on the first morning of the dispute there were some staff who were non-members who were asking to join or rejoin … We signed them all up and they stood firm with us through the dispute so in that respect it had the reverse effect and actually instead acted like a recruiting sergeant and increased the membership.

It was unfortunate that a consequence of this dispute was a major rift between the Wandsworth POA branch and the NEC. That rift took its toll and it took a long time before bridges were built so as to move forward in the best interests of the Association.

None of us involved in the dispute will ever forget the impact it had on us. There was a commitment shown by all POA members involved and it heightened the feeling of camaraderie and support for each other; that is something I will never forget.

I will also never forget the sacrifice that some of our members were prepared to make. A Principal Officer who was weeks from his retirement and who was threatened that his pension would be lost, stood firm and refused to bow to the bully boy tactics that were being used. I can still see him now walking down the steps of the prison after being suspended. He was in tears, but certain in his own mind that he was doing the right thing; he felt he had a duty to consider the staff that were going to follow him. A truly commendable stance.

He was not alone in his consideration of others, and I salute each and every one of those members who stood firm, because they believed they were right and were prepared to fight.

A Special Delegate Conference took place after the event which was attended by many proud, uniformed Wandworth POA members, It was fitting that they received a standing ovation from the delegates there who recognised the important contribution that they had made in defence of the POA and its policies and recognised national agreements.

I say to the Tory administration that was in power and I believe complicit in this debacle – Shame on you … You will never break the determination of the POA to ensure that their members are able to work in a safe and secure environment. They are thoroughly decent men and women who perform a difficult and dangerous task in a most professional manner. To the current administration I give the same message and add, that it is about time that you recognised the asset that you have in prison staff and started treating them with the respect that they so deserve. If you fail to recognise this, you do so at your peril.[13]

'Nobody was Bigger than It'

As this account suggests, the POA leadership were uneasy about the Wandsworth dispute; in fact, they intervened to call the action off. One activist recalled the NEC meeting where the decision was made:

> There was only two [Wandsworth] reps and the rest of the country ... a very stormy meeting when they were told to go back ... Members in Wandsworth wanted to throw bottles and cans at the NEC ... We actually watched full-grown POA reps in tears at having to go out and face their branch and tell them they'd got to go back to work – in tears.[14]

Yet this apparent reluctance to support strike action was counterposed by the POA's 1987 decision to set up an Industrial Action Strike Fund, as indicated in the above account. The activist quoted above also paid tribute to the relative freedom of branches to criticise the NEC:

> If a committee locally wants to have a go at the NEC, which I did – a vote of no-confidence over the 1988 dispute ... you can do that. At the 1989 conference I was due to speak on a vote of no-confidence in the NEC [over] their handling of the Holloway dispute, and I called them a Junta. It was appropriate – they were behaving like a Junta: 'Do as I say not do what I want.' They used bully tactics ....

Rightly, her analysis included the understanding that 'union' can mean different things to members and leadership: 'You have to be careful when you talk about the POA; there's a tendency to say "the POA did, the POA didn't", even when you're POA yourself ... What they usually mean by that is the National Executive.'[15]

Serious internal problems at the head of the union had in fact preceded these examples of relatively healthy dissent. In March 1988, the Association's Deputy General Secretary, Peter Rushworth, and the four Assistant Secretaries, declared they were in dispute with the POA over a pay claim and backed this up by taking indefinite strike action against the union. In response, an NEC meeting on 22 March voted to terminate their employment with immediate effect; there followed a series of allegations and counter-allegations between the parties, with both sides circulating their views among the membership. In May 1988, the NEC convened a Special Delegate Conference to discuss a motion that 'This Conference supports the action of the National Executive Committee in terminating the employment of five full-time officers'. The Conference supported the motion; the five dismissed officials then moved to form a dissident organisation, the Prison Service Union (PSU) (see below). As a retired senior official put it: 'This ... was not the most glamorous moment in POA history but it did show the strength of the Executive and that – irrespective of who and how many challenged the union – nobody was bigger than it.'[16]

While a slightly more successful breakaway effort than the ill-fated 'Prison Force Federation' of 1980, the PSU could hardly claim to be a serious rival to the POA. In 1993, it numbered 1,500 members to the POA's 28,558, but that figure had declined to 1,200 by 1995. Part of the PSU's lack of success was due to the government's refusal to recognise the organisation, a policy unfortunately undermined by the late 1990s with the growth of privatisation (see below), but for the time being the POA held its own. This was despite yet another piece of Tory anti-union legislation, the Trade Union Reform and Employment Rights Act of 1993, which outlawed the TUC's historic Bridlington principles set up in 1939 to prevent 'poaching' by rival trade unions. The same act outlawed 'check-off' of union dues, precipitating the POA into a temporary financial crisis.

In fact, despite the internal problems, membership of the Association grew steadily, in line with the numbers of prison staff. A *Gatelodge*[17] Souvenir Issue for 1989 listed the membership figures over the decades:

1939	2,229
1949	4,100
1959	7,380
1969	12,585
1979	19,638
1989	25,000

The Scottish POA could also record recruitment success. In May 1989, a *Link* editorial noted that:

> In an age where trade union membership is falling, our Association is growing in leaps and bounds. When we became an independent Association in 1971, we had some 1,600 members. Currently there are some 3,700 ... and predictions are that this figure will grow to 4,300 by 1992.

In 1995, the POA in England, Wales and Northern Ireland represented 96 per cent of all prison officer grades. Though not as large as many of the big trade union 'guns', the POA's 'almost continuous year-on-year membership increase' during the period had 'been achieved within its industrial sector and not by extension into other areas of employment',[18] common among other unions through mergers and other methods at that time and since.

Meanwhile, the commitment within the organisation to promoting equal opportunities grew steadily. In the late 1980s and early 1990s, part-time working agreements were increasingly introduced into the Prison Service. As an NEC member put it:

> It sounds sexist but as we got more women in the Service with childcare responsibilities we negotiated a part-time working agreement which helped individuals who were able to go part-time or to job-share. None of that existed in the Prison Service prior to the late 1980s when the POA became very active on equality issues.[19]

Equality issues concerning not only gender but also ethnic minorities and gays were

> pioneered by the union from the mid-90s. We came out with the title Respect – now they've got it under the umbrella of diversity. The Prison Service has a recognised institution for gay staff [GALIPS – Gays And Lesbians In the Prison Service] and the constitution was written by a prison officer.[20]

A 1999 Whitley Committee recorded 'A new Racial Equality Programme for both staff and prisoners, very much in consultation with the POA ...'[21]

'The POA is not a Trade Union'?

Whatever its efforts, the POA was unable to hold back its members' continued unrest, and this began to attract unwelcome attention from the government. As one analysis notes: 'by the early 1990s, the ... Conservative government had decided it was time to tackle the POA'.[22] Revision of the Cubbon formula in 1989 'had not achieved any substantial reduction in industrial action, and industrial relations were in a sorry state'.[23] While yet another new Industrial Relations Procedure Agreement (IRPA) was introduced in 1993, this was almost immediately followed by a threat of national industrial action by the POA over the ongoing issue of staffing levels. Rather than an outright strike, the action threatened was in line with the 'traditional industrial muscle of the POA – adhering to the prison service's own Certified Normal Accommodation (CNA) at each establishment'.[24]

This was coupled with major lockouts by prison officers at Preston and Hull when, as a later General Secretary recalled:

> we took a stand against prison overcrowding. Hull and Preston prisons were the most overcrowded in the civilised world. We found a gun in Preston Prison and we'd had a riot in the visitors' room at Hull, so we locked the gates and said we can't take any more prisoners ... They passed legislation against us to make sure that we opened the gates and crammed people in.[25]

The situation at Preston in late 1993 was one of extreme overcrowding; the prison was operating at 200 per cent of its designed capacity. The inmates were, in the words of Tom Robson, Preston Branch Chairman at the time and later elected to the NEC, 'crammed into an old Victorian prison that had had little spent on maintaining the fabric of the establishment'.

What led to the decision to lock out new prisoners was that:

> We had good security information that there was a pistol and ammunition hidden in the prison. The governor would not close down the jail for a proper search to take place and there was to be further inmates arriving from police cells around lunchtime.

I met with colleagues who were available on the committee and instructed that we would lock up the prisons and accept no more prisoners. Myself and a colleague then went to the gate and turned back coaches arriving with prisoners from police cells; we effectively took over the prison. We had to, with the intelligence we had of a gun in the prison, the overcrowding situation, we could not provide the most basic human decency or ensure safety and the governor would do nothing to help the situation.

As a POA Committee we were served with injunctions at our homes. Disgracefully, the Prison Service also published our names and addresses in the local press. We believe that this was done out of malice and it was extremely dangerous to both us and our families. They even published the names of Committee members who were on leave and had not been party to the lockout.

The membership at Preston stood up to bullying and intimidation from management full square behind the POA Committees locally and nationally. It should also be remembered that some weeks later a pistol was found during a full search of the prisons, but there was never an apology to the prison officers who were placed in extreme danger by a management who just did not seem to care about either their staff or those we were there to hold, protect and care for.[26]

Far from being grateful or apologetic, in fact, the government sought an injunction in response to the dispute. The resulting 1993 case of *Home Office* v. [David] *Evans* resulted in the decision that would deny prison officers their democratic trade union rights to an extent even greater than that posed to the rest of the working population by the Tories' generally draconian anti-trade union legislation. In issuing the extraordinary ruling that there could be no 'trade dispute' between prison officers and their employers because prison officers were not 'workers' (in its turn based on the notion from a previous judgment that prison officers possessed the same powers as constables), the Lord Chief Justice commented that it was 'remarkable that this point has laid dormant for so long'. With corresponding alacrity, he also concluded that the POA was 'not a trade union'.

Unfortunately for his eminent Lordship this conclusion went beyond even what a Conservative government had intended. The ensuing 1994 Criminal Justice and Public Order Act made it clear that the POA was to be reinstated as a trade union. However, the government was no less repressive in its intentions. While the POA was reinstated as a trade union, its right to call on its members to take industrial action became a criminal offence under the Act.

Section 127

The problems and conflict of the period immediately preceding that decision are described vividly by a retired senior POA official:

> The continued attacks on the Association reached new proportions in 1993, resulting from dramatic increases in overcrowding, increased tension inside prisons and dramatic increases in brutality on staff.
>
> Privatisation, contracting-out and market testing were the order of the day, along with management driving through staffing level changes and inadequately supervised regimes. Even worse, management imposed a Code of Discipline and privatised court and escort services.
>
> In addition, the Government and Prisons Agency imposed pay ceilings, even after the delivery of 25 per cent savings over the lifetime of the Fresh Start framework agreement.
>
> In that context the Association balloted for industrial action; the Government and Prisons Agency moved through the High Court and the Criminal Justice and Public Order Bill was the end result.[27]

The Scottish POA also took action. As the Area Secretary recalls: 'In 1993 the threat was from market testing of works functions and jobs like that … There was a long fight, a long period of industrial action … Ian Lang, when he was Scottish Secretary of State, said it was inconceivable that the whole criminal justice system and prison service could be held to ransom by prison officers.'[28] According to a POA NEC member: 'There were a lot of talks, lots of negotiations, threats to go on strike – which led to Michael Howard removing the trade union rights from prison officers.'[29] This removal took the shape of the notorious 'Section 127' within the 1994 Criminal Justice and Public Order Act.

The three key proposals within this Act were contained in Section 127, which banned industrial action,[30] Section 126, which, as signalled above, enshrined in law the trade union status of the POA, and Section 128, which brought in pay review machinery for the Prison Service. While this last might be seen as a relatively constructive move, one commentator accurately points out that 'A … strategy adopted by UK governments to curtail industrial action in certain public services has been the modification of collective bargaining by some form of independent pay determination mechanism, such as a PRB.'[31]

The campaign to remove this unjust legislation continued for years, as shown in the next chapter. Increasingly, the POA began to adopt broader political methods within the labour movement and beyond to remove the yoke imposed by Section 127. As its 1996 Annual Report commented:

> It may transpire that the only recourse would be to change the Criminal Justice and Public Order Act of 1994 as it affects the rights of Prison officers and the removal of their immunities under Trade Union Legislation. The Association is also amending a TUC sponsored motion calling for the restoration of the rights of Prison Officers … The Trades Union Congress will hopefully … assist further the Executive in its fight to restore these rights.

The POA Chairman and General Secretary would also be speaking at the fringe meetings of the major political party conferences, and would be discussing the issue with the Liberal Democrats and with Jack Straw, Labour Opposition spokesman, who, ironically in view of later events, had 'already expressed [his] support for the Association on a broad range of fronts'.[32]

Meanwhile, the government must have hoped that its revised 1993 IRPA would also have had some influence on calming the industrial relations atmosphere. However, this appears not to have been the case. A large number of grievances remained unresolved, mostly due to the very strict time limits of 21 days per stage the agreement imposed on the resolution of unresolved disputes or 'Failure(s) To Agree' (FTAs). Not surprisingly, these were seldom achieved; for example, two disputes registered at one open prison were still awaiting national level meetings over three years later. The time limits were described even by management as 'a joke'.

However, to some extent the system worked for the POA, since a status quo clause could be activated to ensure that conditions remained unchanged as long as the dispute was going through the procedure: 'The POA saw the status quo clause as the only weapon that they could lawfully use after the ban on industrial action in 1994. They could no longer stop a matter by industrial action, but they could delay it by prolonging the procedure.'[33] As one prison governor remarked of the POA: 'Close one door and they'll find something else.'[34]

Nevertheless, the new Prisons Agency did its best to stand in the way of effective union organisation in the workplace. The 1995 POA Report records a letter from the Agency stating its unwillingness to let union meetings go ahead without permission, since this was 'contrary' to the infamous Section 127. As the General Secretary wrote to members:

This is now where we are in the Prison Service. You are not allowed to talk about your imposed pay; additional hours or the disgraceful way staff have been treated ... They threaten the Executive that calling branch meetings is inducing you to break the law. They tell you that you have no right to hold meetings to discuss issues vital to your best interest and that such meetings can only be conducted by permission of the Governor who will decide time and date. They purposely ignore the fact that arrangements for meetings of this nature are always conducted at local level ... This is another disgraceful action by an Agency, which is unable to comprehend how angry POA members are at the incompetence they are witnessing from Service managers and the way they are being treated by an uncaring and hostile employer ... The Executive's position in calling Branch meetings stands, as it is imperative that the membership in general, is afforded the opportunity to discuss these vitally important matters.[35]

By 1998, the Prisons Agency was imposing pay agreements on prison officers; after a POA ballot had overwhelmingly rejected the 1998 'offer', prison officers took industrial action which was then, predictably, prevented by the courts. As the General Secretary commented: 'Again, the Actions of the Agency soured any hope of improving the climate of industrial relations ... Fairness was clearly absent and their actions were devoid of justice.'[36] In its turn, this action affected negotiations on removing Section 127 and establishing arbitration procedures, as well as the progress of the proposed Pay Review Body.

Privatisation ... The Beginnings

As a body, the Prisons Agency not only acted repressively against the union but represented the burgeoning privatisation ideology of the period. Its introduction removed the Prison Service from its previous Home Office status, 'hiving it off' in a process parallel to the increasingly common initiatives of 'contracting out' and 'compulsory competitive tendering' (CCT). The notion of agency status for the Prison Service was first mooted in the 1991 Lygo Report, commissioned to further examine management within the service. Sir Raymond Lygo, noting rather desperately that 'The prison Service is the most complex organisation I have encountered and its problems some of the most intractable', suggested that making the service a Next Steps Agency, that is, a separate entity from the Home Office, would bring benefits of 'autonomy, purpose, and better compliance with headquarters instructions'.[37]

The Criminal Justice Act of 1991 duly introduced 'Agency status [for the] ... Prison Service, together with the market ethos through compulsory competitive tendering and privatisation ... The aim was to have prison boards running their establishments more efficiently, through the threat of competition and the notion of a market discipline.'[38]

As a senior retired official characterised the loss of the Home Office status: 'The Civil Service was an avenue of support for staff problems and grievances. The top tier looked after staff, stuck to rules. The Prison Department lost that status when it became an agency.'[39] The Prison Service in Scotland was also transferred to Agency status in April 1993, after which 'industrial relations tended to become strained ... For the first time in its history, the

Scottish POA balloted in favour of a series of one-day strikes in September 1994 ....'[40]

In 1993, the government had issued a document on 'Court Escort, Custody and Security' which set out its intent to 'reorganise and make subject to competitive tendering the arrangements for escorting prisoners to and from the Court' and proposed that 'responsibility for order and security within the Courts [be] devolved to the private sector'. The POA rejected the document, arguing that 'a privatised Escort System [would be] inefficient, impractical and contrary to the public interest as well as that of the employees who will carry out the work'.[41] However, by this time the government was moving on to the privatisation of prisons *per se*, announcing its intention to privatise Wolds, a newly built remand prison (see below).

The POA summed up the history in its 1993 Annual Report:

> The Government was introduced to the idea of prison privatisation in 1984 by a Consortium headed by the Adam Smith Institute[42] ... [at first] Government and ministers dismissed the idea ... in 1985, [Home Secretary] Douglas Hurd said that he could not envisage the private management of the prison population on ethical and practical grounds. Yet by 1988 he saw no such obstacle ... A fundamental change of attitude had occurred ....

For the POA, one no doubt salient reason for the government's change of heart was 'the belief that privatisation would fragment and weaken the Prison Officers' Association ... In fact it is widely acknowledged that one of the effects ... and purposes of privatising publicly owned industries, services and institutions is the undermining of effective trade unionism therein.'

Industrial relations academics agree: 'Underlining governments' need to reduce union influence was the POA's success in slowing down [Michael] Howard's[43] extensive privatisation programme following complaints to the Central Arbitration Committee over lack of consultation.' Sadly, on that score the POA's own prediction turned out within a few years to be only too accurate; as this account notes, 'In no private prison opened since 1997 has the POA been granted recognition.'[44]

But privatisation was successful in little else. As Black noted in 1995:

> The agency status of the prison service and the recent privatisation offer no guarantee against future disorder in UK prisons. There is already concern over the three existing privatised prisons. There is a high drugs culture at the Wolds Remand Prison (run by Group 4), serious disturbances leading to much damage have ... occurred at Blakenhurst Prison (franchised to UK Detention Services Ltd) and at Doncaster Prison, opened in July 1994 and leased to Premier Prisons Ltd, there have been three suicides of inmates: gangs roam the wings, and intimidation of staff and inmates occurs.[45]

Strangeways

Such problems might have been anticipated four years earlier, with the eruption of the 1990 Strangeways riot, foreshadowed in the concerns expressed by a local MP as long ago as 1985 (see Chapter 3). This led to the Woolf and Tumin inquiry, whose 1991 Report yet again vindicated the POA's position on prison overcrowding and indicated in its every line that privatisation, with its 'modern management principles', was the last strategy which would solve the only too typical problems leading to the riot.

The disturbances in this Manchester prison started on 1 April 1990, when a group of prisoners overpowered prison officers during a Sunday morning church service and, within hours, had mobilised other prisoners to take over most of the establishment. The prisoners gained access to the roof, allowing them to communicate with the media outside the prison walls. It was over three weeks before prison staff regained control, during which the Strangeways riot had sparked off a string of disturbances in 25 more prisons, including Dartmoor, Pucklechurch, Cardiff, Bristol and Glen Parva. The POA noted that at Strangeways itself, 'One prison officer and two inmates died as a result of the disorder, hundreds more staff and inmates were injured and millions of pounds of damage was caused ... The disturbance ... was the worst in the history of the [British] prison system.'[46] Ultimately, the situation was brought under control by the use of 'piercing noise and water cannons', which pressurised prisoners, including the six ringleaders, to surrender. The causes of this spectacular riot were, as mentioned above, the subject of an investigation by Lord Chief Justice Woolf and Judge Tumin, the Chief Inspector of Prisons.

Despite the fact that the Strangeways riot took place at a time when some improvements had been brought into the management of the prison – 'Ironically, when the riots struck ... the Prison Service had already started to tackle some of the worst features of the prison system ... Long term problems were, for the first time, being confronted'[47] – the overall situation in the pre-riot period is most accurately described as one of 'institutional breakdown'.[48] Strangeways had received an unusually large number of hard-to-manage 'dispersal' or Category A prisoners in the months leading up to the riot, and these prisoners, already expelled from other prisons for their capacity for causing trouble, 'severely upset ... the social structure of the prison'. As one senior officer at Strangeways wrote to the Woolf inquiry: 'Manchester was becoming the dumping ground for problem prisoners.' The POA summary described Strangeways as 'a human warehouse doing its best to protect and control too many men in conditions which sap rather than enhance human dignity'.[49]

One unmissable factor in all of this was the extreme shortage of staff at the prison. The influx of Category A prisoners had not only exacerbated staffing problems in its own right, but had also significantly increased the prison population within a very short period from 1,417 at the beginning of the year to 1,658 at the time of the riot – within an establishment built for 970 prisoners. Not surprisingly, staff were unable to cope. As one prison officer put it: 'inmates virtually had [the] run of the prison'.[50] Nor had the promise of improvements done anything to significantly alleviate conditions, which were 'still of a wholly unacceptable standard', according to Woolf. Prisoners were routinely locked up for extended periods in overcrowded cells, the vast majority with no internal sanitation; there was often no change of kit after the weekly shower, and young prisoners were offered no work and few activities. Again not surprisingly, the inmates 'were labouring under an intense sense of grievance'.

Ironically, much of the crisis could be attributed to the optimistically named Fresh Start agreement. Almost every comment on the riot, including the Woolf Report and the POA submission to the inquiry, implicates not only the failure to increase staff in line with the reduction in overtime instigated by the agreement, but also the so-called 'Efficiency Savings' implemented in the aftermath of Fresh Start. Despite the fact that these had not formed any part of the 'formal Fresh Start package', according to Woolf, the savings were expected to achieve 'a targeted improvement of staff efficiency of 24 per cent: 15 per cent over three years and an eventual further 9 per cent'.[51] However, as Woolf and Tumin remarked: 'in order to gain approval [for Fresh Start], the Prison Service was not anxious to draw attention to the extent of the efficiencies involved', and as a result, both governors and staff

> were unaware that 15 per cent efficiencies were to be achieved without any necessary increases in staff. They believed, and told their staff, that staffing complements would be increased. This led to cynicism and disillusionment. The effect of 24 per cent efficiencies to be achieved over five years ... was that promised improvements in regimes could not be achieved.[52]

Hence the far from 'improved' regime at Strangeways.

Other riots followed the uprising at Strangeways and other prisons in April 1990. For example, Wymott Prison, built in the late 1970s, 'suffered serious incidents of persistent discipline throughout the 1980s, which eventually led to its virtual destruction during serious rioting in September 1993'.[53] Further rioting in the early to mid 1990s produced a situation in which Albany prison staff were 'shell-shocked and physically fearful', while at Long Lartin 'the main element ... was fear. Fear of individual cons collectively, fear of a riot, fear of losing the roof'[54] – the latter a reference to rioting prisoners' habit of occupying the prison roof, as at Strangeways, in order to demonstrate their grievances.

A Disgraceful Act by a Discredited Agency

In 1994 the Conservative government exacerbated the situation by imposing that year's pay 'agreement'. As a retired senior official put it: 'Imposing Pay '94 was a disgraceful act by a discredited Prisons Agency.'[55] However, 'keeping the pay offer low and extending the pay period to 15 months ensured rejection by the membership'. The following year, the Prison Agency again imposed a pay increase of only 2.5–2.8 per cent, 'prov[ing] that the Agency was devoid of principle. Their shameful behaviour provoked a membership response, which was fully justified.'[56] Budget cuts and the loss of prison officer posts through compulsory redundancy in the face of an unprecedented rise in the prisoner population also justifiably provoked prison officer unrest. The POA's 1996 Annual Report also expressed concern over the new VERSE (Voluntary Early Retirement and Severance scheme) or 'Voluntary Exit' arrangements in which staff were now denied removal expenses despite the fact that Prison Service management had emphasised that the main aim of VERSE was to achieve head count reductions, and 'as a consequence some staff might have to move around'.[57]

Meanwhile, the Association's anger at the removal of trade union rights continued to be expressed at Annual Conference. While a 1997 Prison Service Review 'accepted that the POA had experienced substantial problems during the 1990s and recognised that recent issues [had made] effective officer representation more important', it 'did not explain in any detail how ... this might occur'.[58] In fact, the Review argued that 'significant investment was required in senior management recruitment' rather than dealing with at least some of the staff unrest by suggesting the recruitment of more prison officers. The recommendation of increased staff at senior management level was made despite the Review's observation that 'One major concern of staff in prisons was the apparent remoteness of those working in Headquarters ....'[59] This was in line with the Review's generally surreal logic: noting that 'the contracting-out of prisons, the involvement of the private sector on running whole prisons, and the POA's loss ... of the right to take industrial action have made good industrial relations harder to achieve', it concluded that these difficulties made such policies 'all the more necessary'.[60]

'Clearly Focused on Performance ... '

The ongoing juggernaut of privatisation was increasingly reinforced by what were known as 'modern management' methods. As long ago as 1982, a new Director General of the Prison Service, Chris Train, had been appointed 'with a clear brief to see through a process of management modernisation'. In 1984, he introduced 'contracts' based on a 'statement of purpose' into prisons, and 'once this idea had been introduced, the next step was to create a coherent management framework within establishments capable of delivering agreed objectives'.[61]

In 1990, the Prison Service was drastically restructured by abolishing the existing regional directors, regarded as 'the four "robber barons" of the Prison Board', and substituting a new area management structure, located in London, which 'symbolised further the ... development of a more "corporate" and centralised organisation'. Some of the ensuing problems mirrored the inherent causes of the Strangeways riot as described above; escapes at Whitemoor and Parkhurst in 1994 and 1996, for example, 'exposed the enduring tensions in and complexity of the relationship between ... headquarters and the "field"', as did a sentence calculation debacle in 1996 which resulted in 542 prisoners being released without warning.

Agency status itself 'marked a new phase in the development of managerialism' in the service. 'Corporate and Business Plans were now regularly published, outlining objectives related to improving quality of service and increasing value for money. The Prison Service was now clearly focused on performance.'[62]

Bizarrely, in signalling this new direction the government decided to 'market test' Strangeways Prison following its reconstruction after the 1990 riot. As Liebling and Price comment: 'The fact that the government accepted that the private sector could be contracted to carry out this grave state function was a severe jolt to a Service isolated from private sector management influence.'[63] In 1999, the prison was subjected to market testing yet again. The POA Annual Report noted that 'The POA branch and all the staff at Manchester were devastated at the re-Market

Testing of the Prison.' A POA representative at a Whitley Council meeting asked the Director General to 'answer the question as to why it should be Market Tested again. There was enough scope in the Service Level Agreement for the prison not to be market tested again for 14 years.'[64]

In another move towards 'modern management' principles, a top manager from no less than Granada Television was appointed as Director General of the Prison Service in 1990 – a major break with tradition which was now beginning to spread throughout public sector employment. The growing obsession with 'performance' was marked by the introduction of so-called Key Performance Indicators (KPIs) in a field where 'performance' is surely beyond the control of most participants. While 'initially these targets were quite loose' and, in the first year of Agency status, management could conjure up no more than six of them, by 2000 there were 15, not to mention a Prison Service 'vision statement'.[65]

During the same period, Scottish prison officers also experienced a 'restructuring' of the Prison Service in the form of a 'Staff and Structure Review'. As the Area Secretary recalled:

> We moved away from Bulletin 8 and Fresh Start to a new way of working which meant moving from grades to roles – two-tier prison officer, residential officer, operations officer, etc. E band was first line manager, F band unit manager etc. There was a new pay-band structure, linked to a performance-based system – we accepted that in order not to get market testing ... This just happened in Scotland. It was a difficult situation where they were bringing in market testing in existing prisons – Michael Forsyth was Scottish Secretary at the time under the Tory regime, 1995–97.[66]

In response: 'We balloted for industrial action, got a positive ballot, there were negotiations [but] we got a letter from Forsyth saying they were going ahead with market testing in other prisons in Scotland.' Presumably as a sweetener, 'Equity shares were allocated'.

Other aspects of 'modern management' continued to dog the Service. To the 'group working' introduced with Fresh Start – similar to the increasingly popular management technique of 'teamworking' – was added one of the 'Investors In People' (IIP) initiatives that were by now dogging the public sector. The worth of such an initiative was demonstrated in the POA's withdrawal, in 1990, of all support for IIP 'due to the continued contempt displayed by the Prison Service Agency to the Health and Safety and conditions of our members'. It was agreed that a meeting be set up to investigate 'any evidence that IIP companies/establishments have lower sick leave figures' than the Prison Service.[67]

Eventually even the government was forced to admit that not everything about 'modern management' worked; escapes by two 'Category A' prisoners from maximum security prisons in 1994 and 1995 resulted in the dismissal in 1995 of the then Director General, Derek Lewis, who had also been recruited from the private sector.

'Step by Step'?

Despite such setbacks, the remorseless drive towards prison privatisation continued. As a number of accounts suggest, this policy was 'profoundly influenced' by US practice and the involvement of American corporations.[68] Even though a 1986 Parliamentary Select Committee examining penal systems in other countries 'had every country in the world at its disposal, the only trip they made was to the United States',[69] and the itinerary included two visits to the Corrections Corporation of America, whose resounding title would eventually be transmuted to the more sober UK Detention Services (UKDS).

Although the development of policy consequent on this expedition was presented in terms of an 'experiment', no evaluation process was put in place, and no such reservations were included in the enabling legislation, the Criminal Justice Bill of 1991. The then prisons minister, Angela Rumbold, pledged firmly that 'if and only if, the contracted-out remand centre proves to be a success will we move towards [further] privatisation', and commented to the *Financial Times* in January 1992 that she was going to take the process 'step by step', but neither of these commitments was kept.[70]

The first private contract was awarded in 1992 to the Group 4 security firm to manage Wolds, a newly constructed remand prison (see above). While a report on Wolds by the Prison Reform Trust in April 1993 concluded that 'there is genuine cause for concern about aspects of the regime', and this was followed by critical reports from the Chief Inspector of Prisons and the National Audit Office, the application of the 1991 Criminal Justice Act was nevertheless extended from new prisons to existing facilities. In 1993, the government announced that *all* new prisons would be privately built and operated. By 1994, two further private prison contracts had been awarded, at Blakenhurst in the West Midlands and Doncaster.

Although academic research on the progress of Wolds Prison, published by the Home Office, found that 'similar and, some might argue, better achievements are to be found in some new public sector prisons, showing that the private sector has no exclusive claim on … high quality regimes', the process continued remorselessly. Within three or four years, 'any notion that prison privatisation was simply an experiment, if that had ever been the case, had long been forgotten'.[71] Yet problems continued to surface. At Blakenhurst, franchised to UKDS in 1992, a major disturbance took place in February 1994 (see above), and in May 1995 a UKDS custody officer at the prison was jailed for 18 months for scheming to have two prisoners beaten up. However, 'perhaps one of the most serious incidents to have taken place at the prison' was when Alton Manning, a 33-year-old black remand prisoner, was 'unlawfully killed by prison staff in December 1995'.[72] On 7 August 1996, when 25-year-old prisoner John Cowley was found hanging in his cell, the tragedy was the fourth death at the prison within ten months. Nor did the prison even conform to the government's management criteria: according to the Prison Service, in 1997–98, Blakenhurst failed to meet its performance targets on four counts (assaults, hours of purposeful prisoner activity, drug testing and percentage of positive test results). In 1999, UKDS received a second penalty when it was fined £25,000 for allowing a prisoner to escape while under escort. Other companies were no better. In 1996 and 1999, Premier Prison

Services topped the Prison Service's league tables for having the most incidents of prisoner self-harm. Yet the company retained its contract in 1999; leaked documents of the tender evaluation process led to allegations of a political fix.[73]

Perhaps the most wounding aspect of the apparently unstoppable progress of privatisation during the 1990s was its wholesale adoption – in fact expansion – by the New Labour government, despite apparently heartfelt promises to the contrary and characterisations of prison privatisation as 'morally repugnant'. In 1994, Deputy Prime Minister-to-be John Prescott pledged to the POA at its 1994 Conference: 'Labour will take back private prisons into public ownership – it is the only way forward.' In 1995, the then shadow Home Secretary, Jack Straw, argued – rightly – that 'It is not appropriate for people to profit out of incarceration. This is surely one area where a free market certainly does not exist [!]' He also pledged that 'at the expiry of their contracts a Labour government will bring these prisons into proper public control and run them directly as public services'.[74] Yet 'Labour's backtracking started soon after the general election on 1 May 1997 ....'[75] We now move on to that historic election and its only too demoralising aftermath.

New Labour in Power

Few Labour supporters – or indeed anyone opposing injustice, inequality and greed – who stayed up to watch Tory heads roll as the results came in on the night of the 1 May 1997 general election will forget the exhilaration of that moment when 18 years of government epitomising exactly those qualities finally came to an end. However, for many the subsequent disillusionment has been equally profound. Prison officers and their Association are among that number.

As a retired senior official active at the time recalls: '1997 saw the election of the Labour Government. Regrettably, the unambiguous commitments made to the Association whilst in opposition were not honoured. Privatisation continued with no restoration of the Trade Union Rights.'[76] A current POA full-timer agrees: 'Despite the Labour party's repeated promises and commitments while in opposition their 1997 election triumph was to mark a sorry day for the POA and many other trades unions who had such high hopes of what a Labour government would deliver after 18 years of Tory attacks on the movement.'[77] The Foreword to the POA 1997 Annual Report was equally sorrowful:

> The election of a Labour Government was long awaited. The unambiguous commitments made to the Association whilst in opposition encouraged the view that the Labour Government would treat us fairly. Regrettably, as the year drew to its close, it was evident that the commitments made were not to be honoured. The privatisation of the Prison Service was to continue and there was to be no restoration of Trade Union Rights for the Association.[78]

The turnaround on privatisation began almost as soon as the new government took office. On 8 May 1997, Jack Straw remarked: 'if there are contracts in the pipeline and the only way of getting the [new prison] accommodation in place is to sign those contracts, then I will sign those contracts'. On 19 June, barely six weeks after the election, Straw announced that he had renewed the much-troubled UKDS contract for Blakenhurst; he then agreed to two further 'privately financed, designed, built and run prisons' and pledged to 'fully consider' the recommendations of the March 1997 Select Committee Report, despite its origins in a wholly alien government. This report had recommended that 'the idea of privately managed prisons … should be allowed to develop further'.[79]

The full extent of the U-turn was revealed in Straw's speech to the 1998 POA Conference, in which he announced, in common with the Conservatives, that new prisons in England and Wales would now be both privately built and privately run. This was supposedly justified by a Prison Service Review commissioned by the government which had concluded that 'the immediate transfer of existing private prisons to the public sector is not affordable and cannot be justified on value for money grounds'.[80] The grand concession announced by Straw at the 1998 Conference was that 'the Prison Service will be allowed to bid for the chance to take over the management of existing privately managed prisons on the next occasion that the contracts expire'. In some ways this 'concession' significantly undermined the government's own case on costs. Within two years contracts for privately managed prisons Buckley Hall and Blakenhurst had been won by the Prison Service on lower cost and higher quality, while a market testing exercise at Manchester prison resulted in the Prison Service successfully beating off bids from the private sector.[81]

Nevertheless, such pyrrhic victories did little to reduce the enormity of a Labour government's betrayal of basic principles of public sector service. As the Scottish Area POA Secretary put it:

> From 1997, there was no difference between Tories and Labour. They just continued with these policies – in fact we were threatened with more privatisation by the Labour government – absolute privatisation as opposed to market testing. That was a great disappointment because we had letters from Tony Blair in opposition stating that as soon as practicable the Labour government would bring private prisons back into the public sector – he called privatisation immoral and reprehensible. We challenged it but their argument was fiscal – they said once you start looking at the books it would not be feasible to bring it back because of the expense to the public.[82]

The bogey of market testing, pressurising prison officers beyond even the threat posed by outright privatisation, continued to dominate in the late 1990s. The 1999 POA Annual Report noted that 'The year ended with the Labour Government re-introducing the Conservative policy of Market Testing.' Ironically, this was in part provoked by the relative success of the Prison Service in 'bidding' for contracts: 'In announcing the return to the Public Sector of Buckley Hall, Government Ministers argued that Market Testing failing prisons was essential.' As the General Secretary commented: 'This was a demoralising blow to staff who had delivered budget cuts for a number of years and achieved every key performance indicator set by the Prison Agency.'[83]

As indicated above, the relentless progress towards privatisation also seriously affected the POA's recruitment and recognition status. The weak reed of the Prison Service Union (see above) was, not surprisingly, receiving sustenance from official quarters. A number of private prison companies such as Premier began recognising the PSU, described as 'defin[ing] itself as a moderate body that accepts privatisation, eschews the POA's political campaigning role, and seeks constructive partnership with private operators'.[84] In this sense it is hardly surprising that the PSU was embraced by the private sector. Nevertheless, the POA responded positively, after initial hesitation, by moving to recruit staff in private prisons. In November 1998, a Special Delegate Conference agreed to recruit within the private sector, from which the Association had already received a number of membership requests.

'In It To Win It'

The arguments against privatisation were spelt out by POA National Chairman Mark Healey in his introduction to the Special Delegate Conference:

> The introduction of the private sector in any industry is there to create competition. That is what it is put there for, with the hope of the economics to drive terms and conditions down both within the private and the public sector. That is what it is there for. That is why it is introduced because if it does not drive down costs, what is the point of introducing the private sector into the industry? There is no point. If you want to play one side off against the other, and that is what has been happening within the Prison Service for the last six years, with a huge amount of success for the Prison Service and the Government – budget cuts, below rate of inflation pay rises and the only thing that is going up is assaults, that is the only thing that is going up, in both public prisons and private prisons, far more in private prisons. The economists, the money men, want this to continue, this continued competition where neither the private sector can win nor the public sector because they are fighting each other to do the job cheaper, the people at the top of the public sector and the people at the top of the private sector, and it is us, our members, the people we represent, who bear the cost of that.

This statement summed up the rationale for the union's continued anti-privatisation policy. But this Conference was now to look at how best the union could move forward in relation to its campaign to bring about the end of the use of private companies in the operation of prisons and at the same time organise prison officers employed by those companies.

Though a number of branches opposed the recruitment of private sector prison officers into the POA, ultimately, with the impending market tests of Buckley Hall and Doncaster, the decision was taken that the POA should be 'in it to win it'. It was felt that with the knowledge of the private sector members providing more detailed information on the working practices of their employers, the union would be better informed and in a better place to challenge the more unacceptable working arrangements.

On these grounds, the decision was taken that the POA would recruit members from private sector prisons. News of the decision spread within days to the private companies and to their staff; within a week, membership forms were being received at an ever increasing rate.

The first private sector branch of the POA was formally agreed by the NEC at its February 1999 meeting at HMP Wolds. Due to the eagerness of private sector officers to join the POA, within three months the POA had over two-thirds of prison custody officers in membership.

Branch status followed for Buckley Hall and Tinsley House the following month, and for HMP Doncaster in April of that year. As indicated above, in October 1999 the government announced that the Prison Service 'in-house' bid for the operation of HMP Buckley Hall had been successful and it would return to public sector management early the following year.

The winning of this contract by the 'in-house' team was seen by many as a justification for private sector membership and was viewed as the first re-nationalisation by New Labour since coming to power, though the leaks surrounding the decision to leave the operation of HMP Doncaster to Premier Prison Service left a slightly sour taste to the victory.

The Blair Letter …

A further betrayal, perhaps even more central to the concerns of the Association, was the new government's determination to retain the Tory provisions banning industrial action by prison officers. This was again despite apparently impassioned promises to restore trade union rights. In May 1994, John Prescott, addressing the POA Annual Conference, pledged that even if the Conservative government pressed ahead with their plans to outlaw strike action under the Criminal Justice Act of that year, 'we will revert and give prison officers the right to be consulted, represented and participate in the decisions that affect their daily lives'. Other Shadow ministers rallied round. As one POA activist put it, while in opposition David Blunkett, later to become Secretary of State for Employment, 'made a big thing of doing the best of his ability, saying I'll withdraw [the ban] if you behave yourself'.[85]

But most significant of all was the infamous 'Blair Letter'. In July 1994, two months after Prescott's speech, Labour Party leader-to-be Tony Blair wrote to the POA General Secretary, David Evans, setting out his position and that of the Labour Party in even more positive terms:

> Dear David,
>
> As you know, we have strongly opposed the Criminal Justice and Public Order Bill on a number of Clauses which represent a wholly unwarranted attack on the working rights of prison officers, the status of the Prison Officers' Association and unwisely introduced an extension of privatisation of the Prison Service.
>
> An incoming Labour Government will want to put this situation right and ensure, once again, that prison officers are treated in the same way and with the same working rights as other public servants, and recognises the status of the Prison Officers' Association as an independent Trade Union …

Yet despite this explicit pledge, and the Labour Party's repeated promises and commitments whilst in Opposition, their 1997 election triumph was to mark a sorry day for the POA and many other trade unions with high hopes of what a Labour government would deliver after 18 years of Tory attacks on the movement.

As the Scottish Assistant Area Secretary summed it up, drawing a parallel with the betrayal over privatisation:

> They said the same thing about our industrial action rights as well. The Criminal Justice Public Order Act of 1994 ... Jack Straw had promised this would be withdrawn but Tony Blair said we don't want to see a Labour government give trade unions power. Labour probably used the Act more than the Tories did – injunctions, threats to sequester, all that.'[86]

A POA activist recalled: 'we always had the power, then the Tories introduced Section 127, said if you do [this] we'll sequestrate you – and now Mr Straw'.[87]

Within months of the Labour government coming to power, Home Secretary Jack Straw had made it clear that New Labour had changed its mind regarding the restoration of POA members' right to take industrial action; there now appeared to be no question of having the Section 127 clause withdrawn. By the time of the POA's 1998 Annual Conference, Straw felt confident enough to spell out aggressively New Labour's opposition on prison officers' trade union rights: 'I have never believed that there was any scope for industrial action or disruptive action within the Prison Service, any more than I believe there is such scope, for example, within the police service.'[88] This outright betrayal of the commitments given by Tony Blair, John Prescott and others was a crushing blow to the leadership of the POA.

The POA Takes Stock

Nevertheless, during his speech to the 1998 POA Conference, Jack Straw had set out what was presented as one way forward for the union: a 'constructive partnership', whereby 'the Prison Service should provide fair and effective pay determination and dispute resolution procedures involving an independent element'. In return, he maintained, 'I want you all in the Prison Service to agree not to take disruptive action.' In presenting this 'partnership' approach, by now a favourite with Tony Blair and many employers, Straw suggested that if the Prison Service could provide what was required, and the POA agreed to a 'no disruption' agreement, 'there would be no need for the legislative constraints introduced by the Conservatives'. Nevertheless, he insisted that he would always 'retain a reserve power to prevent disruptive action'.[89]

To this end, and with the full intention of continuing their campaign for the restoration of prison officers' rights, the POA leadership began talks with the Prison Service and government about the possibilities of moving forward towards the kind of agreement outlined by Jack Straw. Yet, despite all the talk of partnership, this new policy, proposed by the New Labour government, was to 'cause many of the industrial relations difficulties that would arise over the next ten years', according to a POA full-time official.[90]

With the road to the restoration of prison officers' trade union rights now blocked by New Labour, the POA were forced to consider how best to proceed to remove the criminalisation element of strike action from prison officers. After taking stock of the situation, the Association considered adopting a voluntary no-strike agreement and conciliation agreement to be put in place in order to remove criminalisation; this was in fact achieved in 2001.

Conflict continues …

Nevertheless, in the interim, despite the draconian powers of Section 127, industrial action continued. As one academic account notes:

> Although industrial action was rendered illegal, it has taken place. For instance from May 1997 to February 1998, there were six occasions when prison officers locally took industrial action … In three cases, Wormwood Scrubs, Wandsworth and Londholme prisons, the POA was threatened with an injunction. In 1999, an injunction was successfully sought by the Secretary of State to bar the POA from calling meetings in working hours to protest at a below-inflation pay offer.[91]

The POA's indignant response to this ban is recorded above (p. 177).

While the Scottish POA, at least, voluntarily looked for 'partnership' policies from the late 1990s, this approach was itself catalysed by grievances against prison management:

> One of the problems we had at the time was the way the disputes resolution procedure was applied in Scotland because the Prison Service just ran roughshod over dispute resolution procedures ... We always tried to work together but when we fell out there was no method of regulating that – whereas after the partnership we had access to independent binding arbitration through ACAS. That's where we differed from England as well because we had access to pay arbitration as opposed to the Pay Review Bodies in England and Wales.
>
> Partnership has been a better way to regulate industrial relations – we've never had anything imposed on us at all since that time ....[92]

Yet 'partnership' by no means eliminated the underlying problems in Scotland. Some impressive new programmes were introduced in the late 1990s, along with a new post of 'Personal Officer' in which 'the officer manages the sentence'. The new programmes involved 'challenging offender behaviour, anger management – cognitive skills ... Groups of officers specialise in this – it's taught separately during training.'[93] There was also a new 'Throughcare' programme in which prison officers helped prisoners reintegrate into the community, and a 'STOP' programme, involving prison officers, that was introduced to stop reoffending.

Yet despite these commendable policies, 'The prisons are even more overcrowded, so our ability to deliver all this has been reduced. Our main concern is for our members because of the overcrowding. They are always looking for savings ....'[94]

A Peace Agreement ...

Meanwhile, better news was at last to be found in Northern Ireland. While yet another prison officer at the Maze was shot on 1 September 1993 by Loyalist prisoners ('Jim Peacock refused to allow prisoners to cross "the Circle" [at the centre of the H blocks] – Loyalists protested at this, and Jim Peacock was shot in his kitchen'[95]), his was the last name to be carved in the POA's melancholy 'Roll of Honour'.[96] The beginning of the end of the Irish 'Troubles' was signalled shortly afterwards on 15 December 1993, when an Anglo-Irish pact began the long process towards relative peace. It would be almost four more years before the IRA finally declared a ceasefire in July 1997, but on 10 April 1998 New Labour brokered a peace deal, and despite further horrific bombings, December 1999 saw Britain handing over power to the Northern Ireland Assembly. For the time being at least, Jim Peacock would be the last POA martyr to the carnage in Northern Ireland.

5

2000–09: THE FINAL BETRAYAL

Looking back over almost nine years of his leadership of the POA, General Secretary Brian Caton could begin by framing the period in terms of what the Prison Service Agency had termed its 'Decency Agenda'. As he writes:

> The dawning of the new millennium, through the political direction of the new Director General Martin Narey, brought to the forefront of prisons policy the 'Decency Agenda'.
>
> Many of the improvements that this new agenda introduced were welcomed by the POA and were, in fact, in line with many of the policies developed by the union in the preceding decades.
>
> However, the reality behind these new initiatives of liberalising prisons and their regimes was a drive to remove authority from prison officers dealing face-to-face with prisoners and to hand over that authority to a 'new breed' of liberal-minded governor grades, most of whom were fast-tracked university graduates with little experience of working on the landings of a prison.
>
> The combination of these new liberalised policies and the undermining of officers' authority with increases in the volume and types of drugs being brought into and used in prisons – along with an acknowledged increase in the prison population of dangerous and violent offenders – allowed for the development of gang culture amongst prisoners and created an ever more dangerous workplace for staff.
>
> At the same time as prisons were becoming more dangerous places, there were new drives to reduce the number of uniformed staff and an influx of civilian workers into the Service to carry out many of the 'rehabilitation and resettlement' roles previously carried out by prison officers. This was designed to drive down the worth of prison officers and to seriously affect

what they were paid in the longer term. The deskilling of prison officers had commenced.

This liberalisation policy of government was not just confined to prisons; it was also a major factor within the High Security Hospitals. This came to prominence at Ashworth Hospital with a series of high-profile scandals related to paedophile activities by patients, which resulted from the new softer approach that had been developed along with the failure of some NHS managers and medical staff to recognise the levels of danger posed by serious and personality disorders patients.

These events resulted in a major inquiry in which the NHS employed Sir Richard Tilt, ex-Director General of the Prison Service, to undertake a review of security in the high security estate. The recommendations from his report, presented in May 2000, mirrored all the demands that the POA had been making throughout the period of liberalisation.

Thankfully the government, having been embarrassed, accepted his recommendations and on this occasion implemented all of them – unlike those of the Woolf Report on the security of prisons ten years before.

It became evident that the position of the POA's knowledge and understanding of the inherent dangers of the liberalisation policies across both the Prison Service and High Security Hospitals had helped to highlight their dangers and prevent a potential meltdown that could have had disastrous consequences.

Unfortunately, however, though some of the excesses of the liberalisation policies have been slowed, they do continue, with government constantly striving to drive down the potential and professional standards of prison officers in order that they can pay less qualified staff less money to do the same job. This constant cost cutting, driven by the Treasury, continues to have catastrophic potential in the longer term. In the short term it has led to almost nine years of confrontation between the government and the POA.[1]

That confrontation is documented in this chapter.

'The Most Privatised Criminal Justice System ...'

As Britain entered the twenty-first century, a very different world confronted prison officers. Privatisation was now rife. At the end of 2001, there were more than 6,000 adults and young offenders held in private prisons in England and Wales – around 8 per cent of the prison population – while in Scotland the situation was even worse, with 600 prisoners, roughly 10 per cent of all prisoners in the country, held at a single private prison, Kilmarnock. As early as 2002, the UK could be said to have 'developed the most privatised criminal justice system in Europe ... In terms of the number of private prisons, Britain is second only to the United States.'[2]

Nor did the problem stop with the privatisation of prisons alone. The UK was also operating a number of privately run prison-related institutions, including secure training centres (STCs) for young offenders, immigration detention centres, prisoner escort services, electronic monitoring programmes, and provision of a wide range of non-custodial services in state prisons, as well as major programmes for privately financed, designed, built and operated court complexes, police stations and probation hostels – part of the explosion in Private Finance Initiatives (PFIs) now influencing every aspect of New Labour policy in the public sector.

By 2001, seven PFI prisons, each with 25-year contracts, had been commissioned and opened in England and Wales, with two more, Ashford and Peterborough, due to open in 2003 and 2004. The Scottish Executive was also planning three more private prisons in addition to Kilmarnock. The apparently unstoppable growth of one of the largest private contractors in the field, Premier Custodial Group Ltd, was shown by the growth in its end-of-year revenues from £7.52 million in 1994 to £160.9 million by the end of December 2002.[3] Meanwhile, UK Detention Services (UKDS), the British arm of the Corrections Corporation of America, saw its revenues soar from £10.9 million in 1995 to £17.96 million in 2001.

As shown in the previous chapter, the performance of these companies was not all that might have been desired. In 2000, UKDS lost its contract to operate HMP Blakenhurst after a market testing exercise; Group 4, which had won a contract to operate the new Buckley Hall prison in 1994, lost the contract after retendering in 1999; and in June 2000, Buckley Hall reverted to the public sector. Although private companies were invited to put in bids to run Manchester Prison in 2000, none succeeded, and the Prison Service retained the contract. Further failures within the private sector included the enforced withdrawal in March 2000 of Wackenhut UK from a contract to operate prison industries at a publicly-run prison after being shown to have failed to provide adequate services.

Prisons or 'Loft-Style Apartments'?

However, despite the clear evidence that private prisons were in no way superior to the public sector, the contractors continued to win the contracts. In the face of damaging reports on conditions at Wolds, Group 4's contract to run the remand centre was nevertheless renewed for ten years in 2002. The same year, Securicor was chosen as 'preferred bidder' for a new 80-bed Secure Training Centre at Milton Keynes.

New Labour's enthusiasm for 'market testing' in addition to outright privatisation was itself tested in 2002 when an attempt to contract out the management of Brixton Prison attracted not a single bid from the private sector. Charles Falconer, a Minister of State for the Home Office, stated in a parliamentary answer on 25 July 2002:

> The market test for the management of Brixton did not attract bids from the private sector, partly because of its poor physical condition and location ... Therefore ... the prison will continue to be run under existing management arrangements. However, a performance baseline will be set with challenging improvement targets and progress will be closely monitored.

Nevertheless, the failure produced much mockery in the media. One newspaper commented that:

> The refusal of any private security firm to take on HMP Brixton in south London is an embarrassment to the Home Office ... A year after the former prisons minister Paul Boateng announced that the 'failing' prison was to be the first public penal institution to face privatisation, the Prison Service admitted that no company had submitted a tender ....

The unsuccessful outcome of the bidding process was 'a blow for ministers, who had hoped that turning Brixton prison over to the private sector would send a warning message to other underperforming jails'.[4]

Yet the lack of private interest in running the 180-year-old prison is hardly surprising. In a highly critical report in January 2002, the outgoing Chief Inspector of Prisons, Sir David Ramsbotham, said the 'filth and neglect' at Brixton was the 'most disgraceful example of conditions in a prison' he had seen. Conditions in the prison's healthcare centre were described as 'scandalous', and prisoners were locked in their cells under an 'unofficial and unlawful' punishment system called 'Reflections'.[5] Worse, a further report the same week described standards at other jails in England and Wales as falling below even those at Brixton. League tables published by the Prison Reform Trust, based on official Prison Service figures, showed that inmates at Belmarsh Prison, also in South London, spent only 13.3 hours a week in 'purposeful activities'. The press jumped on the bandwagon, labelling Belmarsh 'Britain's laziest jail'. Prisoners at Feltham Young Offenders' Institution (YOI) in West London, the subject of a scathing official report the same week, had only 14.4 hours of activities, while Brixton was fourth in the table with 15.6 hours.

The report also referred to violence in prisons. Castington YOI was rated the most violent, with 93 assaults to every 100 prisoners, against a Prison Service target of 9 per cent. At Brinsford, another YOI in Wolverhampton, where a succession of prisoners had committed suicide, the assault rate was 62 per cent; while Huntercombe YOI, seen as a 'flagship jail', had an assault rate of 61 per cent.[6]

Nevertheless, New Labour continued serenely on course. Prisons Minister Beverley Hughes announced in October 2001 that by 2005 she expected to see a growing proportion of the prison estate privately operated, and at the same time the Director General of the Prison Service endorsed the 'mixed management' model with the remark that 'it is now very possible that, at some point, we will have a prison designed, financed and built by the private sector but run by the public sector' along exactly the lines rejected in 1998 by ... the Prison Service.[7] A few months later, the Prisons Minister said she was considering the closure of up to 28 'Victorian' English prisons, with their land and buildings sold off in order to replace them with a programme of regional 'super jails'.[8] As an article in the POA *Gatelodge* magazine reported: 'the most likely candidates are those in prime inner London locations such as Wandsworth, Pentonville and Brixton. They were likely to attract developers interested in providing loft-style yuppie apartments.'[9]

A month later, the Prison Service published the source of some of these ideas. It emerged that they had originated in a report commissioned by the government on 'how best to develop the contribution of the private sector, particularly PFI,[10] to achieving the objectives of the Prison Service'. As well as advocating continuing with PFI programmes for prisons, this report had also suggested that 'the Prison Service move beyond the traditional choice of public or private prisons and explore the mixed management approach' which had apparently been 'successfully' adopted in France.[11]

In fact, the system adopted in France was one of 'semi-private' prisons, publicly financed and with the prison officers remaining state employees, although the prisons are built by the private sector: a form of privatisation, indeed, but clearly less far-reaching than the US model on which the New Labour government was faithfully basing its policies, despite the 'dearth of independent research to prove that it is as successful as is being claimed'.[12] In fact, the playing-out of the process in the real world suggested the opposite. For example, while one of the many claims made for privatisation was that it would somehow help to reduce prison overcrowding, the ever-growing prison population, leaping from 51,000 in the late 1980s to around 71,000 in 2002 and, at the beginning of 2009, to over 82,000,[13] has consistently exceeded the number of prison places available. Even private prisons began to suffer overcrowding at an early stage. By February 2000, prisons holding inmates two to a cell designed for one included four private institutions, Doncaster, Blakenhurst, Altcourse and

Lowdham Grange, while by 2002, Altcourse and Doncaster were overcrowded by 212 and 303 prisoners respectively.[14]

In general, statements made by the Carter Report, such as 'the results of recent market tests demonstrate beyond doubt the value of the competitive process', and 'it is widely accepted, by management and unions alike [!], that the competition offered by new private prisons ... has made the prisons system more efficient and effective', failed to match the grim reality. In May 2002, the Prison Service removed the Premier Prisons director from Ashfield, a YOI near Bristol, because of concerns over the safety of staff and fears that Premier might lose control of the situation, and on 23 May, the Prison Service Director General reported that 'standards of control and care of prisoners was not as high as I would expect them to be. I considered that the prison was unsafe for both staff and the young people contained there.'[15] Blakenhurst fared no better: in 2001, UKDS, which managed the prison, was reported to be 12 per cent more expensive and 13 per cent lower in quality than the Prison Service bid, while the Chief Inspector of Prisons noted that 'treatment of and conditions for prisoners at Blakenhurst had at best stood still ... and in some respects have become worse'. With typical private sector cynicism, 'many promising innovations [were] stalled until it had become clear whether the contract had been won or lost'.[16] In August 2001, the company lost the contract.

Meanwhile, in Scotland, the first privately-built prison was also provoking controversy. Kilmarnock was described by the Chief Inspector of Prisons for Scotland as 'Scotland's most violent prison'.[17] It was also at Kilmarnock that, as Nathan puts it,

> an incident epitomise[d] how 'commercial confidentiality', extensively used by government and the industry to keep ... information from scrutiny, undermines the public interest. After pressure from both the Scottish Executive and Premier Prisons Ltd, the Chief Inspector was forced to have his first report pulped ... because it included the company's staffing levels at the prison.[18]

Subsequently, Kilmarnock received two further critical reports from the Prisons Inspector. Despite a Scottish Executive review of the prison estate which recommended that three new private prisons be built, a Parliamentary Committee found that 'major questions arise about HMP Kilmarnock ... which mean it cannot be used as a point of comparison. In particular, the committee has serious concerns about the low level of staffing at HMP Kilmarnock.'[19]

Not surprisingly, in view of all this, even prison governors rapidly turned against the policy. In autumn 2000, the president of the Prison Governors' Association wrote in prison governors' journal *The Key*: 'Almost ten years on the private sector provides the most expensive prison places and its performance, in most areas, is well below what the best of the public sector can provide ... The PFI projects are proving so expensive that, quite simply, we cannot afford any more privately run prisons.' The public agreed; in March 2001 an ICM poll for the *Guardian* showed 60 per cent of respondents favouring bringing private prisons back into the public sector. Yet New Labour stubbornly continued with an expensive, destructive policy which every informed analysis had condemned outright.

'A Major Obstacle'

Perhaps the most serious effect of the drive to privatisation, for prison officers at least, was on the strength of their own organisation. By the end of 2001, the POA had failed to win recognition in any one of the then nine privately-run prisons (as against the 126 state-run institutions in which they enjoyed almost 100 per cent membership density). Despite the apparently favourable new legislation on union recognition embodied in the 1999 Employment Relations Act, which encouraged unions with support from at least 40 per cent of the workforce to apply for union recognition, the POA had been unable to use the Central Arbitration Committee (CAC) set up within the Act to enable recognition. This was because the CAC was mandated to 'reject any application for recognition as inadmissible ... if there is already in place a collective agreement in respect of any of the workers in the proposed bargaining unit, even if the union which is party to the agreement is not independent and does not have majority support'. Thus the POA in 2000 submitted an application to the CAC for recognition at a privately-run prison, Parc in Bridgend, where 145 of the 250 employees were already members of the Association, but the CAC would not accept the application as the employer had already signed a recognition agreement with the non-independent Securicor Custodial Services Staff Association.[20]

At first the POA appeared unaware of this clause, which clearly represented a serious loophole preventing the POA and no doubt other public sector unions from gaining a foothold in privatised facilities. In April 2000, in an article headed 'POA, UK, OK!' POA Chair Mark Healey wrote: 'This week the NEC endorsed Parc prison in South Wales and the Court Escort Service in Northern Ireland as Branches of our Association', while in Guernsey, '52 Prison Officers are seeking our help. It is obviously good news that our union continues to grow in size ... Next week another meeting has been arranged with Premier prisons with a view to gaining recognition within Doncaster, and hopefully this will have a knock on effect as regards Kilmarnock.' Further, he commented optimistically: 'In the very near future we will be able to represent our members within the walls of the Private prison estate because of the introduction of the *Fairness at Work* Act.'[21] This was a reference to the Employment Relations Act 1999, which contained the recognition provisions – but also the limitation on CAC recognition procedures. In fact, the POA later began to overcome these barriers (see below), but the implications were only too clear.

The authorities were well aware that an important consequence of privatising a prison was also to rob the POA of recognition. David Ramsbotham, Chief Inspector of Prisons, claimed in late 2001 that part of Feltham, Britain's biggest jail for young offenders, should be privatised both because it was unsafe and because it was 'plagued by the negative and malign attitude' of the POA. This led to the forced transfer of Andrew Darken, local POA Chairman, and a pledge by the Prison Service to put part of the prison out to private tender if conditions did not improve. The POA announced that it would take legal action against the Prison Service over the forced removal of its representative, with POA Chair Mark Healey declaring that 'We have a Government dictating who an independent trade union will have as an elected official.'[22]

As research into the impact of privatisation in Scotland notes: 'Since salaries account for around 60 per cent of prison budgets … eroding pay and conditions and the marginalisation (or exclusion) of unions have been the principal object of the privatisers.'[23] According to Pay Review Body (PRB) figures from 2006, private sector prison officers earned 41 per cent less than those in the state sector, as well as enduring longer hours, shorter holidays, inferior overtime entitlement, poorer pensions and lower staff–prisoner ratios. As Taylor and Cooper point out:

> the source of [private prison companies'] profits, and the cost minimisation that underpins them, lies in the reduction of absolute numbers of staff and the pursuit of the holy grail of labour 'efficiencies' and 'flexibilities' … rhetorical euphemisms used to conceal the harsh realities of labour intensification, lean staffing and inferior pay so vigorously pursued by the privatisers.[24]

Indeed, accountants PricewaterhouseCoopers (PWC) identified the fundamental source of the private sector's cost savings as 'significantly reduced staff levels compared with the public sector achieved mainly by the adoption of different and more flexible working practices'.[25]

As Taylor and Cooper note:

> This leaner, cost-effective and more flexible private model is held up as a virtuous comparator in order to … put pressure on the POA, since it is identified by the state as a major obstacle to privatisation. Industrial relations 'reform' has been central to 'modernisation' of the prison service.

As part of this process:

> successive governments have striven to combat powerful [POA] union organisation, with its 90-per-cent-plus density, and to overcome the legacy of troublesome industrial relations by *inter alia* curbing the right of unions to take industrial action and creating a POA-free segment in which flexibilities could be freely operated.[26]

In Scotland, the POA was formally recognised by the Scottish Prison Service (SPS) to represent prison officer staff, mainly because they still counted the great majority of Scottish prison officers within their membership. A minority of prison officers now belonged, as in England and Wales, to the much smaller Prison Service Union (PSU), but the threat of industrial action by a smaller trade union was not seen as constituting a significant threat to the delivery of services within SPS, because the staff involved in any such action could be relatively easily replaced from the much larger non-membership group. It was also unlikely that significantly large numbers of POA members would choose to become members of another trade union. Yet, according to legal opinion sought by the POA, in such an event, where the collective bargaining power of the POA would be significantly diminished, formal recognition of the POA as the trade union with recognition rights for the prison officer staff group would probably be reviewed by the SPS.

The prognostications were ominous, but by the end of the decade the POA was fighting back. A regular column, 'Strictly Private', was launched in *Gatelodge*, and the Private Sector Committee of the POA became increasingly active. The first 'Strictly Private', written by NEC member Tom Robson, announced that the POA had a voluntary recognition agreement with Tinsley House, a privately managed Immigration Removal Centre, which now had an active local POA Committee and 'hope[d] to engage with the company in the near future'. In May 2007, Tom reported that POA officials had met with members and prospective members at another private institution, Bronzefield: 'Those who attended were very interested in what we had to say ... .We now have a volunteer committee in place and look forward to taking Bronzefield forward eventually to become a *bona fide* branch of the POA.' In fact, by the August 2008 issue of *Gatelodge* it could be reported that 'There is a new branch of the POA in the private sector and the membership numbers continue to rise at the establishment. Welcome Bronzefield into the POA family.' By October 2008 it could be said that 'Membership numbers in the Private Sector continue in a slow and steady upward trend.

More and more individuals in the industry realise that the Union to belong to is the POA.'

Scottish POA activists were also making energetic efforts to recruit in the private sector. The 'North of the Border' column for *Gatelodge* of December 2008 reported a visit to Kilmarnock in which:

> Many uniformed staff told us they were unhappy at the level of support they had received from the union [the PSU] that is recognised by their owners SERCO, and were keen to consider joining the POA ... They were aware that we had already represented some of their colleagues over recent months with good results and were interested in joining.

The doughty POA-ers, Dave Melrose, John Speed and Phil Thomas, had braved 'monsoon weather conditions' to carry out their recruitment exercise, and extended their activities over a number of hours:

> The three of us met and spoke to the night shift as they left and then welcomed the 8–5 staff as they appeared ... as daylight broke the rain and wind calmed down to an acceptable level, and we were joined by some of our existing POA members from Kilmarnock who were off duty and [had] kindly agreed to help ... In the aftermath of our visit to Kilmarnock our numbers there have increased and are continuing to do so.

These POA organisers commented that 'any other organisations that portray themselves as a prison officers' union are nothing other than amateurs who are in management's pocket. Ask yourself why else would a private company be so frightened of giving the POA recognition if they had nothing to fear?'

'What the POA Stands For ...'

The POA had entered the twenty-first century in fine fettle organisationally. As the June 2000 issue of *Gatelodge* signalled with its front cover statement, 'The Beginning of a New Era', after an 18-year stint David Evans was now giving way to Brian Caton as General Secretary of the Association. David received a plaque in honour of his services to the Association at the Annual

Conference of that year, as well as a letter of appreciation from the staff at Cronin House which paid tribute to his sacrifice of 'many interminable hours and weekends of your life' to the Association – and he also received an OBE in the 2001 New Year's Honours List.

In June 2004, the POA joined a growing number of unions in securing government funding for its own Union Learning Fund, which would now go on to develop Learning Centres in establishments across the country; two had already been opened at HMPs Belmarsh and Haverigg, with two more, Moorland and Gloucester, due to open over the coming months. Later in the year, a Union Learning Fund Project was set up in Northern Ireland. In March 2005, the first Learning and Development Professional Conference, run in conjunction with the National Association of Probation Officers (NAPO, the probation officers' union) saw the formal signing of a Learning Partnership Agreement between the POA and the Prison Service.

In May 2005, the POA Annual Conference agreed a name change for the union, carrying a motion which specified: 'The organisation ... is called the "POA" ... Conference also accepts that the Association will in all appropriate documentation use the statement, "The Professional Trades Union for Prison, Correctional and Secure Psychiatric Workers".' POA National Chair Colin Moses commented in *Gatelodge*:

> This historical action may have changed the name but not what the POA stands for. [It] should not be seen in any way as trying to change the history of the Prison Officers' Association, it only gives credence to the fact that we are a Trade Union and not a staff association, as some people believe. The POA has acted as a Trade Union for the past 66 years ....'[27]

A year later, that same trade union was beginning to flex its political muscle – in both a party and an 'extra-parliamentary' sense. Following on the disastrously low PRB 'award' for 2006, Colin Moses asked whether the POA now needed a more explicit 'political voice'. While 'The POA in its history has always maintained a neutral position in regard to a political voice, we must re-examine this position and ... consider political affiliation to one of the major political parties, so that we can have influence in the decisions that affect our daily working life.'[28] Meanwhile, General Secretary Brian Caton had participated in the launch of the cross-union campaigning group Public Service Not Private Profit (PSNPP), launched on 29 March 2006 at the House of Commons. The POA had already been involved in the joint campaign Prisons Not For Profit with probation officers' union NAPO; at the PSNPP launch, Brian called for this cross-union campaign to grow and to ensure that all unions in the public service, including firefighters, health workers, transport workers and others, 'demonstrate to the Government that privatisation and the threat to privatise are unacceptable to public sector workers'.

In their report of the 2007 TUC Conference, two POA delegates commented that 'It is clear to us that the profile of the POA at this Congress was high on the agenda of many of the unions attending; the interest from media, radio and television was quite overwhelming on the first day of Congress.'[29] The delegates reported that in the wake of the union's unprecedented 'wildcat' walkout of August 2007 (see below), there had been 'immense and heartening support' from other TUC delegates.

The POA's membership situation was also improving. In June 2007, NEC member Tom Robson could report not only that 'there continued to be stability in membership numbers in the Private sector', but 'in fact I can report a small but steady increase all round'. The impact of POA organisation in the private sector was growing: 'Our recognition agreement with G4S [Group 4 Security] and those who work with the Custody Escorts contracts continues to flourish.'[30] The August 2007 walkout had played its part:

> The membership of this Union continues to rise and has risen considerably since our one day strike in August 2007. The trend is reflected in the Private Sector albeit at a slower rate. More and more of our colleagues who work for private companies realise the common sense in joining an Independent Trades Union ....'[31]

Along the same lines, Wandsworth branch secretary Stuart McLaughlin reported in the June 2008 issue of *Gatelodge* that 'I was pleased to return from the Annual Conference able to report a far more united union from the floor. Without a doubt, the action on the 29th August was a great success to galvanise the membership.'

Leading the Way on Equal Opportunities

Lastly, the POA's continued efforts to increase diversity and promote tolerance expanded during these years. As a POA activist commented: 'They have done their best to equalise the ethnic minorities – there's still more to do but I think the POA have done the best they can do and they've led the way.'[32]

The appointment of POA National Chairman Colin Moses in August 2004 was itself historic, signalling the election of the first black senior union figure since Bill Morris of the TGWU in the 1990s. He is now the only elected black union leader in the United Kingdom. The POA now had a Race Relations Policy in place, with five points published regularly in *Gatelodge*: part of its brief was to insist that 'race relations training be made more available by the Prison Department in line with its own policy'. In 2000, an appalling racist murder by a white prisoner of fellow cell inmate Zahid Mubarek at Feltham YOI demonstrated only too clearly the need to fight this scourge throughout the Service. A public inquiry into the murder was instigated in 2004, in which POA members at Feltham cooperated fully.

But the continuing realities of racism 'on the ground' remained, poignantly summed up in a poem titled 'Racism – It's in the Way' published in *Gatelodge* in June 2007. As the poem ended:

> It's in the way you get annoyed
> And say I must be paranoid
> It's in the way we have to fight
> For basic fundamental human rights
>
> It's the invasion of my space
> It's how you keep me in my place
> It's the oppression of my race
> IT'S IN MY FACE.

Yet the POA continued to 'do they best they could'. In July 2004, 'a significant milestone in the fight against racism' was notched up with the launch of Parva Against Racism (PAR) at Glen Parva YOI. The ethos behind the initiative was characterised as 'to involve staff and prisoners in activities that challenge racism and promote tolerance and understanding'. The Prison Education Officer who originated the PAR concept, Rob Tinkler, won the Diversity Category at the 2004 Prison Officer of the Year Awards. However, as the report of the launch of PAR in *Gatelodge* makes clear: 'since its inception PAR has been very much a team effort [with] an active committee made up of staff and prisoners'.[33]

In May 2007, the POA Diversity Committee attended the Annual Conference in order to give branch officials and delegates the opportunity to discuss diversity issues in depth. The Committee's exhibition stand at the Conference displayed information 'on various diversity issues such as race, gender, sexual orientation and age'; a far cry from the days of the 'male, stale and pale' image of the POA. The Committee members noted in *Gatelodge* in July 2007 that 'year on year, there has been an increase in interest from Branch Officials and Delegates in the information available on the diversity stand'.

Increasingly, the POA was also taking a stand on the issue of discrimination against gay and lesbian prison officers – and, indeed, prisoners. In April 2000, Pete Allen, the prison officer who was to become Chair of GALIPS (Gays and Lesbians In the Prison Service) wrote to the then Director General of the Prison Service, Martin Narey, suggesting the setting up of the organisation, which is now described on the Prison Service website as a 'Lesbian, Gay, Bisexual and Transgender Staff Support Network'. As Pete recalled in an interview: 'I became involved in GALIPS because of my own experience of being openly gay and what I had witnessed of other people's experience who were gay in the prison service ... That made me realise there was a need for some sort of support mechanism for gay staff.' Asked why staff who were gay often did not openly admit to their sexuality at work, Pete replied, 'I think the first thing is fear ... The Prison Service has a macho culture.'[34]

Pete had himself experienced considerable hostility when he 'came out', which included abusive notes left on his car, abusive phone calls, 'mugs being smashed because I had drunk out of them and generally just being avoided in the office or on the wings'. More difficulties were encountered when Pete became involved in diversity training: 'Although there were a number of people in the training that were very much onside I was also concerned by just how many people questioned, and were resistant to, the idea of diversity and the need for it in the Service.'

While GALIPS had now been in existence for some years, Pete acknowledged that there were still 'no specific mechanisms in place' to support and protect openly gay prisoners, let alone those too intimidated to 'admit' their sexuality: 'It is unfortunately left to individual members of staff to hopefully be on side and understand the issues.' He went on to explain that 'This is where we as a network will come in to support staff to enable them to support prisoners through their sentences.' It was this role which made the organisation 'a support network for all staff and not just for LGTB which is a common misconception'.[35]

The impression of a reluctance to welcome diversity in the Prison Service is unfortunately confirmed by one contribution by a prison officer to a GALIPS website which revealed the extent of racism and other prejudices amongst Prison Service management. In response to the 'diversity' question on an application form, the officer commented:

> I think I just about resisted writing, 'I'm female and bisexual. I've had long-term illnesses, mental and physical ... My best friend's Pakistani, and most of my friends aren't English ... Was there anything else?'
>
> When my diversity-person interviewer said something along the lines of 'I don't like people who aren't English', I stared at her with my mouth open until I could finally say, 'WHAT?!' ....

'New Managerialism' and 'Modernisation' ...

There was need of a strong, diverse and principled union in the Prison Service. During the early 2000s yet more restructuring took place, with a Prison Service Management Board (PSMB) appointed by the Director General to assist in discharging the day-to-day management of the Service. This Board consists of nine executive members, all directors of different functions such as Security, Regimes, Personnel, Finance and Corporate Affairs, amongst others. On his appointment as Director General of the Prison Service in 1999, Martin Narey introduced changes to the PSMB as part of a new 'What Works' agenda which resulted in greater centralisation and a sharper focus on performance. In the process, 'some "robust" and sometimes harsh decisions have been made about improving those prisons seen as "failing" … including time-limited chances to improve and threats of subsequent market testing without an in-house bid'.[36]

In addition, a Strategy Board for Correctional Services (SBCS) was set up under New Labour. This consisted of the Prisons Minister and a number of directors of different departments such as the Home Office Criminal Policy Group, as well as five more non-executive members. Each of the 13 areas into which the prison estate was now divided had its own area manager, reporting directly to the Deputy Director General of the Prison Service. Within this structure, 'The role of the area manager is to establish with the governor of each prison a "service delivery agreement" ….' In this sense, area managers would be 'increasingly concerned with managing performance – as the thrust of much of the new managerialism tends to be'.[37] As Liebling and Price sum up the situation:

> There has been a 'new managerialist' influence on the way the Prison Service operates … with increasing emphasis on setting objectives, measuring achievements in relation to those objectives, [and] stringent financial control … Critics of new managerialism are cynical about these developments, seeing them as … overly concerned with presentation … 'New managerialism' is arguably no more than bureaucracy in a new guise.[38]

As POA Chair Colin Moses noted in the February 2003 issue of *Gatelodge*: 'The current buzz word in industrial relations is "modernisation" … Our employers have already indicated that modernisation will be part of any future pay awards.' He went on, however, to point out that 'there is no public sector service that has provided more modernisation over the last few years than the Prison Service Agency. We are not averse to discussing modernisation, but any modernisation must not endanger the health and safety of our members.' In addition: 'We can expect in the years ahead ... that we will be offered pay awards of a three year duration, linked to modernisation'. Evidently, it was equally 'modern' to expect prison officers to wait three years for a re-examination of their pay levels, whatever might be happening to inflation and other indicators in the interim.

Working Together?

Nevertheless, for two years, since Jack Straw's betrayal of Labour Opposition promises to repeal the anti-union Section 127 clause of the Criminal Justice and Public Order Act 1994, the POA and the Prison Service had tried to move towards agreement on new ways of working together. Despite a number of setbacks and minor disputes, by 2000 there appeared to be growing potential for resolution. The POA agreed to put the joint proposals, which set out a new way of conducting industrial relations and paved the way for the formation of the Prison Service Pay Review Body (PSPRB) proposed under Section 128 of the 1994 Act, to a Special Delegate Conference.

At the same time, Paul Boateng, now Prisons Minister at the Home Office, pledged that 'The Home Secretary intends to use the provisions of the voluntary agreement instead of those in Section 127, while awaiting Parliamentary time to effect the changes in legislation.' This was welcome news, though moderated by the reservation that 'it is clear on all sides that Section 127 would be used in the event of a breakdown of the agreement'. The voluntary measures were seen as 'modernising the way that this key group of public sector workers deal with their employer'. Unfortunately, the 'modernisation' being carried out by New Labour in the Prison Service included elements of only too old-fashioned 1990s Tory policies. At the beginning of July 2000, three weeks before making his statement on Section 127, Boateng had announced his intention to 'market test' Brixton Prison; in August 2000, walkouts and a work-to-rule were staged by POA members at Brixton in protest.[39]

This development was undoubtedly behind the minister's consequent caveat that

> The implementation of this agreement and the delivery of the intentions I have outlined are dependent on my being satisfied that the state of industrial relations within prisons is such as to enable the effective and efficient management of the Service. Such a state cannot be said to have been attained in the light of the current withdrawal of good will by the POA ....[40]

More problems followed. In October 2000, POA General Secretary Brian Caton was expressing disappointment over the delay in setting up the promised PRB a postponement which again appeared to have been provoked, according to the Prison Service, by the 'withdrawal of goodwill by the POA over the market testing of Brixton'. The Deputy Director General had put out an 'open message' in July in which he expressed 'doubts' over POA members' 'commitment' to the Service which made it 'impossible' to proceed with setting up the PRB. The POA action over Brixton was described as 'regrettable ... a blast from the past that will not stop the drive for reform'. The Prison Service was now 'unable to proceed' with setting up an independent PRB due to the POA's 'regrettable and misguided actions'. As the writer of this report concluded: 'So to the Deputy Director General I say take your empty promises you feel unable to offer at this time, put them with the outright lies we have received in the past and bury them six feet deep in the garden with the dolly and teddy you have just thrown out.'[41] The Association, informed that it was unlikely that the PRB would be in place before the early part of 2001 and that it would be unable to deliver a finding before July 2001, argued that there should be an interim pay award to cover the period January–July 2001.

However, in early February 2001, Straw pre-empted this by announcing in Parliament that since the walkout over Brixton:

> There has been a very frank but positive dialogue between the Prison Service, the POA and Ministers on this and a range of other issues. I am pleased to announce ... that I am satisfied that the industrial relations climate is now conducive to proceeding with plans for a pay review body.' He also promised that: 'In order to bring about these important improvements in industrial relations in the Prison Service in England and Wales quickly, I intend to use the provisions of the voluntary agreement instead of those in section 127 ....[42]

Like Boateng before him, Straw warned that 'It is clear on all sides that section 127 would be used in the event of a breakdown of the agreement'; but the government lent credibility to its position by implementing the Regulatory Reform Act 2001, designed to allow the reform of provisions in existing legislation, to remove Section 127 in England, Wales and Scotland, a process finally completed on 21 March 2005 with the Regulatory Reform (Prison Officers' Industrial Action) Order.

As far as the POA NEC were concerned, all this was a significant step towards the ending of the Conservative policy of criminalising industrial action by prison officers, a goal of the union since 1994; and it was in this spirit that the NEC called a Special Delegate Conference on 27 February 2001 to discuss the new Voluntary Industrial Relations Agreement (VIRA).

'Very Naïve Indeed ...'?

While VIRA was largely endorsed by POA delegates, problems with the proposals emerged only too soon. Straw's February 2001 speech had announced a three-strand approach: firstly, the establishment of a mechanism for pay determination; secondly, a new legally binding 'voluntary' agreement; and thirdly, the proposed repeal of Section 127. On the basis of Straw's recognition that 'the issue of revised pay determination arrangements had yet to be resolved', the PSPRB was established as a statutory body on 17 April 2001.

With its usual reasonable and optimistic approach, the POA leadership welcomed the proposed PRB. In the April 2001 issue of

Gatelodge, the then National Chairman, Mark Healey, condemned the recent imposition by the Prison Service Agency of a 2 per cent pay increase as 'an absolute insult', but continued: 'We predict that the Pay Review Body, which starts taking submissions very shortly for the January 2002 pay award, will deliver a far more reasonable settlement.' Even the Agency itself was 'already making predictions that the pay award will be far above the derisory amount awarded this year'.[43]

In October, General Secretary Brian Caton had commented optimistically that:

> the Pay Review recommendations for this year will be the most important pay and conditions related matter to take place in the Prison service since the Wynn Parry recommendation 50 years ago. It is our hope that with the hard work put into the pay submissions and an independent view, that Prison Officers both in the year 2002 and in future years will be treated fairly and appropriately for a job that they do on behalf of Society.[44]

More pragmatically, one speaker at the Special Delegate Conference had greeted the PSPRB proposal with the irrefutable comment that 'We can't do worse on pay that we've done.' Yet even this modest level of expectation was undermined by the eventual outcome. The publication of the PSPRB's first set of recommendations on 1 February 2002 caused applause for the recommendation of a 6 per cent pay increase – and then outrage when the PRB, at the behest of the government, unilaterally decided to stage its implementation.

Attempting to justify the government's decision, Minister of State Beverley Hughes told the 2002 Annual Delegate Conference that:

> the Government has to marry all of those very significant amount of commitments and competing objectives right across the public sector and elsewhere and receiving additional funding from the Treasury for a pay settlement … was, quite frankly, never on the cards and anyone, including the Pay Review Body, who might have thought that was possible, was very naive indeed because that is not the way business is done.

As POA Research Officer Steve Lewis puts it:

> This was not what the delegates, or indeed the POA leadership, wanted to hear. It had been put to the POA negotiators and through them to the NEC, the Special Delegate Conference and the membership as a whole that the PSPRB had been put in place as a compensatory mechanism for the loss of trade union rights. What was now becoming clear was that the PRB was hamstrung by the amount of funding that HM Treasury were prepared to let the Prison Service have.

The General Secretary reported in the February 2002 issue of *Gatelodge* that 'branch officials attending outside the Prison Service Conference in Nottingham spoke directly to the Minister who, after some pressing on the point, agreed that prison officers should have the full 6% but the money could not be found.'

From this time on, the POA looked on the PRB mechanism with suspicion, concerned that it was no more than a further tool of Government and the Prison Service to keep pay disputes outside of any future industrial relations agreements or conflicts. As POA Chair Colin Moses commented, noting that the mechanism had the full title of Prison Service Pay Review Body, 'the pretence that it is INDEPENDENT has even been dropped from its name'. He reported that:

> On 30th July 2003, the Home Secretary wrote to the Prison Service Pay Review Body outlining the DEMANDS of the Government in regard to pay for 12 months ... beginning April 2004 ... The Home Secretary goes on to DIRECT the Prison Service Pay Review Body ... The thrust of the remit letter from the Home Secretary is more for less.

Significantly, 'The direction of the Prison Service Pay Review Body is clearly being pointed at regional pay.'[45]

The New World of NOMS ...

Also in early 2004, a new and ominous entity with the acronym NOMS (National Offender Management Service) entered prison officers' vocabulary. As Colin Moses wrote in the April 2004 issue of *Gatelodge*: 'From 1st June, we enter the new world of NOMS. This new world seems to be built on the premise of contestability and the Prison Service being one competitive element in it.' The new initiative raised 'more questions than answers'. One disturbing feature was that these proposals for a seamless service from arrest through trial, imprisonment and release stemmed from the same (Lord) Patrick Carter who had been responsible for many of the new privatisation initiatives surveyed above. In the words of NEC member Steve Gough: 'I deliberately have not used the words CARTER or NOMS up to this point but we have to be honest and admit that the attack on ... terms and conditions is gaining momentum.'[46]

A letter in the October 2004 issue of *Gatelodge* summed up the dangers:

> I have been hearing more and more of my colleagues talking about NOMS and the introduction of contestability and market testing ... I can see them wanting to hand as much of the Service to the private sector as they can. They will not do it all at once, they will do it bit by bit. But if they can do it they will. They will see it as a way of breaking the POA.

And indeed, by the end of 2004, POA Chair Colin Moses could report that American companies were being 'courted by NOMS', including Correctional Services Corporation (CSC), which had been seeking UK private sector contracts since 1998, and Management and Training Corporation, which had recently been reported as 'having links with the running of the infamous Abu Ghraib prison in Iraq'.[47]

In March 2005, an early example of this process was threatened at the Isle of Sheppey cluster of prisons, which had been 'put up for sale' under the NOMS proposals. POA members from the three prisons met the NEC and confirmed their support for the POA policy of refusing to participate in the 'market testing' process. By June 2005, Brian Caton could report that:

> the NEC have been able to change the minds of the Government in regard to the market testing of the three prisons on the Isle of Sheppey ... [T]he market test has been delayed until September to allow further work, [but] we are convinced that by using the knowledge of our membership and the resolve of the Union we can win through.[48]

In fact, as NEC member Steve Cox reported in the December 2005 issue of *Gatelodge*, the POA had achieved this result by:

> holding a national ballot asking you, the membership, if you wanted to take part in another round of Market Tests. The result was … the largest turnout in a ballot for many years and 85% of those who voted rejected the Market Test. The POA then called a Special Delegates' Conference with a motion to ballot for action up to and including strike action, if the [Sheppey] test was to go ahead. This prompted an urgent meeting with the Home Secretary where our concerns were laid out … [and] convinced him to defer the Market Testing of Sheppey ….

As so often, the NEC's actions were backed up by the support and the potential power of the POA membership as a whole.

Finally, in the February 2006 issue of *Gatelodge*, POA Chair Colin Moses was able to report 'Success born out of unity'. The Home Secretary had announced in December that the three Sheppey prisons, Elmley, Standford Hill and Swaleside, had been granted a Service Level Agreement (SLA) for three years, thus keeping them in the public sector and 'avoiding the corrosive effects of a Market Test … The branch officials and members on the Isle of Sheppey should be applauded and congratulated for their valiant efforts and hard work' – which, as shown above, had been backed by the support of the POA as a whole.

The Swing of the Pendulum …

The second plank of the government's new approach to industrial relations in the Prison Service was what was termed its Voluntary Industrial Relations Agreement (VIRA), though the characterisation of the same agreement as 'legally binding' would appear to be something of a contradiction in terms. The new procedure agreement not only included the clause that 'the parties intend that that this agreement shall constitute a legally enforceable contract' – wording which made it 'unlike most collective agreements' – it went further than outlawing strikes *per se* to outlawing any kind of 'disruption'.[49] The agreement specified in its Clause 13 that 'In the event of a dispute between the parties as to whether action …

would have the effect of disrupting the operations of the Prison Service, the question will be decided by the Secretary of State whose decision will be final ....' If such disruption was judged to have taken place, 'the Prison Service may take action in court, including seeking injunctive relief'.

Given their awareness of the crucial security role they play, most forms of industrial action taken by POA members involve tactics such as working to rule rather than outright strike action. Yet the 'disruption' clause could easily be applied to any such action; and the potential for such rulings became clear at an early point in the operation of the agreement. Thus, according to a POA full-time official: 'From the instant of coming into operation the Voluntary Agreement (VA) was, in the view of the POA, undermined by Prison Service officials. Repeatedly disputes raised by the union were unilaterally ruled out of scope ....'[50]

As one commentator remarks: 'A key question is why did the POA ... agree to legally binding no disruption arrangements?'[51] An answer is suggested in terms of the 'sweeteners' offered not only by the (initially attractive) PRB but also by the agreement's offer of unilateral access to arbitration. The new agreement included provision for both conciliation and arbitration, and also a status quo clause, though it was specified that this would not apply 'in cases of clear operational emergency'. The conciliation and arbitration proposals were themselves hedged about with qualifications; for example, 'the Secretary of State has the power to overrule the award of the arbitrator for reasons of national security or public interest'.[52] Thus, although the new procedure agreement set out to avoid many of the pitfalls of the old, in particular the long wait for resolutions of FTAs (disputes registering a Failure to Agree), it also contained an overwhelming number of disadvantages. Even though FTAs would now proceed automatically to conciliation within 14 days, in the event of no resolution the next stage would be a unilateral reference to arbitration; however, this would require the consent of either the POA or the Prison Service, and if one party refused consent, 'the management's position [would] be deemed to have been accepted'.

Moreover, the type of arbitration used was to be the 'pendulum' variety, in which the arbitrator chooses one position out of those on offer, with no compromise available. The inflexibility of this form of arbitration, and its failure significantly to prevent disputes by comparison with conventional 'split the difference' arbitration, has been noted by industrial relations researchers.[53] For all these reasons and more, the arbitration proposals which had initially been welcomed by the POA proved less than useful. In the event, the POA were prevented from progressing numerous disputes to independent arbitration.

When is a Voluntary Agreement Not a Voluntary Agreement?

The progress of the third strand of the agreement, despite all that had been hoped from it, also ultimately proved disappointing. While in early 2001 Straw had signalled his intention of repealing Section 127 of the 1994 Act and had undertaken to use the provisions of the procedure agreement, this change was 'largely cosmetic'[54] due to the legally binding nature of its 'no disruption' clause – it is difficult to think of a form of industrial action which does not, by definition, involve disruption. In addition, Straw specified that he was replacing Section 127 with a 'reserve statutory power' and specified that Section 127 would itself be used in the event of a breakdown of the new procedure agreement. In every way, it looked like a set of stipulations which would justify the question 'When is a voluntary agreement not a voluntary agreement?' As one letter-writer put it in *Gatelodge* in December 2001: 'With regard to Section 127, [the government] have withdrawn from any agreement which would make it unlawful for the POA to take industrial action, as long as the POA "agree not to induce, support or authorise industrial action". Isn't this the same thing, I ask?'

Nevertheless, according to plan, the government eventually began consultations on the amendment of Section 127. As NEC member Andy Darken put it in the October 2003 issue of *Gatelodge*: 'Yippee! We may get our right to strike back.' However, he cannily observed that:

> Of course Blair and his mates made it clear they would return full trade
> union rights to the POA when they came to government and that it was
> unacceptable for prison officers or union members to be criminalised for
> taking industrial action. Well it's taken them six years to do nothing, so
> I suppose another year or so will make no difference, will it? ... Yes, we
> have been persecuted, maligned and treated as industrial slaves and better
> sooner, rather than later that it stopped ....

By 2002, one commentator could already remark that
'Undoubtedly the new agreement has come under strain', mainly
due to the twin factors of the staging of the PRB award and the
fact that 'the prison population has continued to rise without
corresponding staffing increases'.[55] In April 2001, *Gatelodge*
reported that the present prison population of 63,000 was
projected to increase to 70,800 by 2002 and 78,500 by 2007.
Despite 24 new prisons and 12,000 extra places in ten years, 'the
system remains seriously crowded. It holds today more inmates
per head of the population than any other country in Europe
apart from Portugal ....' Prison population had grown by 36
per cent since the first PFI contract in the late 1990s. As the new
Home Secretary David Blunkett put it on a visit to Leeds Prison
in August 2001, holding more than 1,200 inmates in a prison
designed to take 770 was like 'trying to get a quart into a pint
pot'.[56] Yet less than two months later, Prison Service Director
General Martin Narey was warning that the prison population
had risen by more than 1,200 since Blunkett had become Home
Secretary.[57] As an indication of the 'strain' on the agreement
caused by such factors, further industrial action had continued
sporadically, with staff at several prisons leaving their work
during lunch breaks, and injunctions had been duly granted. As
one prison officer put it at the time: 'The [procedure] agreement
is still in place – just.'[58]

But prison officers' patience was becoming exhausted. Finally, on
25 January 2004, only three years after its introduction, the union
decided to give the required twelve months' notice of termination
of the agreement. POA negotiators and the Prison Service rapidly
began work on a new agreement which could eliminate what a

full-time official calls 'the detested "scope" question' – the process whereby the resolution of POA disputes could be unilaterally ruled as being out of the scope of the voluntary agreement. Within a year, a new legally binding collective agreement, the Joint Industrial Relations Procedural Agreement (JIRPA) was ratified by membership ballot and signed on 11 November 2004 by POA and Prison Service representatives. This would replace the existing agreement in January 2005.

More good news followed; the process of removing Section 127 was finally completed on 21 March 2005 through the Regulatory Reform (Prison Officers Industrial Action) Order. As the full-time official quoted above recalls:

> Despite the Government's failure to remove Section 127 for prison officers in the private sector and Northern Ireland, along with the fact that it had only been removed in England, Wales and Scotland due to the existence of 'no strike agreements', this was seen as a major advance in securing the full restoration of full trade union rights for all POA members across the whole of the United Kingdom.[59]

However, yet more trouble was to follow. JIRPA had been intended to provide the POA and the Prison Service with 'a fair and equitable mechanism to resolve disputes', but 'unfortunately the Prison Service from top to bottom … mismanaged and abused the JIRPA since its introduction, in an attempt to undermine the POA and introduce new policies without full and proper consultation or negotiation', according to the POA full-timer. Like so many other attempts, 'JIRPA faltered', and little more than a year after its introduction, on 11 January 2006, the NEC decided that due to the 'intransigent position' shown by the Prison Service on interpretations of the agreement, the Association would withdraw from the joint training of management and POA reps specified in the agreement. With the POA's effective lack of participation in JIRPA, the remainder of 2006 and indeed 2007 saw almost constant conflict between the POA and Prison Service senior management.

Two Years of Dispute

A major dispute in 2006, for example, took place over the operations of the PSPRB. Since its introduction, the POA had maintained that awards made by the Review Body had not provided sufficient compensation for the loss of prison officers' trade union rights, a loss so significant that it had been condemned by the ILO in 2004. The ILO had also questioned the adequacy of the PSPRB as an alternative arrangement for establishing prison officers' pay levels. Unlike the composition of a typical joint industrial relations body, designed to afford reasonable impartiality through a tripartite structure of one-third employer, one-third independent and one-third trade union representation, the current PSPRB lacked any formal representation from a trade union side. These concerns came to a head in 2005 when a leaked letter to the PRB showed that the Prison Service was intent on manipulating and interfering with PRB decisions to achieve its own aims.

Comments by prison officers invited to express their views on Prison Service pay submissions in 2005 exposed the scandalous levels of the so-called 'awards' made by the PRB. As one officer wrote, referring to the comment by Prison Service Director of Personnel, Gareth Hadley, that 'At first our proposals may seem somewhat low': 'Low is not the word I would use – 0.5 per cent increase in pay would not even cover my yearly rise in council tax let alone my living costs.'[60] As Colin Moses commented later: 'I do not think below inflation awards are fair, just or right and when you know that some staff are on income support or holding down two or three jobs to make ends meet a rise of 10p an hour isn't right.'[61] The 'offer' had also denied any increase at all to prison staff on Long Service Increments (LSIs). As another commentator wrote:

> I have just had the pleasure of reading the recommendations to the PSPRB
> of our kind and generous employer. The breathtaking arrogance of those
> who have no dealings whatever with prisoners never ceases to amaze me
> ... We are shafted on an annual basis and have come to expect no less,
> however the grossly insulting half of one per cent offer they have put

forward this time takes the biscuit … On top of that they have decided that those on the L.S.I.s are already well rewarded and as such are not deserving of a pay rise … Do Home Office ministers and others in high places really believe that an average of three hundred pounds a week is a fair reward for working in these miserable places and dealing with some of the most difficult and dangerous people in the country?[62]

The size of the 'award' looked even more pitiful by contrast to the increase gained by the Scottish members of the POA who, outside the PRB's brief, had received a standard public sector payout of 2.3 per cent.

In March 2006, a meagre 1.6 per cent increase was granted to the vast majority of prison officers covered by the PRB. As the April 2006 issue of *Gatelodge* commented: 'More than 50% of Prison Staff will receive a pay cut in real terms as a result of this year's recommendation by the Pay Review Body. Is this fair, reasonable and just?' In response, the 2006 POA Annual Conference passed an emergency motion instructing the Association to ballot its members for 'industrial action up to and including if necessary a national strike'. The ballot, held between 31 July and 13 August, resulted in an 83 per cent vote in favour of action. POA General Secretary Brian Caton said his members were 'infuriated' by the proposed pay increase, and accused the Prison Service of trying to influence the independence of the PRB. The General Secretary reported that he was seeking talks with Home Secretary John Reid and Prisons Officer Gerry Sutcliffe, but warned that strike action could begin within a fortnight if discussions were not successful.

As the POA recognised it would, the size of the strike vote caused great concern to the Prison Service and the government; so much so that talks aimed at finding an 'amicable resolution' began almost immediately. By 1 September, the NEC believed that they had an agreement they could recommend to the membership. The following week, a Special Delegate Conference was called to consider the NEC's proposed terms of settlement, with a POA motion recommending acceptance carried by the Special Delegate Conference on a card vote. However, throughout the debate a number of delegates voiced concern over what they considered potential loopholes that could and probably would be manipulated by the Prison Service to undermine the agreed changes.

They were proved right when, on 8 September, Director General Phil Wheatley sent out an email to all staff which further exacerbated these fears through the use of phrases like 'strive to' and 'may', seen as undermining what had been thought to be clear and definite commitments by the Prison Service. The NEC felt compelled to seek further commitments as to the legitimacy and authority of the agreement. To this end, leaders of the POA joined Home Office minister Sutcliffe and Prison Service Director General Wheatley at a meeting convened by the Deputy General Secretary of the TUC, Frances O'Grady. Here, Sutcliffe gave his full commitment to the agreement and promised to confirm it in writing. At the end of the meeting, however, Wheatley raised the matter of a POA Circular regarding staff working voluntary overtime beyond 'contract supplementary hours' (CSH). While Sutcliffe commented that this was 'a matter for another day', the following morning, POA leaders, much to their surprise, were served with a 'letter before action' from Treasury solicitors regarding the POA Circular. The next day, Friday 15 September, the Prison Service was granted an interim injunction at the High Court, and on Monday 18 September, during an NEC meeting, further letters were served on the union by Treasury solicitors acting on behalf of the Prison Service.

At this point it became evident that in serving these papers on the union, Prison Service management had no intention of seeking an honourable settlement with the union on the question of either the operation of the PRB or overtime within the Service. In response, the NEC passed a motion instructing the POA membership to take strike action on Friday 22 September 2006, 'unless the Prison Service and Government enter into meaningful discussions with this Union and the injunction is set aside'.

On behalf of the NEC, the POA Chairman contacted the Director General of the Prison Service and the Home Office to inform them of this decision and call on them to enter into meaningful dialogue with the union directly and not by recourse to the courts. The response from the Prison Service, while swift and immediate, was not sympathetic; at 2 p.m. on 19 September, a number of POA leaders, including the General Secretary and the National Chairman, were called to the High Courts of Justice to face charges of contempt. The dramatic implications are summed up in the recollection of General Secretary Brian Caton that 'We expected and were ready for the Prison Service to go all the way and for them to push the Judge into finding us guilty and handing down a custodial sentence. Some of them were determined to break the union.'[63]

Before attending the court, the POA leadership again met with the General Secretary and Deputy General Secretary of the TUC, who agreed to contact the Home Office on behalf of the union. Later, both officials met with Prisons Minister Sutcliffe at the Home Office. In the meantime, POA representatives met with Damien Brown QC, representatives of the union's solicitors, and members of the Wakefield Branch Committee, who had been held to be 'in contempt of court' for having instructed their members not to go beyond their CSH.

The importance of the CSH issue is demonstrated in a letter to *Gatelodge* in September 2006 from the Birmingham POA branch recounting that prison officers had been accused of 'refusing to do suicide watches'. This accusation was based simply on the fact that staff were exercising their right not to work additional hours. Imposition of these extra hours had meant in the past that 'Staff had had their domestic and social lives turned upside down ....' While 'the Governor enjoyed telling us that Jails just up the road were doing business as usual – Why Birmingham? he asked', in fact 'of course it wasn't just Birmingham it was Wakefield, Stafford, Woodhill, Holme House and Liverpool. We are proud to stand shoulder to shoulder with you ....' The letter also made 'Special mention to Blakenhurst who were recently a Private prison but also heard the call to arms' in the dispute.

Whatever the rights and wrongs of the situation, the POA's lawyers were forced to inform the leadership that the charges laid against them were 'extremely serious'. There was a distinct possibility that the court could order sequestration of all POA funds and property. Treasury solicitors and the Prison Service were now vigorously pursuing this matter in an attempt to break the union. As Steve Gillan, POA Finance Officer, put it in the October 2006 issue of *Gatelodge*:

> no one could have prepared me for the scenario that faced this Trade Union on Tuesday 19th September 2006, when the union faced the prospect of National Officials along with a Branch Official from Wakefield being held in contempt of court ... the penalty being potentially one of the following: Officials being sent to Prison; the Union being fined; Union assets being seized. This was truly a baptism of fire for me ... [but] Our message is clear: 'You will never rule us by fear'.

In fact, ten minutes before the POA representatives were due to appear in court, phone calls from TUC General Secretary Brendan Barber and the Home Office minister brought the welcome news that all legal proceedings against the POA had been withdrawn. Although Gareth Hadley, Prison Service Director of Human Resources (HR), insisted that the case was to continue, less than one minute before they were due back in court the delegation was informed, once again, that all legal proceedings against the POA had indeed been withdrawn. Hadley had been mistaken.

Now that the injunction had been withdrawn, POA leaders joined the TUC General Secretary and Deputy General Secretary at the Home Office for tripartite negotiations which ultimately secured a commitment from the Home Office to undertake meaningful discussions on JIRPA, the PRB, the operation of supplementary hours and payments and the establishment of a joint project to look at how best to improve industrial relations within the Prison Service. These commitments were made by both sides with the full knowledge and understanding of both the TUC officials and the Prisons Minister.

Back at Court Again

It seemed that the POA had won an unconditional victory. Yet any genuine progress was still hampered by the fact that Prison Service officials had put forward a so-called 'agreement' on the reform of the PRB as viable, despite the fact that, as they were well aware, other government departments had not been consulted. This was confirmed when Prisons Minister Gerry Sutcliffe wrote to POA leaders on 23 November 2006 notifying them that the government had forced them to withdraw this provisional agreement. As a result, Gareth Hadley, who had been Prison Service HR Director since 1999, resigned his position on Monday 13 November 2006.

Little further progress was made in ensuring that the system could hold the confidence of the POA. The union decided that the next step would be to take the matter to the European Court of Human Rights in order to force the government to introduce necessary changes to prison officers' compensatory mechanisms – or, even better, return their trade union rights. A second Special Delegate Conference was held to discuss the current disputes and in particular the independence of the PSPRB. As was expected, the delegates at the Conference were not inclined to accept what they saw as the totally unsatisfactory 'commitments' provided since the previous Special Delegate Conference. Anger at the evident betrayals was clear from every delegate who spoke from the rostrum.

Not Quite Getting its Tackle in Order …

Yet another legal threat to the POA arose shortly afterwards. In January 2007, due to total lack of progress in the negotiations over CSH, the POA issued a Circular to branches reminding members of the union's policy that 'CSH is not an acceptable way to staff our jails and working CSH is not acceptable conduct for POA members.'[64] In response, on Friday 29 January, the Prison Service once again issued further threats of court action unless such circulars were withdrawn, and on the 31st the Prison Service and Home Secretary duly took the union once more to the High Court, where the judge ruled in favour of the Prison Service. In order not to enter into yet another dispute with the court, the union issued a Circular complying with the court order. The following day the POA leadership was informed that the Treasury solicitors did not accept their efforts to comply, and reserved their right to seek further court action against the POA by an order of contempt of court.

Finally, however, common sense began to make an appearance. At a hearing in the High Court on 2 February, the judge rejected the Prison Service position and set a date for a further hearing on 13 March; here, to everyone's relief, the courts rejected the suggestion that the National Chairman, the General Secretary or the POA itself were in contempt of court over any of these matters.

Yet the legal offensive did not end there. When, later that March, the Stoke Heath POA branch decided to investigate 15 of its members who had signed up to work contract hours in contravention of POA policy, Treasury solicitors' letters began arriving the following day. On the 8 May 2007, the leadership of the POA were in court once again to defend themselves once again against charges of contempt. This time, the judgment was clear and favourable: 'There was no wilful intention on the part of the union or any individual, so far as the evidence discloses, to act inconsistently with what it perceived to be its obligations.' The judge went on to say: 'In the circumstances, the Prison Service, if I may say so, did not quite get its tackle in order in launching contempt proceedings against the appropriate parties.'[65] Justice, against all odds, appeared for once to have prevailed.

POA Win JIRPA in Court

In late 2006 the POA had taken out proceedings against the Prison Service through the High Courts of Justice for what the union believed were a series of breaches by management of JIRPA. The Prison Service had been, in the opinion of the POA, abusing the agreement in a deliberate attempt to reduce its effectiveness and run the Prison Service without engaging with the POA in 'partnership', as had been stipulated within JIRPA. As the POA had commented as long ago as November 2001, in a report of a meeting with the Home Secretary:

> The Prison Officers' Association would not sign a partnership agreement with the Prison Service until they saw the good faith necessary from the

Prison Service to form a solid and sustainable partnership arrangement ... The Home Secretary agreed that partnership is more than just words on paper and requested the Prison Service Agency to action this as soon as possible.[66]

However, it seemed that the Prison Service never did 'action this'. In June 2005, a letter from a POA member urged: 'Do not quote JIRPA to me because in my eyes there is only one party in this so called partnership adhering to it – I will let you guess ... It's not you lot!!!!' By December 2006, after POA officials had been found guilty of 'contempt of court', POA Chair Colin Moses could comment that 'The events of the 19th September 2006 once again prove that [although] the Prison service management in England and Wales talk of partnership working, their idea of partnership is one steeped in the ... employer style of the 1970s.'[67]

Because of the abuses of the JIRPA by Prison Service management and their actions during the contract hours dispute in trying to use the courts rather than joint agreements to run their industrial relations, on 8 May 2007 National Chairman Colin Moses wrote to the Director General of the Prison Service, Phil Wheatley, terminating the agreement:

Dear Phil

JOINT INDUSTRIAL RELATIONS PROCEDURAL AGREEMENT BETWEEN THE PRISON SERVICE AND THE POA

We write following a decision made at a Special NEC meeting held at POA Headquarters on Tuesday, 8th May 2007 and in accordance with paragraph 6 of the Principles of the Joint Industrial Relations Procedural Agreement (JIRPA) to inform you that with immediate effect we issue 12 months notice of termination of the above Agreement. That notice period starts at today's date 8th May 2007.

We ask that you inform appropriate political officials of this decision.

Yours sincerely

COLIN MOSES
National Chairman

The decision of the NEC to issue twelve months' notice of the termination of JIRPA was endorsed by speaker after speaker at the POA Annual Conference two weeks later.

National Walkout

Frustration and anger over the Prison Service's continued obduracy broke out in spectacular fashion when 20,000 prison officers at 140 jails across England and Wales walked out in an 'illegal' and unofficial strike at 7 a.m. on Wednesday 29 August 2007. The immediate response by Gordon Brown, now Prime Minister, was to call for an injunction against the strikers. In reply to a question about the action, he recited his usual mantra that 'public sector pay must be held down as an essential part of tackling inflation'. However, most prison officers remained on strike for several hours after the injunction was served, and looked set to continue the action until 7 a.m. the next day. The strike forced Brown and Jack Straw to the negotiating table, with Straw promising emergency talks by the end of the week. While General Secretary Brian Caton denied the action was illegal, stating, 'I believe every officer has human rights, and they include the right to withdraw their labour', the POA Executive decided to take its members back to work that evening 'in the light of the offer of meaningful discussions regarding the staging of pay'.

This mass action was sparked after the PSPRB had announced a pay rise of 2.5 per cent for the year; the government had then yet again ruled that the increase should be staged, with an initial 1.5 per cent rise followed by a 1 per cent rise six months later. This would keep the prison officers' pay rise well below even the meagre 2 per cent public sector pay limit. At the time, prison officers' starting salary was £17,500, rising to £25,000 over ten years. Meanwhile, prison governors, who already received salaries of up to £78,000, had received increases of £4,000 a year. Not surprisingly, these disparities and the injunction to stop the action inflamed feelings even further. As one Birmingham prison officer pointed out in an internet forum: 'Our pay awards are meant to be according to performance. The fact that the prison population is increasing without increases in staff means our performance in increasing … When they tried to serve an injunction on me this morning, I refused to take it.' A POA shop steward from Liverpool responded to the injunction by telling fellow-strikers: 'Tell [the government] to shove it up their arse, we're sitting it out.' In *Gatelodge*, a POA representative from Aylesbury reported that 'The day passed by with huge support shown by the public and passing traffic in the form of honks and beeps'; from Wandsworth, Stewart McLaughlin reported that 'It was my proudest day as Branch Secretary to see the unity and loyalty shown to the POA.'[68]

During the strike, a lively internet forum, mentioned above, presented prison officers' views. For example:

> In twenty years as a prison officer, I have never known staff morale as low as it is now. This is due to rising staff assaults, management bullying and pay cuts. We will gladly let Jack Straw through the picket line to pick some keys up and give reality a try. I am proud to be a striking prison officer.

Another added: 'Enough is enough. This should have happened long ago', to which a further post agreed: 'Most staff consider this action long overdue.' Another striker recalled:

> I went to work this morning and yes I stayed outside on strike … I stand by the decision as I believe it has to make the government look not just at officers' pay but also the budgets that prisons are forced to work on … I believe I am worth much more than the £18,908 that I am paid … I accept that is my wage but when an independent pay review body recommendation is ignored by this government something has to be done.'

These views had been borne out in a ballot earlier that August in which 87 per cent of members endorsed action up to and including a strike.

As Colin Moses reported in the September 2007 issue of *Gatelodge* under the heading 'A Great Day in the History of the POA', the POA received massive support for its action at that year's TUC: 'The POA is now seen as a member of the Awkward Squad.'[69] There were some reservations, nevertheless, on whether the POA leadership had been quite 'awkward' enough. As one letter to the October 2007 *Gatelodge* put it:

> Our NEC did a great job, but, Was it enough? Did we stop too soon? I believe that we did, why? Because we did not have the right assurances in place to warrant the cessation of the strike and I believe that the right outcome was not achieved … The Prison Office were scared and unsure what to do … our NEC should have capitalised on that and instructed them that if our legitimate concerns were not met, further action WOULD follow.

Anger against the treatment of staff by the Prison Service continued:

> As the fall out of our first ever national strike rumbles on, there is growing anger towards the prison service and the current way it's treating its staff … Prison Staff today are more akin to social workers than prison officers and staff at the coal face are rapidly reaching burn out. What does the Service think such loyalty/dedication should be rewarded with? You guessed it … *'A Zero per cent pay recommendation for the bulk of staff'*. Thanks for nothing![70]

Yet despite the obvious unrest, by 2008 Jack Straw was seeking reintroduction of the draconian Section 127. On 7 January, in what POA Chair Colin Moses referred to as 'a black day for this union and the Trade Union movement', Justice Secretary Straw announced in Parliament his intention to return Section 127 to the statute books. According to a report in the *Guardian* on 8 January 2008, Straw blamed the move on the wildcat strike the previous August. Arguing that he had 'no alternative' but to reinstate Section 127, Straw maintained that the measure, tabled in the form of an amendment to a Bill currently going through Parliament, would be held in reserve and only used if the government and the POA failed to arrive at a new voluntary no-strike agreement. POA General Secretary Brian Caton reacted angrily, insisting that his members would not be 'intimidated' by the government. In his February 2008 *Gatelodge* column, Caton could report that 'The reintroduction of Section 127 to the House of Commons on 9th January 2008 created the biggest rebellion for the government since the wasteful and dangerous commitment to a new Trident Missile system.' Section 127 was nonetheless reintroduced on 8 May 2008.

In response, a Special Delegate Conference on 19 February 2008 mandated the NEC 'to take any action, including strike action, should any Government launch an attack on the Union's finances, their membership, their pay [and] conditions', and resolved that 'any further agreement must not constitute a "no strike agreement" nor should it prevent the campaign to fight for full trade union rights'. In the May 2008 issue of *Gatelodge*, a prison officer from the Mount wrote urging united action across the movement to regain the POA's right to strike:

> We proved we could make them listen to us after the 29th August 2007. Imagine how they would shake in their boots if we had up to a further 6 or 7 unions joining us in a coordinated action or even a threat of [it] ... Colleagues let us warn our colleagues in the Fire Brigades union ... they will come after you with the same sort of legislation regarding public safety etc. ... I have just read that the Coastguards are about to take industrial action for the first time, I find it amazing that with a Labour Government (?) in power public sector workers are taking more industrial action than ever before ....

And in fact, on 8 September 2008, prison officers found themselves once again threatening strike action on a national scale after a private contractor, EDS, employed by the Ministry of Justice, admitted it had lost a hard drive containing the personal details of 5,000 staff. In response, POA Chair Colin Moses stated that unless the government could provide assurances about the safety of staff, 'strike action would follow'.

'Modernising' Pay and Conditions ...

More threats to prison officers' conditions came shortly afterwards with Workforce Modernisation (WFM) proposals which, predictably, set out to intensify prison officers' working practices and cut down on staffing still further. The POA was reluctantly forced to participate in negotiations on the basis that the proposals would put more money into the Prison Service; at the 2008 POA Annual Conference, Jack Straw had promised an extra £50 million for the prisons budget if the proposals were accepted. There was also a strong suggestion that the ongoing programme of 'market testing' in prisons would be slowed or withdrawn on that basis.

The first indications of the WFM initiative emerged in the Chairman's column of the April 2008 *Gatelodge* magazine, where he reported on yet another recommendation from Carter, this time to build three 'Titan Prisons' housing around 2,500 prisoners each. At the same time as this 'highly controversial proposal' was being introduced, 'the Prison Service wish to introduce workforce modernisation. This whole process could initiate the biggest change in working practices seen by POA members in over a decade.'

The same issue carried an article by the Swaleside branch Chairman, Dave Cook, headed 'Workforce Modernisation or the Demise of a Public Service?' which repeated the Prison Service statement that 'At the current trend by the year 2015 the prison service will only have the finances to pay our staff and … nothing else', and argued that 'Workforce Modernisation is about cutting the wages bill … aiming to achieve competency based progression … [and] introduc[ing] performance related pay to all manager grades' which included Senior and Principal prison officers.

In May 2008, nevertheless, the Annual Conference passed a motion accepting that 'Workforce Modernisation is inevitable' and mandating the NEC 'to enter into meaningful discussion with the Prison Service in order to achieve the best possible deal for the members of the Association'. However, in late 2008 a pre-budget report indicated that yet more market testing of 'failing' prisons would be ongoing, cancelling out the hope that accepting WFM would mean an end to this menace, and in January 2009 the policy was overturned by the POA, with a Special Delegate Conference voting against WFM in principle.

Better News North of the Border?

Meanwhile, a very different set of events was playing out in Scotland. The Scottish Prison Officers' Association had re-merged with the POA nationally in 2000; POA Chair Mark Healy reported in the April 2000 issue of *Gatelodge* that SPOA members had voted overwhelmingly, by 92 per cent, in favour of the merger. But conditions in the country remained different in a number of respects from those in England and Wales, or indeed Northern Ireland (see below). In April 2001, the POA (Scotland) took strike action across the country when the Scottish Prison Service (SPS) imposed new attendance patterns on POA members at Noranside Prison during the course of negotiations. The instigation of Scotland-wide action ultimately led to a VIRA, similar to that in England and Wales, between the SPS and the POA in December 2001.

In comparison to England and Wales, the agreement appears to have run relatively smoothly. The POA in Scotland has at no time given notice to withdraw from the agreement, even though it was similarly legally binding in the sense that the POA are obliged not to induce, authorise or support any form of industrial action by its members. Since entering into this agreement, the SPS and the SPOA have also signed a partnership agreement based on the TUC's 1997 'Partners for Progress' document. The progress of the partnership agreement was described as late as 2008 by the Scottish Area Assistant Secretary as 'very positive – there's been the odd hiccup [but] it's how you manage the falling out and get back on an even keel'.

As the Assistant Secretary noted:

> There's some resentment from people in the field because they don't understand – you try and tell them you're working in partnership and it's not always understood exactly what it means. It's a political concept for both the trade unions and the management because management can no longer say we're the management and we're going to do this and the union says we're the union and we're going to stop you. There's got to be give

on both sides – different agendas, common ground. See if a compromise can be achieved ....[71]

Yet the POA in Scotland was also facing many of the issues causing conflict in England and Wales, as described above. The same POA official described how 'The Market Testing System is still in place to some extent. Part of the Modernisation agenda.' Some initially positive results had been gained on pay and hours: 'In 2001 the Bichard and Mackeson Report commissioned by the Labour government reduced our pay scales – it used to take up to 20 years to get maximum pay, was now reduced to five years – we negotiated a 37-hour week as well.' However, part of the new arrangements was that the 'top 10 per cent' of the organisation was now to be rewarded for 'excellent' performance.

This didn't work – it became so corrupt – you either got patronage from your manager to get put on 'sexy' projects that meant you were taken away from the mainstream or you had to cover that's person's work – at one stage there was anecdotal evidence that it's 'your turn this year' so it was getting allocated on that basis rather than by worth.[72]

All prison officers were now expected to 'contribute through Key Performance Indicators – every governor's got a set of KPIs to meet – this was brought in about the same time to do with the private prisons – we were supposed to be competing with them'. As the Area Secretary pointed out:

The only way you could compete was by setting the same kind of standards they were set. This was madness because they're governed by profit. They've got access to capital through the banks. We have to go to the government.[73]

Change had come, however, with the rule of the Scottish National Party (SNP):

The biggest change was the SNP government ... They promised more prisons in the public sector, although some private prisons like Addiwell had been commissioned by Labour before they lost office. We had faith in the SNP ... There was a prison, Low Moss, inside an RAF camp, which had been condemned by the fire service – it was supposed to be in open competition with the private sector. The SNP stopped this as soon as they came in – they said no – and it was built as a public sector prison.[74]

The 'North of the Border' column in *Gatelodge* confirmed this report in October 2007:

Scotland's Justice Minister ... announced that he was suspending the procurement process for the replacement prison on the Low Moss site in Bishopsrigg ... the new prison [would be] publicly run ... In making the announcement the Minister stated that they were committed to a publicly owned and run prison service with more investment ... and that both the Low Moss and Peterhead prisons would be run by the public sector, for the public good, not for private profit.

A Regime in Crisis ...

This was glad news, but in the meantime the hulk of Kilmarnock still loomed as a private prison under a 25 year contract between the SPS and Premier Prison Services (PPS). Research into the experience of working at Kilmarnock reveals the harshness of the regime. Prison officers laboured under 28 targets or Key Performance Indicators (KPIs) – none of which, as the researchers point out, measure staff welfare. Staffing levels were about 25 per cent lower than in the public sector, and savings were also made from 'radical adjustments to pay', made possible because the private sector 'operates local recruitment and pays regional market rates for all grades of staff', thus delivering 'competitive pay rates for prison custody officers'.[75]

In making this case, the Scottish Executive was signalling its intention to extend local pay determination to all proposed new prisons, thus implying threats to national pay bargaining and to the role of the POA in Scotland. While the managing director of PPS defended the localised pay with 'evidence' based on low turnover at the prison, management was forced to respond to charges of 'high attrition undermining performance' in 2002; in fact, the Prisons Inspectorate found turnover levels, at 32 per cent, to be 'significantly higher than any other Scottish prison'[76]

Even the 'scab union' PSU General Secretary, Phil Hornsby, gave evidence attributing Kilmarnock's recruitment and retention difficulties to what was described in a Parliamentary Report as 'the ferocity of the tendering system [which] means that every new private prison that comes on stream does so with fewer staff on lower pay, because the wage bill is the big cost of running a prison. He claimed that an average [increase] of around 20% would be required at HMP Kilmarnock to bring the level up to proper staffing complement'.[77] As Taylor and Cooper point out, 'the irony is that that Hornsby is gesturing here towards a critique of the privatisation process upon which his union depends for its existence'.[78] However, as demonstrated, even the PSU was becoming more militant: despite the union's commitment to privatisation and 'embrace of the partnership concept with Premier' (a statement made by Hornsby in November 2001), the organisation was forced into an 'oppositional posture'. In 2002, Hornsby commented: 'My own Executive council and ... membership are now calling for me to adopt a much more vigorous and robust stance on perceived employer abuses in the private sector custodial service.'[79]

Clearly, the concrete experience of the horrors of privatisation, apparently unmediated by 'partnership', had forced even a company union into a stance much closer to that of the 'old-fashioned' POA; all the more bizarre that it attempted to retain its management-oriented position. At a 2002 court hearing investigating Kilmarnock, PSU Secretary Hornsby reported that 60 per cent of PSU members at Kilmarnock received income support. Also in 2002, Consultants MCG reported that staff at the prison 'receive less pay than many security guards and about the same as supermarket shelf-fillers and checkout operators, though less than some'. Given the stresses of the job, a stint in Tesco's would be seen by many as a relief. Thus it was not only low pay which lay behind the high turnover; 'exit interviews showed that rather than the attractions of rival employers being the cause ... it was dissatisfaction with working conditions.'[80]

By 2002, Kilmarnock was experiencing problems so intense that 'to describe [it] as a regime in crisis is not to indulge in hyperbole'.[81] The principal factor in the growing storm was understaffing, with a torrent of complaints highlighting shortfalls against ASLs (Agreed Staffing Levels) which, despite the name, were the 'ideal' levels of staff defined by the contract. Meanwhile, levels of staff turnover began to exceed even the figures cited above, being estimated by consultants at 39 per cent, while even Kilmarnock's HR department gave the figure of 34 per cent. That management had fabricated its own figures was admitted by the prison director in an email to a PPS director;[82] but even PPS was unable to ignore the growing problems. The clinical manager briefed senior management in May 2002 on the 'chronic shortage of staff' illustrated by vacancies for five out of twelve qualified nursing posts; staff in general were 'at breaking point' because of poor pay and stress caused by working as many as 70 hours a week.[83]

Prison officers themselves gave vivid accounts of the stresses of working at Kilmarnock, citing the main causes of staff turnover as 'the terrible, terrible wages', the 'terrible staffing levels' and the 'drastic' shift patterns. Officers reported working up to 30 hours a week over their contracted 44 hours, but received no overtime pay and, of course, were rarely able to take the time off in lieu accumulated. One recalled working 16 ten-and-a-quarter-hour shifts 'on the trot', and officers often had to perform additional unpaid work at the end of a shift. For example, in changing from a late to an early shift:

> Although you are paid until 10.15 pm, you don't get away till maybe 11.15. There are eight wings and you have to do a count on all of them, and if there is one wrong you are held back ... By the time we get home, it's 12.30 ... You have got to be back for 6.30, so you have to get up at 5.30. Four hours' kip, and then I'm back in and dealing with ninety-two prisoners.[84]

Prison officers were angered by the falsification of statistics and failure to report assaults by prison management. In one particularly shocking incident:

> A personal alarm went off ... and it was an officer who had a pen plunged into his neck ... he was actually staggering down the stairs, on his own,

holding a bandage with blood pouring out of it. I read a couple of weeks later that the assault was 'nothing', he was 'barely scratched' ... they had definitely downgraded that.[85]

Significantly, despite their widespread anger and unrest, prison officers at Kilmarnock 'did not see the PSU as being able to represent their interests, largely because it was seen as, in one prison officer's words, "in Premier's pocket"'. For all these reasons, prison officers at Kilmarnock could see no way out other than, literally, walking out from the troubled institution and seeking equally low-paid, stressful but perhaps less dangerous work elsewhere in the area.

An Angel from Heaven ...

While Section 127 remained in force throughout the period in Northern Ireland, the 'Troubles' of the province continued to extend beyond even the crucial matters of pay, conditions and union organisation. The cessation of outright murder in Northern Irish prisons was sustained, yet by late 2002 the situation had worsened to the extent that prison officers were threatening industrial action that November over threats to their security. As National Chair Colin Moses wrote in the December 2003 issue of *Gatelodge*:

> Our members in Northern Ireland have withdrawn their goodwill and are refusing to perform overtime. This is as a direct result of the Northern Ireland Office's failure to put in place adequate and appropriate security measures which meet the needs of our members and their families.

Part of the issue was meagre compensation: POA members 'receive approximately £17,000 compared to approximately £50,000 which is afforded to other public servants in Northern Ireland facing similar threats'. As Area Chairman (NI) Finlay Spratt put it in the same issue: 'The situation regarding current and retired members in Northern Ireland is that they are still facing constant threats by paramilitary organisations whose campaign for segregation is leading to damage to property and injury to staff.'

At about the same time, in the autumn of 2003, a more positive move was seen with the official launch of the Prison Service Trust, which aimed to support prison staff and families who had suffered as a Result of the 'Troubles' with healthcare, life planning and support services. As *Gatelodge* reported in October 2003:

> The signing of the Good Friday Agreement and changes within the Prison Service have not prevented our colleagues and their families suffering. Jane Kennedy, Prison Service Minister, stated that the launch of the Trust was in recognition of the dedication of former prison staff and families owed a great debt of gratitude for carrying out a very difficult job often in the face of serious threats, intimidation and murder.

The Northern Ireland POA commented in the same issue: 'We know these threats are still live today and our colleagues still suffer at the hands of terrorists.'

In October 2008 it could be reported in *Gatelodge* that June Robinson, Area Secretary (NI), had been awarded an MBE for public service 'in recognition of the commitment ... given to Prison officers in the Province for the past 23 years' through her voluntary work with the Prison Service Trust. In particular:

> the threat made by the Provisional IRA against [prison] staff did not deter her from carrying out her duties. She has dealt with many families over the years who were intimidated and threatened out of their homes ... She assisted families in their endeavours to rejoin the community after their terrible experiences ... There are many families who are grateful to her; one even described her as 'Their angel from heaven' ....

On 7 November 2008 a memorial service was held under the auspices of the Northern Ireland Prison Service for POA members killed during the conflict in the province. A retired senior officer from Liverpool, representing the POA, recounted:

> The Last Post was sounded ... [Then] the Reveille ... followed by a Lament. The names of our colleagues from the Roll of Honour were then read out, also remembering other members of the Northern Ireland Prison service who have died. The words of the Supreme Sacrifice were then read out ....[86]

Later, the same officer was introduced to the daughter of Brian Armour, 'a very close friend before he was murdered by terrorists (04.10.88)'. That simple phrase perhaps says as much as any about the impact of the Northern Ireland 'Troubles' on so many innocent people's lives.

Choose Freedom. Break These Laws

As the POA approaches its 70th birthday, it has increasingly been at the forefront of campaigning against the evils of a system which creates criminals at both its highest and lowest levels.

It was at the TUC Conference of 2008, the same year its right to strike had once again been removed by a 'Labour' government, that the POA leadership distinguished itself by leading the way against the longstanding anti-trade union legislation which had now crippled the movement for almost 30 years. Speaking in two debates, General Secretary Brian Caton called for strikes not only in support of low-paid local government workers, who had received no pay rise that year, but also against the anti-trade union laws themselves. Referring to the POA's own loss of trade union rights in 1993–94, he went on to express the union's sympathy for the rest of the British trade union movement as 'more oppressed than anyone else in the Western world'.

The General Secretary continued:

The trade union movement was born of struggle, but not just struggles you wave a flag at. The history of Tolpuddle and other historic acts of resistance is about those who stood tall and said 'We will not'. We would not be here today if they and others had not withdrawn their labour. Trade unionists before us have been thrown in jail and have starved for our right to be here. Not just in the history books, but now and in the future.

You can have your rallies, yes, we can have campaigns to try and change the legislation, but let's show we mean business and withdraw our labour. We are now worse off than at any time in recent history. You expect the Tories to kick you to bits but Labour? These are laws, and normally laws serve society, but these are bad laws ... Choose freedom. Break these laws.

With the usual TUC vacillation, delegates clapped and cheered Caton's speech and that of Bob Crow of the Rail, Maritime and Transport (RMT) union, as well as the NUM's Ian Lavery, both of whom supported the POA; yet the vote was lost. In reply, Caton told the delegates: 'We feel sorry for you, because we, the POA, will break these laws. You can take our money but you can never take away the heart and soul of our members.' Coming from a union often patronised as somehow failing to share in the 'left' culture of the movement, this stood as clear class leadership.

Along similar lines, in October 2008, the General Secretary, in an article in *Gatelodge* headed 'A Strike – The Forgotten Concept', reported on the strong support the POA had received at the TUC: 'The POA's reputation as a fighting campaigning union could not have been more prominent ... It was a great honour to move the amendment on Public Sector Pay, calling for strike action against the Government's unfair ... and unacceptable pay restraint on public sector pay.' Caton regretted the fact that the TUC committee in charge of compositing motions 'did not agree to have the word "strike" placed before Congress'; nevertheless, 'it was with great delight and pride that congress delegations overturned this view'.

The General Secretary continued:

> The Trade Union Movement was born out of adversity, struggle and determination to gain freedom, liberty and fairness for working people. It does no good to substitute and re-model trade unionism into a skills provider, where those skills bring little financial reward and a continued threat of loss of living standards and redundancy. Being skilled, poor and unemployed can never be what this movement is about ....

The amendment fell, due to 'the President's card vote and confusion amongst the leadership of Unite's delegation'; Caton's motion on strike action against the anti-union laws also went down due to ... well, what can only be described as 'loss of bottle'. Yet the POA General Secretary concluded his report with the words:

The POA will continue its campaign and fight to get the whole of the Labour Movement to straighten their spines and stand up for new laws that take away the restrictions on strike and industrial action.

Our simple message to other unions is 'Don't think that your members cannot deliver on strike action – they can.'

Please recognise that if you don't ask them – they never will.

CHOOSE FREEDOM – BREAK BAD LAWS.

It is in this way that the POA stands proud today as a union which has given true leadership to the whole working-class movement.

NOTES

Introduction

1. J.E. Thomas, *The English Prison Officer Since 1850: A Study in Conflict*, Routledge and Kegan Paul, 1972. See also Joy Cameron, *Prisons and Punishment in Scotland from the Middle Ages to the Present*, Canongate, 1983.
2. Thomas, *English Prison Officer*, p13.
3. Ibid., p42.
4. The 1888 Matchgirls' and 1889 dockers' strikes were highlights in the development of a 'New Unionism' which took union organisation beyond craft workers to the much larger groups of the unskilled and semi-skilled.
5. Thomas, *English Prison Officer*, p68.
6. Quoted in Thomas, *English Prison Officer*, p86.
7. Ibid., p89.
8. Quoted in ibid., p110.
9. Ibid., p140.
10. Quoted in ibid., p112.
11. Ibid., pp118, 122.
12. Steven R. Thomas, 'The Alienation of the English Prison Officer, 1877 to 1980', BA dissertation, Manchester Polytechnic, 1984.
13. Thomas, *English Prison Officer*, p142.
14. This and other parliamentary questions were evidently asked at the instigation of the famous *Prison Officers' Magazine* editor, 'E.R. Ramsay' (see below).
15. Thomas, *English Prison Officer*, p144.
16. 'The Late E.R. Ramsay', *Prison Officers' Magazine*, May 1961.
17. Thomas, *English Prison Officer*, p144.
18. Ibid.
19. 'The Late E.R. Ramsay', *Prison Officers' Magazine*, 1961.
20. Thomas, *English Prison Officer*, p145.
21. A.V. Sellwood, *Police Strike 1919*, W.H. Allen, 1978.
22. Ibid., p10.
23. Quoted in Thomas, *English Prison Officer*, p145.
24. Sellwood, *Police Strike*, pp10–11.
25. Ibid., p12.
26. Ibid., p7.

27. 'The *Prison Officers' Magazine* and its Editors – 1910–1985 (Seventy-five Years On)'. Mimeograph (no date).
28. Ibid.
29. Thomas, *English Prison Officer*, p147.
30. Ibid.
31. 'The Late E.R. Ramsay', *Prison Officers' Magazine*, 1961.

Chapter 1   1919–39

1. Harley Cronin, *The Screw Turns*, POA, 2004, p41. The 1967 memoir of the POA's first General Secretary, Harley Cronin, was republished by the POA in 2004.
2. Ibid., p40.
3. See A.V. Sellwood, *Police Strike 1919*, W.H. Allen, 1978. Unfortunately this account makes no mention of prison officers.
4. J.E. Thomas, *The English Prison Officer Since 1850: A Study in Conflict*, Routledge and Kegan Paul, 1972, p146.
5. Ibid., p153.
6. Prison Commissioners, Annual Report.
7. Thomas, *English Prison Officer*, p155.
8. Ibid., p156. See also *Report of the Committee of Inquiry into the United Kingdom Prison Services*, October 1979 (the 'May Report'), p15, for an almost identical assessment.
9. Thomas, *English Prison Officer*, p159.
10. Ibid.
11. *Prison Officers' Magazine*, April 1938.
12. Ibid.; emphasis in the original.
13. Ibid.
14. Ibid.
15. Ibid.
16. Thomas, *English Prison Officer*, p141.
17. Ibid., p170.
18. PORB Minutes, June 1927.
19. PORB Minutes, July 1928.
20. Fred Castell, 'The Prison Officers Association – Northern Ireland'. Mimeograph (no date).
21. *Prison Officers' Magazine*, April 1938.
22. Editorial, *Prison Officers' Magazine*, November 1938.
23. Cronin, *The Screw Turns*, p39.
24. Ibid., p40.
25. Ibid., p41.
26. *Prison Officers' Magazine*, April 1938.
27. Cronin, *The Screw Turns*, p42.

28. Ibid., pp42–3.
29. Ibid.
30. Ibid.
31. Editorial, *Prison Officers' Magazine*, April 1938.
32. Cronin, *The Screw Turns*.
33. POA, *A Short History of the Association and a Copy of the Rules and Constitution*, POA, 1959.
34. *Prison Officers' Magazine*, May 1938.
35. Editorial, *Prison Officers' Magazine*, July 1938.
36. Ibid.
37. 'Board Matters', *Prison Officers' Magazine*, July 1938, p196.
38. *Prison Officers' Magazine*, August 1938.
39. 'Progress Continues', *Prison Officers' Magazine*, September 1938.
40. *Prison Officers' Magazine*, October 1938.
41. This system is now defunct, undermined by Thatcherism and largely replaced by Pay Review Bodies under New Labour.
42. *Prison Officers' Magazine*, October 1938.
43. Castell, 'The Prison Officers Association – Northern Ireland'.
44. *Prison Officers' Magazine*, November 1938.
45. *Prison Officers' Magazine*, December 1938.
46. *Prison Officers' Magazine*, November 1938.
47. Castell, 'The Prison Officers Association – Northern Ireland'.
48. Written note at end of letter to Miss Curtis, 8 December 1938.
49. Note on Conference held at Prison Commission, Home Office, 18 January 1939.
50. *Prison Officers' Magazine*, May 1939.

Chapter 2   1939–79

1. 'A Great Jubilee', *Prison Officers' Magazine*, Volume 52 No. 11, November 1962, p1.
2. Ibid.
3. *Prison Officers' Magazine*, November 1939, p352.
4. F.G. Castell, 'The Prison Officers Association – Northern Ireland'. Mimeograph (no date).
5. Correspondence between F.G. Castell and L.C. White, POA Northern Ireland Correspondence and Minutes, 1940–49.
6. J.E. Thomas, *The English Prison Officer Since 1850: A Study in Conflict*, Routledge and Kegan Paul, 1972, p178.
7. Harley Cronin, *The Screw Turns*, POA, 2004, p264.
8. Thomas, *English Prison Officer*, p178.

9. Whitley Committee, Departmental Minutes and Correspondence, 10 April 1945.
10. Whitley Committee, Departmental Minutes and Correspondence, 23 May 1945.
11. POA, *A Short History of the Association and a Copy of the Rules and Constitution*, POA, 1959.
12. Ibid., p7.
13. Ibid., p10.
14. *Prison Officers' Magazine*, July 1945.
15. POA, *Short History*, p21.
16. See 'A Great Jubilee', p1.
17. Interview with Dave Turner (see below), June 2008.
18. Confidential Report from the Labour Party of a Study Group on Crime Prevention and Penal Reform: Memorandum received from the POA, 1964.
19. POA, 'The Late W.J. Brown', *Twenty-second Annual Report*, 1960.
20. Cronin, *The Screw Turns*, p79.
21. Steven R. Thomas, 'The Alienation of the English Prison Officer, 1877 to 1980', BA dissertation, Manchester Polytechnic, 1984.
22. Thomas, *English Prison Officer*, p181.
23. Ibid., p184.
24. Ibid.
25. POA, *Twenty-second Annual Report*.
26. Thomas, *English Prison Officer*, p188.
27. Cronin, *The Screw Turns*, p80.
28. Ibid., p88.
29. Thomas, *English Prison Officer*, p189.
30. *Prison Officers' Magazine*, August 1958.
31. Prison Commissioners' Report, 1952, cited in Thomas, *English Prison Officer*.
32. Thomas, *English Prison Officer*, p191.
33. Cronin, *The Screw Turns*, p89.
34. Confidential Report from the Labour Party of a Study Group on Crime Prevention and Penal Reform: Memorandum received from the POA.
35. POA, *Short History*.
36. POA, 'Pay', *Twenty-second Annual Report*.
37. Whitley Council Bulletin, 21 December 1960.
38. POA, 'Special Hospitals', *Twenty-second Annual Report*.
39. Confidential Report from the Labour Party of a Study Group on Crime Prevention and Penal Reform: Memorandum received from the POA, 1964.

40. Thomas, *English Prison Officer*, p206.
41. Ibid.
42. Confidential Report from the Labour Party of a Study Group on Crime Prevention and Penal Reform: Memorandum received from the POA, 1964.
43. Thomas, *English Prison Officer*, p199.
44. Bill Driscoll, BBC Radio 4, August 1997, quoted in Alison Liebling and David Price, *The Prison Officer*, Prison Service Journal, 2001, p161.
45. Report of General Secretary's Speech to 1985 Annual Conference, *Prison Officers' Magazine*, August 1985.
46. Interview with John Boddington, November 2008.
47. *Report of the Inquiry into Prison Escapes and Security* (the 'Mountbatten Report'), 1965.
48. For comparison, the figure in June 2008 was 83,100.
49. D. King and K. Elliott, *Albany: Birth of a Prison, and of an Era*, London, 1977.
50. Interview with John Boddington, November 2008.
51. Thomas, 'Alienation of the English Prison Officer'.
52. General Secretary's column, *Prison Officers' Magazine*, June 1965.
53. *Prison Officers' Magazine*, July 1965.
54. Interview with John Boddington, November 2008.
55. Interview with Dave Turner and Angela Burgess, June 2008.
56. Interview with Finlay Spratt, Northern Ireland POA Area Chairman, September 2008.
57. Letter to *Prison Officers' Magazine*, October 1979.
58. Report of the Committee of Inquiry into the United Kingdom Prison Services, October 1979 ('May Report'), pp222–3.
59. Susan Corby, 'On Parole: Prison Service Industrial Relations', *Industrial Relations Journal*, Volume 33 No. 4, 2002.
60. Thomas, 'Alienation of the English Prison Officer', p45.
61. Interview with retired senior full-timer who wished to remain anonymous, September 2008.
62. Ibid.
63. Ibid.
64. Interview with retired senior full-timer, September 2008.
65. Interview with John Boddington, November 2008.
66. Interview with retired senior full-timer, September 2008.
67. Interview with General Secretary, *Prison Officers' Magazine*, October 1972.
68. Interview with retired senior full-timer, September 2008.
69. Thomas, 'Alienation of the English Prison Officer', pp42–3.

70. *The Times*, 24 August 1972, cited in ibid.
71. Hull Prison Riot: Submissions, Observations and Recommendations of Mr John Prescott, MP ... Presented to [the] Chief Inspector of Prison Services, Hull, 1977.
72. *Prison Officers' Magazine*, October 1977.
73. J. Kay, Letter to MP, Lincoln, 1977, cited in Thomas, 'Alienation of the English Prison Officer', p51.
74. Thomas, 'Alienation of the English Prison Officer', p45.
75. 'London Weighting' refers to the extra payment allocated to those living and working in London and reflects the increased costs of living in the London area.
76. POA Circular 56, 23 October 1978.
77. POA Circular 64, 9 October 1978.
78. POA Circular 45, 28 November 1977.
79. POA Circular 57, 23 October 1978.
80. John Black, 'Industrial Relations in the UK Prison Service', *Employee Relations*, Volume 17 No. 2, 1995, p71.
81. Email communication from John Renton, December 2008.
82. Email communication from John Renton, December 2008.
83. Jimmy Boyle, *The Pain of Confinement*, Pan, 1985, pp7–8.
84. Joy Cameron, *Prisons and Punishment in Scotland from the Middle Ages to the Present*, Canongate, 1983, p227.
85. Boyle, *The Pain of Confinement*, pp15, 28.
86. Cameron, *Prisons and Punishment in Scotland*, p226.
87. Quoted in Cameron, *Prisons and Punishment in Scotland*, pp195–6.
88. Ibid., p208.
89. Report of Special Delegate Conference, *Link*, April 1979.
90. Ibid.
91. Cameron, *Prisons and Punishment in Scotland*, p228.
92. Letter in Northern Ireland POA file, 1999.
93. Interview with Finlay Spratt, September 2008.
94. May Report, p208.
95. May Report, p280.
96. Ibid., p283.
97. Ibid., p284.
98. Ibid., p288.
99. Thomas, 'Alienation of the English Prison Officer', p52.
100. May Report, p237.
101. Thomas, 'Alienation of the English Prison Officer', p84.
102. POA circular, December 1979.
103. Thomas, 'Alienation of the English Prison Officer', p56.

Chapter 3   1980–87

1. *Guardian*, 25 March 1980, cited in Steven R. Thomas, 'The Alienation of the English Prison Officer, 1877 to 1980', BA dissertation, Manchester Polytechnic, 1984, p56.

2. POA, *Forty-Second Annual Report*, January–December 1980, p5.

3. 'Parliamentary Discussions', *Prison Officers' Magazine*, January 1981, p4.

4. General Secretary's address to SPOA Conference, *Prison Officers' Magazine*, November 1981, p346.

5. POA Circular, March 1984, in POA *Annual Report*, 1984, Appendix D(i).

6. Although this was published before the Tory victory in 1979, it was sponsored by the Conservative Shadow Cabinet.

7. Parliamentary Report, *Prison Officers' Magazine*, January 1981.

8. *Prison Officers' Magazine*, January 1981.

9. POA Circular, 12 February 1980.

10. Interview with Dave Turner, June 2008.

11. Ibid.

12. Ibid.

13. Earlier in 1981, the National Union of Mineworkers (NUM) had threatened strike action over proposed pit closures. Aware of widespread support within the movement, the government had backed off in order to 'fight another day'.

14. Interview with Angela Burgess, June 2008.

15. *Prison Officers' Magazine*, November 1981.

16. 'News and Jottings', *Prison Officers' Magazine*, December 1981, p398.

17. Interview with retired senior full-timer who wished to remain anonymous, September 2008.

18. Ibid.

19. Ken Daniels had been forced to retire through illness.

20. *Report of Inquiry into Civil Service Pay*, July 1982, Chairman Sir John Megaw.

21. POA, *Forty-Fifth Annual Report*, January–December 1983, Appendix A (Pay).

22. *Report of Inquiry into Civil Service Pay*, p102ff.

23. Interview with Dave Turner, June 2008.

24. Interview with retired senior full-timer, September 2008.

25. Ibid.

26. POA, *Annual Report*, 1983, section J(i) (Management Structure).
27. POA, Chair's Address to 1983 Annual Conference, *Annual Report*, 1983, Appendix D (Industrial Action).
28. POA, General Secretary's Address to 1983 Annual Conference, *Annual Report*, 1983, Appendix D (Industrial Action).
29. OME Report, March 1984, cited in POA, *Annual Report*, 1984, Appendix A (Pay).
30. These related to allegations of excessive force used by prison staff against inmates.
31. POA, *Annual Report*, 1984, Appendix G (Parliamentary Questions) and Appendix D(iii) (Working Party on Communications between Management and Staff).
32. POA, *Annual Report*, 1984, Appendix L(iv) (Code of Discipline).
33. 'News and Jottings', *Prison Officers' Magazine*, July 1985.
34. Cited in POA, *Annual Report*, 1984, Appendix G (House of Lords Debate), 21 March 1984).
35. Letter to *Prison Officers' Magazine*, October 1985.
36. 'Lifting Our Parliamentary Profile, *Prison Officers' Magazine*, September 1985.
37. Interview with retired senior full-timer, September 2008.
38. Interview with POA activist Angela Burgess, June 2008.
39. POA, *Forty-Fourth Annual Report*, 1982, Appendix E.
40. Interview with retired senior full-timer, September 2008.
41. Interview with John Boddington, November 2008.
42. Hansard, 30 March 1983.
43. 'News and Jottings', Ashford, *Prison Officers' Magazine*, February 1985.
44. *Prison Officers' Magazine*, February 1985.
45. *Prison Officers' Magazine*, March 1985.
46. Ibid.
47. Interview with Dave Turner, June 2008.
48. Interview with John Boddington, November 2008.
49. Letter to *Prison Officers' Magazine*, February 1985.
50. *Prison Officers' Magazine*, February 1985.
51. 'News and Jottings', *Prison Officers' Magazine*, March 1985.
52. Letter to *Prison Officers' Magazine*, March 1985.
53. 'News and Jottings', *Prison Officers' Magazine*, July 1985.
54. *Prison Officers' Magazine*, April 1985.
55. Interview with Angela Burgess, June 2008.
56. *Prison Officers' Magazine*, May 1985.
57. Ibid.

58. *Prison Officers' Magazine*, April 1985.
59. *Prison Officers' Magazine*, August 1985.
60. *Prison Officers' Magazine*, November 1985.
61. *Prison Officers' Magazine*, April 1985.
62. General Secretary's comments, *Prison Officers' Magazine*, May 1985.
63. 'News and Jottings', *Prison Officers' Magazine*, July 1985.
64. Ibid.
65. 'News and Jottings', *Prison Officers' Magazine*, November 1985.
66. A reference to the proposals for 'Compulsory Competitive Tendering', or contracting-out of basic services, in the National Health Service (NHS).
67. 'News and Jottings', *Prison Officers' Magazine*, October 1985.
68. David Evans, 'Comment', *Prison Officers' Magazine*, August 1985; emphasis in the original.
69. As recounted in the next chapter, a catastrophic riot took place at Strangeways in April 1990.
70. 'News and Jottings', *Prison Officers' Magazine*, May 1985.
71. 'News and Jottings', *Prison Officers' Magazine*, August 1985.
72. Ibid.
73. Ibid.
74. This, of course, far outweighed the Home Office's 1984 prediction of 47,000 prisoners by 1990; see above.
75. 'News and Jottings', *Prison Officers' Magazine*, September 1985.
76. 'News and Jottings', *Prison Officers' Magazine*, October 1985.
77. Ibid.
78. Ibid.
79. Ibid.
80. John Black, 'Industrial Relations in the UK Prison Service: The "Jurassic Park" of Public Sector Industrial Relations', *Employee Relations*, Volume 17 No. 2, 1995, p72.
81. Interview with John Boddington, November 2008.
82. POA, *It Need Never Have Happened*, POA 1986/87, p40; emphasis in the original.
83. Interview with John Boddington, November 2008.
84. Ibid.
85. Black, 'Industrial Relations in the UK Prison Service', p72.
86. Interview with retired senior full-timer, September 2008.
87. Susan Corby, 'On Parole: Prison Service Industrial Relations', *Industrial Relations Journal*, Volume 33 No. 4, 2002, p287.
88. Black, 'Industrial Relations in the UK Prison Service', pp72, 74.
89. Corby, 'On Parole', p287.

90. Interview with John Boddington, November 2008.
91. Interview with Derek Turner, Scottish POA Area Assistant Secretary, November 2008.
92. Interview with Dave Turner, June 2008.
93. Interview with Angela Burgess and Dave Turner, June 2008.
94. Interview with Derek Turner, November 2008.
95. Interview with John Boddington, November 2008.
96. Interview with Derek Turner, November 2008.
97. Ibid.
98. John Hall, Assistant Secretary, Northern Ireland POA, Statement by POA (NI) on events leading up to 'Escape from Lawful Custody of 38 Inmates on the 25th September 1983 from HMP Maze Cellular'. Mimeograph, POA (NI) Office.
99. Ibid.
100. Ibid.
101. Ibid.
102. *Prison Officers' Magazine*, January 1985.
103. Interview with John Boddington, November 2008.
104. *Prison Officers' Magazine*, August 1985.
105. Interview with John Boddington, November 2008.
106. Interview with Angela Burgess and Dave Turner, June 2008.

Chapter 4   1988–2000

1. Interview with John Boddington, November 2008.
2. Lord Chief Justice Woolf, *Prison Disturbances*, HMSO, 1991, pp287, 343.
3. Bob Riddell, 'A Personal Point of View', *Link*, May 1988, p23.
4. Letter to members from Finlay Spratt, Northern Ireland POA Area Chairman, 23 June 1988; emphasis added.
5. 'Prison officers' leaders back Home Office deal', *Financial Times*, 18 April 1987.
6. Letter from J.G. Pilling of the Prison Service to David Evans, POA General Secretary, 18 May 1988.
7. Quoted in POA, *Forty-third Annual Report*, 1989 (Privatisation).
8. Letter from J.G. Pilling to David Evans, 18 May 1988.
9. Interview with Angela Burgess, June 2008.
10. Interviews with Angela Burgess and Dave Turner, June 2008.
11. John Black, 'Industrial Relations in the UK Prison Service: The "Jurassic Park" of Public Sector Industrial Relations', *Employee Relations*, Volume 17 No. 2, 1995, p74.

12. Now retired, Mr Goodman is an Honorary Life Member of the POA and holder of the 'Cronin Clasp', the honorary insignia granted by the POA to its most committed members.

13. Communication from Bryan Goodman, January 2009.

14. Interview with Angela Burgess, June 2008.

15. Ibid.

16. Interview with retired senior full-timer who wished to remain anonymous, September 2008.

17. *Gatelodge* replaced the *Prison Officers' Magazine* in 1986.

18. Black, 'Industrial Relations in the UK Prison Service', p76.

19. Interview with John Boddington, November 2008.

20. Interview with Dave Turner, June 2008.

21. POA, *Fifty-third Annual Report*, 1999, p120.

22. Alison Liebling and David Price, *The Prison Officer*, Prison Service Journal, 2001, p168.

23. Susan Corby, 'On Parole: Prison Service Industrial Relations', *Industrial Relations Journal*, Volume 33 No. 4, 2002.

24. Black, 'Industrial Relations in the UK Prison Service', p83.

25. Brian Caton, *Gatelodge*, December 2006, p7.

26. Communication from Tom Robson, January 2009.

27. Interview with retired senior full-timer, September 2008.

28. Interview with Derek Turner, Scottish POA Area Assistant Secretary, November 2008.

29. Interview with John Boddington, November 2008.

30. This clause was criticised by the International Labour Organisation (ILO): see John Hendy, Damien Brown and G. Watson, *The Prison Officers' Association and the Right to Strike*, Institute of Employment Rights, 1999.

31. Corby, 'On Parole', p293.

32. POA, *Fiftieth Annual Report*, 1996, Appendix I: Industrial Relations, p110.

33. Corby, 'On Parole', p289.

34. Ibid.

35. POA, *Fiftieth Annual Report*, Appendix J: Industrial Relations, p77.

36. POA, *Fifty-second Annual Report*, 1998, Foreword.

37. Liebling and Price, *The Prison Officer*, p180.

38. Black, 'Industrial Relations in the UK Prison Service', p73.

39. Interview with retired senior full-timer, September 2008.

40. Black, 'Industrial Relations in the UK Prison Service', p81.

41. POA, *Submission to the Woolf Inquiry*, September 1990, p60.

42. A right-wing think-tank which promoted 'neo-classical economics' as the basis for government policy.

43. Howard was Conservative Home Secretary between 1993 and 1997.
44. Phil Taylor and Christine Cooper, '"It was Absolute Hell": Inside the Private Prison', *Capital and Class*, Volume 96, autumn 2008, pp10,11.
45. Black, 'Industrial Relations in the UK Prison Service', p86.
46. POA, *A Summary of the Report of the Woolf Inquiry*, POA, 1991.
47. Woolf, *Prison Disturbances*, p1.
48. Arjen Boin and William A.R. Rattray, 'Understanding Prison Riots: Towards a Threshold Theory', *Punishment and Society*, Volume 6 No. 1, January 2004, p57.
49. POA, *Summary of the Report of the Woolf Inquiry*.
50. Ibid.
51. *The Woolf Report: A Summary of the Main Findings*, Prison Reform Trust, 1991, p26.
52. Ibid.
53. Black, 'Industrial Relations in the UK Prison Service', p72.
54. R. Sparks, A.E. Bottoms and W. Hay, *Prisons and the Problem of Order*, Clarendon Press, 1996, cited in Liebling and Price, *The Prison Officer*.
55. Interview with retired senior full-timer, September 2008.
56. POA, *Summary of the Report of the Woolf Inquiry*.
57. POA, *Fiftieth Annual Report*, Appendix I: Industrial Relations, p96.
58. Liebling and Price, *The Prison Officer*, p168.
59. Quoted in ibid., p183.
60. Prison Service, *Prison Service Review*, London, 1997.
61. Liebling and Price, *The Prison Officer*, pp177–8.
62. Ibid., p177ff.
63. Ibid., p180.
64. POA, *Fifty-third Annual Report*, p147.
65. Liebling and Price, *The Prison Officer*, p181.
66. Interview with Derek Turner, November 2008.
67. POA, *Fifty-second Annual Report*, p140.
68. Taylor and Cooper, '"It was Absolute Hell"', p9.
69. Stephen Nathan, 'Prison Privatisation in the United Kingdom', Chapter 14 in Andrew Coyle, Allison Campbell and Rodney Neufeld (eds), *Capitalist Punishment: Prison Privatisation and Human Rights*, Clarity Press/Zed Books, 2003, p162.
70. Ibid., p163.
71. Ibid., p164.

72. Ibid., p173 ('HMP Blakenhurst: A "Snapshot" of Fines and Failures').

73. Cf. 'UK: Competition Shrouded in Secrecy', *Prison Privatisation Report International*, No. 31, October 1999, and 'Documents Reveal Tender Facts', *PPRI*, No. 32, November 1999, both at <www.psiru.org/justice>; cited in Nathan, 'Prison Privatisation in the United Kingdom'.

74. 'Labour gives pledge to end prison privatisation', *The Times*, 8 March 1995, quoted in Nathan, 'Prison Privatisation in the United Kingdom', p168.

75. Nathan, 'Prison Privatisation in the United Kingdom', p168.

76. Interview with retired senior full-timer, September 2008.

77. Communication from POA Research Officer.

78. POA, *Fifty-first Annual Report*, 1997, Foreword.

79. Cited in Nathan, 'Prison Privatisation in the United Kingdom', pp168–9.

80. Prison Service, 'Public and Private Prison Management, Considerations on Returning Privately Managed Prisons to the Public Sector', unpublished document, April 1998, cited in ibid., p169.

81. Nathan, 'Prison Privatisation in the United Kingdom', p169.

82. Interview with Derek Turner, November 2008.

83. POA, *Fifty-third Annual Report*, Foreword, p1.

84. Taylor and Cooper, '"It was Absolute Hell"', p11.

85. Interview with Angela Burgess, June 2008.

86. Interview with Derek Turner, November 2008.

87. Interview with Angela Burgess, June 2008.

88. Report of 1998 Annual Conference, *Gatelodge*, August 1998.

89. Ibid.

90. Communication from POA Research Officer.

91. Corby, 'On Parole', p288.

92. Interview with Derek Turner, November 2008.

93. Ibid.

94. Ibid.

95. Interview with Finlay Spratt, Northern Ireland POA Area Chairman, September 2008.

96. A brass plaque, hung in the POA Headquarters, that commemorates 30 prison officers killed in the course of their duties.

Chapter 5   2000–09

1. Communication from Brian Caton, POA General Secretary, January 2009.

2. Stephen Nathan, 'Prison Privatisation in the United Kingdom', Chapter 14 in Andrew Coyle, Allison Campbell and Rodney

Neufield (eds) *Capitalist Punishment: Prison Privatisation and Human Rights*, Clarity Press/Zed Books, 2003, p165.

3. Ibid., p166.
4. Ian Burrell, *Independent*, 2 August 2001.
5. *Gatelodge*, March 2002.
6. Ibid.
7. Nathan, 'Prison Privatisation in the United Kingdom', p169.
8. Ibid.
9. 'What the Papers Say', *Gatelodge*, February 2001, p23.
10. Private Finance Initiatives, in which buildings required for the public sector, such as prisons, hospitals and schools, are built by private companies on the basis of government loans.
11. Patrick Carter, *Review of PFI and Market Testing in the Prison Service*, 2002.
12. Nathan, 'Prison Privatisation in the United Kingdom', p170.
13. *Prison Service Bulletin*, January 2009.
14. Nathan, 'Prison Privatisation in the United Kingdom', p171.
15. Ibid., p172.
16. Ibid.
17. Ibid.
18. Ibid.
19. Ibid., p173.
20. Susan Corby, 'On Parole: Prison Service Industrial Relations', *Industrial Relations Journal*, Volume 33 No. 4, 2002, p292.
21. *Gatelodge*, April 2000, p5.
22. 'What the Papers Say', *Gatelodge*, October 2001, p13.
23. Phil Taylor and Christine Cooper, '"It was Absolute Hell": Inside the Private Prison', *Capital and Class*, Volume 96, autumn 2008, p9.
24. Ibid., pp25–6.
25. PriceWaterhouseCoopers, *Financial Review of Scottish Prison Service Estates*, PWC, 2002.
26. Taylor and Cooper, '"It was Absolute Hell"', p11.
27. *Gatelodge*, October 2005, p4.
28. *Gatelodge*, May 2006.
29. *Gatelodge*, October 2007.
30. Tom Robson, 'Strictly Private', *Gatelodge*, June 2007.
31. Tom Robson, 'Strictly Private', *Gatelodge*, September 2007.
32. Interview with Angela Burgess and Dave Turner, June 2008.
33. *Gatelodge*, February 2005, p30.
34. *Gatelodge*, December 2008, pp30–1.
35. Ibid.

36. Alison Liebling and David Price, *The Prison Officer*, Prison Service Journal, 2001, p176.

37. Ibid., p175.

38. Ibid., p176.

39. Corby, 'On Parole', p288.

40. *Gatelodge*, September 2000.

41. 'DG Throws Dolly Out', *Gatelodge*, October 2000, p40.

42. In Scotland and Northern Ireland also, a Voluntary Industrial Relations Agreement was based on the government's commitment to remove the provisions of Section 127 from officers working there.

43. Mark Healey, 'A Long and Winding Road', *Gatelodge*, April 2001, p4.

44. *Gatelodge*, October 2001, p4.

45. *Gatelodge*, October 2003, p4.

46. *Gatelodge*, June 2004.

47. *Gatelodge*, November 2004.

48. *Gatelodge*, June 2005.

49. Corby, 'On Parole', p291.

50. Communication from POA Research Officer.

51. Corby, 'On Parole', p292.

52. 'Industrial Relations Procedure Agreement between HM Prison Service and the Prison Officers' Association' (unpublished), 2001.

53. 'Pendulum Arbitration: The First Decision', *Industrial Relations Review and Report*, No. 370, June 1986.

54. Corby, 'On Parole'.

55. Letter to *Gatelodge*, January 2002.

56. *Independent*, 9 August 2001.

57. *Gatelodge*, December 2001.

58. Corby, 'On Parole', p293.

59. Communication from POA Research Officer.

60. *Gatelodge*, September 2005.

61. *Gatelodge*, December 2005.

62. *Gatelodge*, September 2005.

63. Communication from POA Research Officer.

64. Branch Chairman, Ashworth, 'Cheap Labour', *Gatelodge*, June 2007, p11.

65. Communication from POA Research Officer.

66. *Gatelodge*, February 2002, p36.

67. *Gatelodge*, December 2006.

68. *Gatelodge*, September 2007.

69. The term 'Awkward Squad' was coined by the press in 2003 to refer to left union leaders such as Bob Crow of the RMT (Rail, Maritime and Transport workers' union), Andy Gilchrist (then) of the FBU (Fire Brigades Union) and Mark Serwotka of PCS (Public and Commercial Services union), along with others who were in one way or another putting up resistance to New Labour.
70. Letter to *Gatelodge*, December 2007.
71. Interview with Derek Turner, Scottish POA Area Assistant Secretary, November 2008.
72. Ibid.
73. Ibid.
74. Ibid.
75. Scottish Executive, *Consultation on the Future of the Scottish Prison Estate*, 2002, cited in Taylor and Cooper, '"It was Absolute Hell"', p12.
76. HMIP, Her Majesty's Inspectorate of Prisons for Scotland, Intermediate Report on HM Prison Kilmarnock, HMIP/Scottish Executive, cited in Taylor and Cooper, '"It was Absolute Hell"', p14.
77. Scottish Parliament, 2002, cited in Taylor and Cooper, '"It was Absolute Hell"', p15.
78. Taylor and Cooper, '"It was Absolute Hell"', p15.
79. Ibid., p20.
80. Cited in ibid., p17.
81. Ibid., p15.
82. Ibid., p17.
83. Cited in ibid., p18.
84. Ibid., p22.
85. Ibid., p23.
86. England and Wales POA representative at the 7 November 2008 memorial service.

INDEX